NAMING
JACK THE RIPPER

NAMING
JACK THE
RIPPER

New crime scene evidence
A stunning forensic breakthrough
The killer revealed

RUSSELL EDWARDS

Lyons Press
Guilford, Connecticut
Helena, Montana
An imprint of Rowman & Littlefield

First published 2014 by Sidgwick & Jackson
an imprint of Pan Macmillan, a division of Macmillan Publishers Limited
Pan Macmillan, 20 New Wharf Road, London N1 9RR
Basingstoke and Oxford

First Lyons Press edition, 2014

Lyons Press is an imprint of Rowman & Littlefield
Distributed by NATIONAL BOOK NETWORK

British Library Cataloguing-in-Publication Information available
Library of Congress Cataloging-in-Publication Data available

ISBN 978-1-4930-1190-2 (hardcover)

∞™ The paper used in this publication meets the minimum requirements of American National Standard for Information Sciences—Permanence of Paper for Printed Library Materials, ANSI/NISO Z39.48-1992.

For Sally,
Alexander and Annabel

* * * *

CONTENTS

INTRODUCTION

It was Saturday, 17 March 2007, St Patrick's Day. Not that I was even aware of the saint's day: the date had a much greater significance for me. It was the day that I attended an auction, the first I had ever been to. A day that started with great excitement and determination, and ended in desperate disappointment.

Why was this auction so important to me? To a casual observer, the catalogue produced by Lacy Scott & Knight, a firm of auctioneers, for the sale that day in Bury St Edmunds, Suffolk, was fairly standard: antiquarian books, ceramics, jewellery, clocks, paintings, plenty of Victorian and Edwardian mahogany furniture. At another time in my life, when I was dabbling in antique furniture, I would have enjoyed browsing through the lots.

But today there was only one item I was interested in, and it was definitely the star item of the day, with an entire page of the catalogue devoted to it. It was an old, silk shawl, damaged, with pieces missing. I'd been to see it the day before, and had been struck by how beautiful it was, much more so than I expected: the centre panel was plain silk, and at either end there were broad panels intensely patterned with flowers, Michaelmas daisies predominantly, in gold and red. On one side it was brown with patterned edges, and a wide border at each end of blue with the flower pattern, and on the other side a lighter brown with blue ends. Even to my untutored eye it was clearly very old.

But its significance was far more than its age. This is what the catalogue listing said:

Lot 235: A late 19th Century Brown Silk Screen Printed Shawl decorated with Michaelmas daisies, length 8ft (with some sections cut and torn).

Unlike the tables and pictures that filled the rest of the list, there was no estimated price given. It simply read: 'Est: please refer to auctioneers.'

I had done just that. When I saw the shawl on the previous day, when auctions normally hold a viewing day for potential buyers, the auctioneer had told me the reserve price, and I had been surprised by how low it was: definitely within my budget.

On another page, with a large photograph of the shawl, the catalogue read:

Provenance: According to the vendors' family history this shawl is purported to have been removed from Jack the Ripper victim Catherine Eddowes body by his great great uncle, Acting Sergeant Amos Simpson, who was based near Mitre Square in the East End of London. However, there is some controversy surrounding the authenticity of this story and interested parties are advised to do their own research before bidding. The shawl spent some time in the

Metropolitan Police Crime (Black) Museum and in 2006 was subject to inconclusive forensic testing for a programme on Channel 5.

The story of the shawl is discussed at length in Appendix One of Kevin O'Donnell's book The Jack the Ripper Whitechapel Murders based on research by Andy and Sue Parlour: a copy is available on demand in the office.

So there you have it. If genuine, this was one of the few physical remains from the scenes of the crimes committed by Jack the Ripper as he terrorized the streets of London, and carved his way into the British psyche. Everyone has heard of Jack the Ripper. Not many know the full story, but everyone has a vague impression of dark, foggy streets in Victorian London with a mad serial killer on the loose, attacking and viciously mutilating his prostitute victims. It is perhaps the greatest, most famous unsolved crime in the world, the one that draws tourists from across the globe to the streets of London's East End.

Of course, the catalogue was careful to make sure that the claims for the shawl were muted. There was no proof it had belonged to the victim Catherine Eddowes, just a long family history. But, still, there was a good chance. I had done some research, I believed it was genuine, and I wanted it. I wanted it very badly. I was nursing a nugget of information about the shawl that only I knew, a secret that made it much more important to me, and one I believed would add a great deal to what little we know about Jack the Ripper.

I set off for the auction early. It started at 10 a.m., and my wife Sally and I were living with our toddler son Alexander in Newmarket, only twenty-five minutes away. She didn't come with me: she doesn't share my fascination with the Ripper story. I dressed casually, keen not to draw attention to myself, but smartly enough to show that I was serious. I expected a large crowd, and I was right: the huge barn of an auction room, the size of a football pitch and crammed with furniture, was packed with people, and I guessed at least some of them were there for the same item as me. National and local newspapers had carried stories about the auction, so there was bound to be a high level of interest. Before the sale started a bemused assistant from the auction firm was holding the shawl up high so that a crowd gathered round him could look at it: he clearly could not understand the massive interest in this old, damaged piece of material.

I felt a mixture of excitement and apprehension. The auction started, and as lot after lot went by I realized nothing much was being sold: clearly, not just some, but the bulk of people in the crowded room were there for the shawl. I was worried, I felt sure it would soar way above its reserve, and in my mind I saw it reaching a sum of £150,000 or more. Was I prepared to go that high? Yes, I wanted it so badly I would have paid whatever it took to get it.

As the morning dragged on, I noticed that Stewart Evans, one of the world's leading authorities on the Ripper case and a collector of true-crime ephemera, was there. I had seen him on television being interviewed in various documentaries about the subject so I decided to ask him for his opinion on the shawl, without revealing my own interest. He chatted happily about the Ripper story, but seemed to be dismissive about the authenticity of the shawl.

'It's not for me,' he said, 'I'm only here to see who it goes to. Nobody should buy it.'

I felt he might be bluffing, trying to throw me, and anyone else who was drawn to listen to him, off. He looked at me keenly, and I was sure he was sizing up whether or not I was going to rival him in the bidding.

With half the auction lots sold, a lunch break was called. I wasn't interested in eating: my stomach was lurching at the thought of what was to come. I made my way to the office to have a look at the book that was mentioned in the catalogue. When I got there I found a small group of people gathered round a very tall man who was holding up the book, and expounding on the shawl and its history. I realized this was Andy Parlour, whose research for the appendix was the crucial part of the book in terms of the shawl. He was enjoying telling everyone about it, so I asked a few superficial questions: I didn't want to show my hand, but I wanted to hear everything he could share. Luckily, like Stewart Evans, Andy did not need much encouragement to talk. Every so often I said something like, 'That's interesting, mate,' just to keep him going.

I found it hard to believe that I was actually in the same room as this man, who was a specialist on the shawl, and Stewart Evans, a top expert on the whole Ripper story. And every so often I reminded myself that I knew something about the shawl that everyone else had missed, even the guys who had given years of research to the subject.

When the auction resumed I decided to stand at Stewart Evans's shoulder, thinking that he was definitely going to bid, and I'd wait until he did before I joined in. The auction room had been noisy all morning, people chatting and moving about, but when 'Lot 235' was bellowed across the room, a deep hush fell. The assistant gestured to the shawl, now locked in a glass cabinet at the front of the room.

I cannot remember the first bid: who made it or how much it was for. But bids were soon coming from all parts of the room and the price was shooting up. I couldn't see who was bidding. There were three phone lines accepting bids, and the auctioneer was going with practised speed between the phones and the room. I can remember thinking, 'This thing is going to go for millions.'

Every now and then the auctioneer, who knew of my interest, would glance at me to see if I was going to join in. But I was hooked on waiting for Stewart Evans to bid, and kept watching him. The auction rapidly ran through, and before I realized it the auctioneer was saying, 'Final bids.' Again he looked at me, again I wavered and did nothing. I was still expecting a bid from Stewart Evans, and when none came I froze. A combination of nerves, and a fear that, if he was not bidding perhaps he was right to believe the shawl was worthless, gripped me.

'No more bids. The item remains unsold.'

There were groans around the room. Despite the frenzied bidding, the reserve had not been met. People had waited all day for this, and now they were disappointed. The spectacle was over, and the whole event had been a waste of everyone's time.

'Lot 236' the auctioneer called, as a rosewood tea caddy went under the hammer. But nobody was paying any attention. Little knots of people drifted out of the saleroom, sharing their frustration with each other. Others pushed past and left alone, the feeling of being let down etched on their faces.

Nobody was more disappointed than I was.

What had I done? Had I just lost out on owning one of the most vital pieces of tangible evidence from the most famous murder mystery of all time? Or had I had a narrow escape, saving me from spending thousands on what was little more than a whim?

When I had told Sally how much I was prepared to put up for the shawl she had laughed, and made me promise that if it turned out to be worthless, I'd give her exactly the same amount of money to spend as she wished. At least I was spared that!

But the money I had saved did nothing to make me feel better. Like everybody else, I headed wearily towards my car empty-handed; I felt defeated. All I could think was 'What have I done? What kind of idiot am I, to be struck dumb at the vital moment?'

It affected me badly and that night I didn't sleep. The terrible feeling of failure stuck with me through the following Sunday and I continued to beat myself up over it. I talked to Sally, who sympathized, but could not really understand my pain.

But when Monday morning came, I had a revelation: perhaps all was not lost. I had tried hard to convince myself that buying the shawl could have been a mistake: Stewart Evans didn't want it, nobody else was willing to pay the reserve and perhaps they were right – the shawl was just a pointless piece of old fabric that had been imbued over many years with a family myth.

But I knew something they didn't. As I've said, I had my own reason for believing the shawl was hugely significant, perhaps the key to the whole Ripper case. I could not talk to anybody about it because at this time I knew nobody who shared my interest, and I certainly did not want to alert the 'Ripperologists', people like Stewart Evans who devote themselves to studying the case, and are acknowledged experts. What I knew was too precious to share with the world at this stage. So despite my doubts, the importance of the shawl would not be challenged: I still believed in it.

I decided that morning to call the auction rooms to see what would happen to the shawl. Thankfully the auctioneer remembered me and told me that it was to be returned to the vendor. I asked him if he thought the owner would be interested in selling it to me if I offered to pay the reserve price. I was told to wait by the phone. The auctioneer wanted to call the vendor there and then. A few tense minutes later, the phone rang and the auctioneer's voice came through.

'You're in luck,' he said. 'If you can meet our fee and pay the reserve, the shawl is yours.'

I was elated. It had crossed my mind that somebody else might have tried the same thing, but it seems I was the only one. I had, provisionally, bought it. The relief that flooded through my body was immense.

'I'm going to need a letter of provenance. I need the history of this from the owner, in writing,' I said.

It was very important for me to establish as much information as possible about how the shawl had come down through his family.

But the deal was done, and I put the phone down in a much happier mood than I had been in since the auction.

I had to wait for the letter to arrive with the auctioneer, which took a few days. It was a strange feeling, knowing that this thing was mine, but I could not confidently believe it until it was there in my hands. As I waited in limbo I was riddled with doubt – what if the vendor had changed his mind? I couldn't stop going over my secret, and wondering what would have happened if somebody else had stumbled on it before I did. As it turned out, my life would have been a whole lot different.

I went to collect the shawl on 2 April 2007, just over two weeks after I first saw it. I picked up a banker's draft from a branch of my bank in Bury St Edmunds, and walked to the auction house, aware of my own heartbeat. As I saw the people of Bury St Edmunds going about their daily lives, it felt surreal that I was going to collect something that meant so much to me and that could have so much historical significance, and yet nobody else shared my excitement.

I was kept waiting at the auction house, they weren't ready to hand over my precious purchase. The auctioneer asked why I hadn't made a bid for the shawl on the day, and I explained I felt too nervous, with all eyes focusing on the item, and I was waiting for the right moment, but that moment never came.

He smiled, no doubt used to customers suffering auction nerves, but also possibly thinking that I had played a long game, and never intended to put myself out in public as the purchaser of the shawl. I wish I had been that clever! Eventually he passed me a large piece of card folded in half and taped with yellowing Sellotape.

Within it was the shawl, wrapped in red tissue paper. On the card was the name and profession of the previous owner, David Melville-Hayes, along with the inscription: 'Shawl in two pieces (1) approx 71ins by 24ins, (2) approx 24ins by 15 ins.' I was also handed the letter from Mr Melville-Hayes, and was immediately struck that it was written on an old typewriter, which somehow added to the huge sense of history I already had.

'Keep in touch and let us know how you get on with the thing, won't you?' the auctioneer said as he shook my hand.

'Of course I will, my pleasure,' I replied.

I walked back to my car, carrying the inauspicious-looking parcel, and feeling immensely pleased with myself.

I knew I was only at the beginning of my own personal crusade to unmask the Ripper. But the journey had begun.

CHAPTER ONE

FROM BIRKENHEAD
TO BRICK LANE

The story of Jack the Ripper is well documented. Whole libraries have been written about it, countless theories have been expounded, television documentaries and feature films have been made. It is the greatest true crime mystery ever, world-renowned, lingering in the collective imagination, a constant source of fascination. There are serial killers with much bigger death tallies, even some just as vicious in the way they dispatched their victims. But none, ever, has held the public interest in the same way as this case. In a short killing spree in 1888, Jack the Ripper carved his way into history as surely as he carved up the unfortunate women he came across as he prowled through the Whitechapel alleys and passageways.

Many people have tried to solve the case, both at the time and in the years since. I am the latest in that long line: but unlike anyone before me, I believe I have incontrovertible proof, the kind of proof that would stand up to any cross-examination in a courtroom today.

I am not the most likely of candidates to solve this puzzle: in fact, I stumbled into it almost by chance. But I believe it was my ability to think laterally that helped me to see a link that nobody else had spotted. With no background as a researcher, I have had to learn as I go along, and I have been down countless blind alleys. I have been rebuffed, discouraged, and at times I have given up entirely. But the project niggled, and I never completely let go of it.

I don't come from London's East End, so I have no direct connection with the history of the crimes: I was born and grew up in Birkenhead. We started out as a regular family: Mum, Dad, me and my sister living in a council flat in a tower block in a tough area. But by the time I was four my parents had split up. They both went on to marry again, and through Mum's new partner I acquired a stepbrother and a stepsister, and through Dad's I gained another stepbrother, stepsister, and then a half-sister. So it was always a complicated, fragmented upbringing, and the greatest stability in my childhood came from my grandmother, who lived across the road from us when we moved, when I was five, to a two-up, two-down terraced house, with a toilet out the back, and weekly trips to the public baths for a bath.

After my stepfather accidentally set fire to the house while cooking, we were rapidly moved to a council estate. But I always gravitated back to my grandmother, and by the time I was thirteen I was staying with her every Tuesday night and from Friday through to Sunday. I am sometimes asked how I first became interested in crime, and I believe it dates back to my early childhood. My mum and stepfather were often working: they ran market stalls. My sister and I were looked after by a succession of teenage babysitters, and my grandparents, and they didn't insist on early bedtimes: we stayed up watching *Frankenstein*, *Dracula*, *The Mummy*, *The Wolfman* and other horror movies. At the same time I was collecting and painting small plastic models of monsters and characters from horror movies.

When I was ten, the news was dominated by the Yorkshire Ripper, and I followed the case closely, with no idea that his nickname derived from an earlier murderer. It became an interest as I moved into my teens: I was fascinated by TV programmes on American serial killers like Ted Bundy, John Wayne Gacy, and then the British killer Dennis Nilsen.

It wasn't a serious obsession: I didn't go out of my way to study murderers. But I was always intrigued by the big question: what makes someone become, not just a murderer with a clear motive, but a serial killer, who strikes again and again, seemingly randomly? Where does that urge to kill come from?

I did well at school, working hard for my O levels, putting up with the bullies who dubbed me 'Half Mast' because my trousers were always too short: my parents didn't have enough money to buy me new ones each year. I was in the O-level class with the posh kids, but I was on free school dinners: I didn't really fit in. I did my revision at my grandmother's house, my favourite refuge. It was then that I realized nobody would ever fight my battles for me, and I developed a strong sense of having to look after myself.

I wasn't encouraged at home, where schoolwork wasn't particularly valued. I started doing A levels in Chemistry, Biology and Music, but a spectacular row with my mother and stepfather sent me running to North Wales to live with my dad at the guest house he ran in Rhyl, North Wales. I was even unhappier living with my stepmother, so I went back to Birkenhead and went to college to carry on studying. My mother and stepfather had moved from the council house into a shop in Wallasey, and then when I was eighteen they returned to the terraced two-up, two-down opposite my grandmother. There was no bedroom for me, so I slept on a camp bed underneath the stairs in the living room, still spending a lot of time with my grandmother, whose health was declining (she died when I was 21). I was also playing the saxophone in a band, and devoting more time to this than to college work: I took two A levels, in Biology and Chemistry, and when the results came out I had an F (fail) for Biology and an O (O-level grade) for Chemistry. I stared at them: FO. At that moment, I felt the letters were spelling out a message to me, to give up my academic hopes and just get on with life.

One thing that both my parents unconsciously handed to me was a desire to be my own boss. My dad ran his own guest house, my mum and stepdad made and sold soft toys on market stalls. I'd been helping them since I was thirteen, I knew everything I needed to know about making teddy bears and other popular stuffed toys, and I was soon running two market stalls of my own. It was my first taste of business success. I was nineteen, I had seven outworkers (women who made the toys), two stalls, and a business supplying soft toys as arcade prizes to all the concessions along the seafront at Rhyl.

With my girlfriend, I was also soon buying property, jumping at the chance to buy a rundown place in Toxteth, Liverpool, then another one in Birkenhead, where we lived, then another one. The band took up all my spare time: we were punk rockers, and we went by the name of Dust Choir, which makes me cringe today. But it was good fun.

Then I crashed and burned: I lost it all. My girlfriend split with me, and I was devastated because I did not see it coming. At the tender age of twenty-two I couldn't deal with the rejection. I needed to get away, and with a mate we left Merseyside in an old red Escort van which I bought for £200 from a bloke in a pub, which needed a pair of pliers to keep the choke out, and which I had to rev up at traffic lights in case it stalled. I had £130, a suitcase of clothes and a tent. We more or less stuck a pin in a map and decided to go to Cambridge, because it sounded like it would be a beautiful place, which it is. But what I saw for the next few months was not the lovely city, but potato fields, where we worked as pickers, a car components factory, where I worked on a production line, and a campsite where we pitched the tent.

Even the campsite did not last: when my mate bailed out and went back home, I couldn't pay the site rent and I wasn't allowed back to get my tent and my possessions. The van had been towed away by the police as it had no tax and MOT, and was, after the journey down, undriveable. I was, for a short time, truly homeless. I switched my shifts at the factory to mainly nights, and during the day dozed on a bus shelter seat, and occasionally in a trench halfway from the town centre to the factory. I was washing at the railway station and walking to work. In desperation one cold night I asked a couple of policemen in a police car to arrest me, just so that I could get warm: they declined. I was so rundown and filthy that I actually caught scabies, which was horrible, and I felt ashamed because to me scabies meant dirt and poverty. I must have been a bit smelly because my workmates at the factory showed me where there was a shower to clean myself up.

It was a very bleak time, but when I look back it was important. It reinforced my need to be successful, to make something of myself, and my strong feeling that I would always have to do it myself, without any help. It also gave me a great empathy with people who find themselves at the bottom of the heap, with nobody to turn to and nowhere to live: eventually, years down the line, this helped me understand the dire poverty of the Ripper victims. I knew, as they knew, the overpowering drive for the basics of life: shelter and food.

Luckily, I kept on working and with my wages could afford a bed and breakfast. I was soon back on my feet, raising the deposit to rent a house, which I shared with my new Spanish girlfriend. Eventually, I got some money from the properties in Birkenhead and decided to get back into studying, but this time a subject that would be relevant to me: Business Studies. I applied to various seats of learning, and in the end landed a place at the Polytechnic of North London in Holloway Road, a complete contrast with the tranquillity of Cambridge and my first introduction to the metropolis. For the first couple of weeks I commuted from Cambridge: a ridiculously long journey. I would doze on the four-hour coach journey and wake as it came into London down Commercial Road, through the heart of the East End. This was my first impression of the area, and I remember thinking it looked sad and rundown.

I was soon living in London and having a great time, making good friends, girlfriends, finding the college work easy. I decided to go on to do a postgrad course in Management Studies at the Polytechnic of Central London (now the University of Westminster), funding myself with grants and casual work. I was, like all students, permanently broke and always with an eye out for a cheap place to eat.

That mission to eat cheap, often in the middle of the night after strumming guitars or arguing pretentious philosophy with my student friends, took me for the first time into the

East End. We patronized the famous twenty-four-hour Beigel Bake at the north end of Brick Lane, where we could have, in those days, a delicious, filling, cream cheese bagel for the princely sum of 40p. And as we discovered this manna, at the same time I discovered the whole area, a place I knew nothing about but where, for some inexplicable reason, I felt at home. It was rough back then – it still is, in parts. But I loved the buzz, the coolness of the place. It spoke to me in a way no other area has ever chimed with me before. There were hookers and their pimps, knots of dodgy-looking men outside the pubs, and spicy, exotic smells drifting from the Asian restaurants and cafes. I was used to the rougher areas of Liverpool, but this was different in a way it is hard for me to explain. I loved the place, still do, and if it was not for family reasons I'd live there today.

I can remember one particular evening when I went with my best mates Andy and Paul to celebrate Andy's birthday with a curry in Brick Lane, our idea of the best possible night out. We'd had a tankful, we somehow got separated, and in my inebriated state I had no idea how to find my way back to Liverpool Street station. For some reason which now seems surreal, I found myself talking to a Spanish prostitute in Spanish (thanks to my Spanish girlfriend I knew a smattering of words) and she took me back to the station, where I dodged the barrier and ended up back at the flat where I was living. Her friendliness and willingness to help somehow typified the area for me.

I knew nothing about Jack the Ripper at this stage. Yes, like everyone else in Britain I'd heard the name. But I had no idea that I was walking the streets where his crimes took place. That would all come later. There was, though, a very strange moment in 1991, nine years before I first heard the Ripper story. I was walking down Commercial Road and at the junction with White Church Lane I had a very strong feeling that something had happened there. It was powerful enough to make me stop for a few seconds, and just absorb the feeling: I had no notion what it meant until years later.

My life was going well. While I was at college I met a lovely girl, Lyndsay, and we became engaged, and even got to the stage of sending out the wedding invitations, and paying for the dress. But I realized that we had drifted apart, with her concentrating on her teaching career and me, after leaving college with my master's degree, flat out pursuing a lucrative career with a software company which I helped to establish. I was greatly relieved when, after plucking up the courage to tell Lyndsay I didn't think I could go through with the wedding, she sighed with relief and told me she felt exactly the same . . . I will always be grateful to her and her family, because they showed me, for the first time, what a normal happy family life can be like. They welcomed me into their home, and it was very different from my own childhood, with everyone getting on well and caring about each other.

Soon afterwards, with business going great guns, I met and married my first wife, Feiruz, who was Ethiopian. It didn't last: we were only married for three-and-a-half years.

During this time I was still frequenting the East End, making it my regular stop to entertain the corporate clients of our business who flew in from Holland, Denmark, Africa and other countries, as well as from other parts of the UK. A curry in Brick Lane was a popular choice, as they always enjoyed seeing the East End of London, and I was happy for any excuse to go there.

The business became the third largest supplier of software in the country, and I will give you a couple of examples of the way my brain works – not because I am bragging, but to illustrate how I think in a lateral way, seeing opportunities that others have failed to spot. This quirk, which has helped me so much in business, eventually helped me when I first encountered the shawl and started thinking deeply about the Ripper mystery.

One Sunday afternoon I went to the Tate Gallery, purely as a visitor. I noticed that while they sold prints and souvenirs in the shop, they had no software. The following day I spoke to the buyer and did a deal to supply CD-ROMs of art and artists. In the same way, I read a news item about government plans to put computers into all schools, started work on it the following day and we became a major supplier of educational software to schools. Another time one of our customers told me he had acquired a large collection of titillating, but perfectly legal, photographs of semi-naked girls. I encouraged him to put them on disks, and I sold them into the Virgin and HMV stores on Oxford Street – but only after sitting up late into the night obscuring the nipples on the covers with a marker pen.

When I decided to leave the company, I set up a software brokerage company. For three-and-a-half years we were very successful, but 9/11 put paid to it overnight, as some of our customers were badly hit. By then my marriage was foundering, I was in the process of buying a beautiful seventeenth-century malting house in the country, and I was considering setting up my next venture, a company running care homes for the elderly. I was on the brink of big changes in my life, but even bigger ones were in store . . .

The first and most important (she'd kill me if I didn't say that, and it's true) was meeting my second wife, Sally. I went for a day out with a mate of mine, Mark, and he promised to take me somewhere interesting. Unlike half the population of London, I'd never heard of the restaurant School Dinners. How I'd avoided all the publicity about this place, where the waitresses dressed as if they were off the set of a St Trinian's film and the food was all traditional British grub, I don't know.

But what first struck me about the place was not the ambience, but the woman who was at the reception desk who, when I remarked it felt a bit chilly in there, looked up and with a straight face said: 'That's because you've got no hair.'

I laughed at the insult, and we spent the rest of the evening laughing and talking together. Sally McMullen owned the restaurant with her ex-husband, and they had seen every star you can name pass through, it was such a unique and popular venue.

As we chatted I discovered that she came from a part of North Wales I knew well, and she had even been in the same school as my sister, at the same time. There was an immediate feeling that we were right together. Later that night, Sally suggested we go to a club in the Kings Road and as she and I danced together, another club-goer tried to make a play for her. She said: 'Excuse me, I'm dancing with my future husband.'

It was a prescient remark. In 1999, in the space of three weeks there had been big events in my life: I bought our golden retriever Goldie on a Friday, the following Friday I met Sally, and exactly a week later I moved to the malting house. Sally and I were so sure we belonged together that she moved in with me straight away. Shortly afterwards I was in the middle of buying my first care home, a stressful business.

Then the next, vitally important, event happened. It was, on the face of it, nothing more than a pleasant night out, a trip to the cinema with Sally. We went to the Vue Cinema in Cambridge to see *From Hell*, a Johnny Depp movie in which he plays a police inspector who investigates the Jack the Ripper killings in Victorian London. The film shows some of the key locations in the Ripper story, notably Christ Church in Spitalfields and the Ten Bells pub. I had never realized until I saw it that my favourite area, the East End, was the location of these grisly murders about which I had only the vaguest idea.

'How come I didn't know about this?' I asked myself.

The strange feeling that I had been walking the same streets as this mysterious killer without knowing it, coupled with my inherent interest in crime, made me want to know a lot more. That night, watching the film, my continuing fascination – obsession, even – with the Ripper case was born. There have been four or five massive moments for me in the quest for the Ripper and this was the first.

I started to read books about the case, and soon after seeing the film Sally and I went on a two-hour-long 'Jack the Ripper' walk around Whitechapel, one Saturday afternoon. We were conducted around the area and heard the story of the crimes, told by a Ripper expert who made a very good job of stoking my enthusiasm for the mystery, even if Sally made no attempt to hide her boredom: she was rolling her eyes, folding her arms, looking up at the sky. But for me, it was all fascinating. Yes, here was the Ten Bells pub I had seen in the film, here was the church, here the places where each of the victims' bodies were found: real streets, real places.

We were in a group of assorted people, including American tourists, but despite the varied company I could feel the deep affinity I had always felt for the East End, but now coupled with something darker, more intriguing. This was the biggest unsolved murder case ever: surely there had to be a key to it somewhere, some door that nobody yet had opened? I had a feeling, born I suppose of ignorance and arrogance, that I was going to find that door, that it was simply a matter of thinking about it all in a fresh way.

Looking back, I'm astonished at my presumption. I now know that much better qualified people than me, professional historians, genealogists, forensic psychiatrists, senior policemen, have all tried and failed to give definitive answers to the big question: whodunit? But I have always enjoyed and risen to challenges, and this was a huge one.

By the time I had bought and was running three care homes I was under a lot of stress: it was a fraught business, dealing with staff and, more importantly, making sure the needs of the residents were met. I was working long hours, and there were other worries in my personal life. I'd never wanted children before in any of my other relationships, but when Sally fell pregnant I was overjoyed. We were putting roller blinds up when she told me: 'I think I'm pregnant.' I felt such a surge of joy. Tragically, within a week of the great news, she had a miscarriage and we lost the twins she was carrying. We then embarked on a frustrating round of IVF. To our lasting delight, she became pregnant with our son Alexander naturally, between IVF cycles, and we were thrilled when he made his appearance on my birthday in 2005.

For me, Jack the Ripper was an escape route. I could shut off from the problems of the business and the worries about our battle for a baby by immersing myself in books and research. I didn't take much notice of the books which expounded wild theories, but stuck to the ones that laid out the facts. I even rang Scotland Yard's Crime Museum, thinking they would have all the official paperwork on the case, but they told me the material was at the National Archives in Kew. I went there and viewed everything they had on microfiche. I even once handled some original documents, including a photograph of one of the victims, Elizabeth Stride. Seeing the grainy black and white image of her brought the case to life more than anything had before: this was a real person. But it's true to say that I was much more fascinated by the detective work than I was about the social history of the area, and the plight of the women victims, at this stage. What drove me on was a deep-seated conviction that something, somewhere along the line, had been missed.

But to understand my quest, it is vital to know the whole story of Jack the Ripper's crimes.

CHAPTER TWO

A MURDERER STRIKES
IN WHITECHAPEL

As I've said, the East End became a special place for me as soon as I got to know it. It is a fascinating area, a distillation of its own rich, evolving history. It feels like it's constantly in flux, bending and changing with the waves of different people who have lived there, the new and the old rubbing along together, old tenements and warehouses holding their own against the new glass and steel skyscrapers I have watched going up over the last twenty-five years I have been going there.

If you look hard, you'll see old alleyways and cobbled streets, narrow, dimly lit, just as they were in Victorian times. I have seen rats scuttling along Gunthorpe Street, off Whitechapel High Street, and felt transported back to the nineteenth century. And like them, I feel at home in these dingy streets.

Nowadays the area is enjoying a renaissance as a trendy hangout, but when I first went there it was more squalid, the streets often strewn with rubbish, much quieter than it is today, with transactions between pimps and prostitutes openly conducted on street corners. The lights were dimmer, the sound of music more muted, and the others who hung around the area were locals or, like me and my friends, poor students who liked the lack of pretension and the cheap food.

Today there are two contrasting East Ends. There is the area around Brick Lane where the most recent immigrants are Asian, and where the shops and restaurants cater for them and the outsiders who come in search of a good curry, where the old synagogues are now mosques. Then there is the area around the four streets that have survived and been preserved: Princelet Street, Hanbury Street, Wilkes Street and Fournier Street, where the beautiful four- or five-storey houses built for the Huguenots (themselves religious refugees, escaping persecution in France) and dating back to the seventeenth century now sell for millions of pounds each. In Victorian times these were crumbling, rat-infested tenements with whole families in one room, sometimes with a couple of pigs for company. When I first visited, a quarter of a century ago, those now-restored houses were still slums, many of them in a terrible state of disrepair, the rooms sub-let to a polyglot mix of tenants, only slightly more salubrious than in Victorian times.

Now they attract artists like Tracey Emin and Gilbert & George, the actress Keira Knightley, there are bustling cafes with well-heeled clienteles, pubs that attract a young, right-on crowd, fashion mavens tottering along cobbles in their preposterous shoes. The gentrification is creeping, with lofts on sale for seven figures in Commercial Street and Brick Lane.

Over the years that I have been going to the East End, I have seen the architechural landscape change drastically. I've watched warehouses become galleries and restaurants and the old buildings being dwarfed by new and modern office blocks and apartments. Hoardings and cranes are a familiar sight, as every small space between the old and new buildings is developed as prime real estate. I have also seen the Ripper 'industry', which has existed since a few years after the murders, grow into a big business, with upwards of ten different walking tours a day being escorted around the area, some in daylight and others at dusk, to add to the atmosphere. Some tours have as many as forty people, others as few as ten; some are in Spanish, German, French. Small coaches struggle round the tight corners, as guides tell the stories of the crimes on their intercoms. Early in the twentieth century the tours were fewer and sparser, but still attracted the curious, reputedly including Arthur Conan Doyle and Charles Dickens's son, also called Charles. Nowadays, with tourism and more leisure time, the tours have become so popular that the East End streets swarm with them, guides swerving down side streets to avoid mingling with other tours.

It is just another phase: the East End has been through so many incarnations over the centuries. But the most interesting time to me is the 1880s, the era that spawned the Ripper Murders. In those times the neighbourhoods of Whitechapel and Spitalfields, as well as nearby districts like Bethnal Green, St George in the East and Poplar, had some of the most scandalously poor living conditions in London. The East End was, in parts, a vast, dirty, overcrowded slum, struggling to cope with the sheer number of people choosing to live there. Much of this was down to the fact that it was home to many of the so-called 'stink industries', such as breweries, slaughter-houses and sugar refineries, which had attracted many migrant workers to the area during the industrial revolution.

The City of London refused to allow such noxious trades

within its walls, so instead they went to the outlying districts. This resulted in a polluted East End, dirty with soot and other industrial residue that blackened the walls of buildings and the lungs of its inhabitants. Its proximity to the mighty Thames and the growing docks ensured that immigrants arriving in London would find their first point of entry in places like Wapping, Poplar and of course Whitechapel: the French Huguenots in the late seventeenth and eighteenth centuries (who built those amazing town houses), the Irish fleeing the potato famine in the mid-1800s and, later, eastern European Jewish refugees. The Jewish incursion into the East End is vital to the story of the Ripper, so let's look at what caused it.

When, in March 1881, Tsar Alexander II of Russia was assassinated, there were unfounded rumours that the perpetrators were Jewish, and this led to a wave of maltreatment and persecution against the Jews in Eastern Europe, known as 'pogroms' (the word comes from Russian Yiddish, and means 'destruction'). Thousands of Jewish Russians, Germans, Hungarians and, significantly, Poles, fled their homelands in the hope of setting up a newer and safer life elsewhere.

One of the places they chose was London, the largest and most powerful city in the world at that time, and cheaper to reach than America, where many of them dreamed of settling. The area of London outside the old walls of the City already had small Jewish communities and there were a number of synagogues which had been established for many years such as those at Duke's Place, Aldgate and Bevis Marks at the edge of the East End. Although the Jewish community already living there tried to discourage immigration because of the lack of housing and jobs – even advertising in newspapers in Russia and Poland telling Jews not to come – the dire conditions in

Eastern Europe left no choice. However difficult life in the slums of the East End was, it was better than the constant threat to their lives in countries under Russian domination.

The influx was persistent and dramatic – by 1887, Whitechapel was home to 28,000 Jewish immigrants alone, amounting to almost half of the entire population of Jews in the East End. Ten per cent of the total East End population were eastern European, settling into culturally confined 'ghettos' and finding work where they could, mostly in sweated trades like tailoring. But it was not easy, for regular work was already difficult to come by, and the swelling population made unemployment a problem for many. The arrival of the Jewish immigrants caused resentment among the indigenous population and the smaller number of other immigrants who had long ago been assimilated into the fabric of the East End. The Jews, willing to work all hours for poor pay (out of necessity) were blamed for pushing others out of the job market, for aggravating the precarious housing situation and for all the other ills of the area.

For centuries the East End had been a great melting pot, and until this massive flood of immigrants it had dealt well with incomers, but now it was stretched to breaking point, and anyone who could afford to move away did, leaving a population who were, by and large, scraping by. Survival was the key, food and lodging the most important aims. Typhoid, cholera and venereal disease were rife, and the area had the highest birth rate, the highest death rate and the lowest marriage rate in the whole of London.

Housing was the big problem. Whereas parts of Whitechapel and Spitalfields had once been prosperous and semi-rural, demand throughout the early to mid-1800s resulted in gardens being built over to provide accommodation, often only accessible from narrow alleyways and courts. These squalid dead ends were the preserve of the desperately poor and the criminal element, who could use the anonymity of an enclosed passageway to hide from the law. Sanitary facilities were appalling: for example, in one Spitalfields tenement near Brick Lane, sixteen families shared a single outside lavatory which did not seem to be cleaned regularly and which, shockingly, was next to the only source of running water for the inhabitants, a single water tap.

Children were born and brought up here, although 20 per cent of them failed to reach their first birthday. They worked to earn money as soon as they could, sweeping pavements, cleaning windows and scavenging food from the rubbish in the streets, until they were big enough to work in the 'sweaters' (sweat shops) doing tailoring and other work for long hours and very low pay. Some of them formed small bands of skilful pickpockets.

More prosperous Victorians never ventured to the area they nicknamed 'the dustbin'. The writer Jack London called it 'the Abyss'. When he went undercover to write about the poverty of the East End in 1902 he wrote of the filth and vermin, and that when rain fell 'it was more like grease than water.'

A major scourge in the area was the Common Lodging Houses, or 'dosshouses' as they were commonly called, properties owned by private landlords and catering for the transient and the homeless. Spitalfields in particular had a great concentration of such houses and their owners, who lived elsewhere and appointed 'wardens' or 'keepers' to run them, were happy to take money from any available source.

Each lodging house had to be licensed and was subject to

police supervision, and had to display a placard of how many beds were available. Men and women were supposed to be housed separately, paying four pence for a bed in a dormitory, and there were double beds for 'married' couples, in effect a place for prostitutes to take clients, costing eight pence. Some stories suggest that for as little as two pence, the desperate could sit on a bench and sleep upright, supported by a rope stretched across the room in front of them, although this was not part of the official licence. A house, which today would comfortably house a family in four bedrooms, would regularly have more than 50 beds for rent, and larger buildings crammed in as many as 300, with children sneaking in to sleep with their mothers.

Each person rented their bed for one night at a time, and unless they could guarantee their next night's rent there was no provision for them to leave their belongings: men and women put all the clothes they owned on their backs in the morning. Each day was a battle to scrape together the money for a bed. The law said that every bed had to have clean sheets once a week, and that every day the windows would be opened at 10 a.m. to clear the fetid air, but even if the lodging-house keeper stuck to the rules, you can imagine how unpleasant it was by the standards of today.

Food was for sale from the dosshouse wardens, making more profit for the owner, and there were communal cooking facilities in the grubby kitchen, and in the better ones there was a stove or fire for warmth. There were frequent fights and squabbles over food.

The neighbourhood around Commercial Street, which had been built in the 1850s and ran from Whitechapel, through Spitalfields, to Shoreditch, was particularly notorious and names like Thrawl Street, Flower and Dean Street and Dorset Street would become synonymous with the three vs: vice, violence and villainy. There were 700 beds for rent in Dorset Street alone, and 1,150 in Flower and Dean Street. It's hard to imagine today the desperation that the population of these places felt, struggling every day to find the pennies to survive.

The men looked for casual work; many were involved in petty crime and others in serious lawbreaking, attacking passers-by and making the area dangerous after dark. The women tried to eke out a meagre existence on a day-to-day basis, perhaps selling flowers, embroidery, matches or, when things were really harsh, themselves. Without anywhere to take their clients, they would use dark, secluded alleyways and courts, and they charged as little as four pence for their services, the money for a night's sleep. Prostitution was illegal, but the police turned a blind eye, believing that if they routed it out of the East End it would spread into more respectable areas. The women were sitting targets for street robbers and were often victims of violence.

Two of the women whose stories I would come to know well, the Ripper's victims Mary Ann Nichols and Annie Chapman, were effectively sent to their deaths, having been turned away from the dosshouses where they wanted to sleep because they did not have enough money. The punter who went with them into the dark alleys that night should have been their ticket for a night's rest: instead he sent them to a permanent rest, in his own horrific way, leaving his trademark on their malnourished, neglected bodies.

The prostitutes were known collectively as 'the unfortunates', and that's the name I prefer to use, because most of them were not full-time vice workers, they preferred other work, but they were sucked into it when the choice was selling their bodies or starvation and sleeping on the streets. At the time the Ripper struck there were an estimated 1,200 women available for hire in the East End.

As well as the dosshouses, there were rooms to be rented, and here some of the women of the East End managed to keep their children. But most of the unfortunates had lost their families, and at times spoke wistfully of children and husbands. Being abandoned by the men in their lives was a common theme, and frequently the cause of the abandonment was drink: a very large proportion of the women plying their trade in the East End were alcoholics.

So another important feature of the area was the pubs – many of the dosshouse owners, always out to make as much money as they could, ran the pubs as well. Seeing the Ten Bells in the Johnny Depp film jumped out at me: I had passed it many times. Other pubs in the area date back at least as far as the Ten Bells, which is now a trendy haunt for City workers, but even more have been demolished or closed and the building changed to become shops or cafes. There were, in the Ripper's day, literally pubs on every street corner and more in between. Alcohol was as important to the men and women at the very bottom of the poverty ladder as food and lodging. Getting drunk – and alcohol was cheap – was an easy way out of the misery of life, and the pubs were a good source of trade for the prostitutes, who would trawl from one to another looking for punters. We know that at least some of the Ripper's victims had imbibed a plentiful amount of strong liquor before their deaths: I can only hope it helped to anaesthetize them a little from the savage attack he made on them.

*

So what about the victims themselves?

The first two murders in the sequence known as the White-chapel Murders are generally thought not to be the work of Jack the Ripper. For years it has been debated as to whether they are his handiwork, but most experts accept that, in fact, there are five Ripper deaths, and these two are not among them. I, for one, am not convinced: I think the second of the two may be his first killing, even though it does not conform completely to his later pattern. Whoever was responsible for these murders, they were both violent, horrific deaths, and they sparked the fear and hysteria which began to stalk through the East End, meaning that by the time of the five 'official' Ripper deaths the area was on high alert.

They also shone a light on conditions for the very poor in the East End, stirring an underlying concern for the welfare of those who lived below the poverty line and raising urgent questions about what should be done to sort out the problems: perhaps the only good legacy of the Ripper is that a society that had turned a blind eye to the horrors of poverty was forced to confront it.

The victims of these first two murders both lived in the dark heart of the Spitalfields dosshouse district and died close by in mysterious and appalling circumstances. They were typical of the type of women the Ripper would later choose to murder, so their stories are important.

Between 4 and 5 a.m. on the morning of 3 April 1888, the day after a particularly wet and cold bank holiday Monday, Emma Smith stumbled into her lodging house at 18 George Street. She was in a terrible state; her face was bloodied, one of her ears had been torn and was hanging off, and she was suffering excruciating pain from an injury to her abdomen. She had hobbled back with her shawl stuffed between her legs to soak up the blood.

She managed to tell Mary Russell, the deputy of the lodging house, that she had been set upon by a gang of three men who had assaulted her and robbed her of what little money she had. Even though she did not describe her attackers, she did say that one of them looked to be about nineteen years of age. Mrs Russell, together with another lodger, Annie Lee, convinced Emma that she needed to go to the London Hospital on Whitechapel Road. As they made their way there, with the two women supporting Emma, they passed down Brick Lane to Osborn Street. Emma pointed out the spot where the attack occurred, by a cocoa and mustard factory at the corner of Wentworth Street and Brick Lane. It is a junction I had crossed many times as I walked along Brick Lane, oblivious to what had happened there. Then, as now, the spot was hardly secluded: it was at a crossroads and at the time of the assault it would likely have been busy with people returning home after their bank holiday celebrations.

Emma, who was forty-five at the time, must have been a powerfully strong woman to have made it back to the lodging house and then on to the hospital. There she was attended by Dr George Haslip and she told him in more detail what had happened to her. She had been walking by the church of St Mary Matfelon on the Whitechapel Road at about 1.30 a.m. and, seeing a small group of men ahead, had crossed the road to avoid them, probably because they appeared unruly or threatening. Unfortunately, they followed her up Osborn Street, a reasonably spacious thoroughfare that segued into Brick Lane. They attacked her outside the factory. Dr Haslip's examination revealed the horrific extent of Emma's injury to the lower abdomen: a hard instrument, probably a stick, had been thrust into her vagina with such force that it had ruptured the perineum.

Emma's condition worsened, and she eventually lapsed into unconsciousness. There was little the hospital could do and at 9 a.m. the following morning, 4 April, she died, the cause of death being peritonitis, a direct result of that brutal injury.

Three days later, a coroner's inquest was convened, the purpose of the proceedings being to find the cause of death (rather than the identity of the perpetrator). It was here that the last hours of Emma Smith were brought to light. On the evening prior to the attack, the Easter bank holiday Monday, she had left the George Street lodging house at about 6 p.m. which was not unusual, for Emma was a woman of regular habits. At some point she had made her way to Poplar, near the docks, where she was seen on Burdett Road by fellow lodger Margaret Hayes, who was leaving the area after being punched by a man in the street a short while before. It was 12.15 a.m. and Emma was apparently talking to a man of medium height, who was wearing a dark suit and white silk handkerchief round his neck. The next time she was seen was when she arrived at the lodging house in distress. The inquest lasted a day and the coroner recorded a verdict of 'wilful murder against some person unknown'.

The police were not informed of the attack on Emma until the day before the inquest, when there was little hope of finding the perpetrators – some reports suggest this was because Emma herself asked for them not to be told. The official reports into what was obviously now a murder case have since gone missing, but notes were taken from some of them prior to their disappearance, notably by Detective Inspector Edmund Reid of the Metropolitan police's H, or Stepney, Division.

In his notes, Reid recorded some biographical details about Emma Smith; she apparently had a son and daughter living in the Finsbury Park area of north London. She had been lodging at 18 George Street for about eighteen months and was in the habit of going out at around 6 p.m. every night, often returning to the dosshouse very drunk. Newspaper reports at the time stated that when drunk she could sometimes behave like a 'madwoman' and on one occasion came home to the lodging house claiming to have been thrown out of a first-floor window. She often had cuts and bruises from drunken brawls. Although these accounts reveal a belligerent and boisterous character, it is about as much as is known about Emma Smith, apart from the suggestion that she was a widow and that more than likely she was a prostitute. Other women who knew her had the impression she had known better days. Inspector Reid noted that there was a touch of culture in her speech, unusual in her class.

Naturally, the death of Emma Smith was covered by the press, where it was described as the 'horrible affair in Whitechapel' and that Emma had been 'barbarously murdered'. In his summing up at the inquest, even coroner Wynne Baxter was moved to comment that, 'It was impossible to imagine a more brutal and dastardly assault.' However, Emma's attackers were never caught. Her story is a mysterious one, with a number of questions that remain unanswered. Why did it take her so long (about three hours) to travel the 300 yards from the scene of her attack to her lodging house? Why did none of the policemen on the beat in the area see or hear anything about the attack at that time? And why did Emma appear reluctant or unable to describe the men other than mentioning that one was quite young? Was she telling the truth?

One theory is that the men who attacked her worked for her pimp, or that she had failed to pay them protection. Another version is that they were one of the gangs of youths who roamed the East End, always willing to use violence to rob their victims. The gangs were nicknamed 'High Rip' gangs, a name originally adopted by a gang in Liverpool, but which had become common coinage across the whole country. The High Rip gangs were known to use extreme violence for the sake of it, regardless of whether or not they intended to rob their unfortunate victims – but even by their standards, the attack on Emma was particularly vicious.

It has been suggested that the Ripper was part of the gang that carried out the attack, choosing later to work alone, but it is merely supposition unsupported by hard evidence, and it flies in the face of what we know about serial killers, who are almost always loners. The suggestion by some researchers that Emma Smith may have been attacked by the Ripper working alone, and that she used the gang story to deflect attention from the reality that she was soliciting that night, doesn't add up: why, at death's door, would she go out of her way to fabricate a cover story? I'm very keen to stick to the facts and not get involved in wild supposition: I believe that Emma Smith was attacked by a gang of youths, as she claimed, and that this attack had turned into a murder, probably not intended – the use of the stick may have been intended to humiliate her rather than cause death.

Perhaps the answers to all or some of the questions about Emma's murder would be revealed if the original investigation reports were still available. But I believe we know enough about it to discount any involvement of the Ripper.

The next murder, a few months later, is harder to understand, and it is the one I am happy to accept, despite the opinions of many of the Ripperologists, as the first excursion of Jack the Ripper.

Bank holidays were clearly a time when prostitutes could easily find punters from among the large number of men who, enjoying a rare day off from the grind of work, would frequent the pubs and the music halls. Loosened up by alcohol and a sense of freedom, these men could have the pick of the local unfortunates who solicited along the streets, the pubs and the riverside areas of the East End. Criminals also profited by the number of prostitutes around, who offered easy pickings, especially after they had been drinking. The women had to have their wits about them to avoid being robbed of their pennies or ill-used by their clients. It is therefore unsurprising that the next Whitechapel murder took place, like the first, after a bank holiday Monday.

The victim was Martha Tabram, found dead in the early hours of Tuesday, 7 August 1888. Her body was found only thirty seconds walk from where Emma Smith was attacked four months earlier: I know, because I have walked all the sites of the Ripper's crimes and timed all his routes. I have walked them quickly and slowly, and recorded all the possible variations. But this of course came later, when I found out who he was and where he most likely lived . . .

Martha Tabram was thirty-nine years old at the time of her death. She was born Martha White in Southwark in 1849 and she had married Henry Tabram, a foreman furniture packer, in 1869, when she was twenty. He worked steadily and provided for her and their two sons. But after only six years of marriage the couple separated because of Martha's continuous heavy drinking. Henry initially supported his estranged wife financially, and reasonably generously, at twelve shillings a week, but he dropped the amount to two shillings and six pence after she drunkenly accosted him in the street. He stopped supporting her completely when he discovered that she was co-habiting with a carpenter named Henry Turner, a man with whom she lived, on and off, for twelve years. He was described as short, dirty and slovenly in appearance.

To earn their living, Turner and Martha hawked trinkets at the markets and on the streets, and by 1888 they were living in a room in a house at Star Place, Commercial Road. But Martha's drinking affected this relationship too – she was given to fits when very drunk – and sometimes she and Turner would separate, during which time he had no idea how Martha conducted herself. With no other way of supporting her serious drink habit, she probably turned to casual prostitution. In July 1888, the couple parted for the last time. After Turner left her, Martha left the house in Star Place without paying the final rent and took up lodgings in Spitalfields, at 19 George Street, the dosshouse next door to where Emma Smith had been living.

At the time of her murder, Martha was described as plump, 5 foot 3 inches tall with a dark complexion and dark hair. At approximately 4.50 a.m. on 7 August 1888, she was found by

John Reeves, a dock labourer, lying on her back in a pool of her own blood on the first-floor landing of a tenement block where he lived, known as George Yard Buildings. This was in Whitechapel's George Yard, which today is called Gunthorpe Street, and is still one of the narrow cobbled alleyways that survive from the old East End.

When he saw the body, with her skirt pulled up to her waist and her stomach exposed, Reeves ran to find the nearest policeman, who turned out to be PC Thomas Barrett, on duty in Wentworth Street close by. After rushing to the murder scene, PC Barrett immediately sent Reeves to fetch Dr Timothy Killeen from his surgery at 68 Brick Lane. The doctor arrived at 5.30 a.m. and pronounced Martha dead at the scene.

The body was soon taken to the mortuary in Old Montague Street, where a photograph was taken and a post-mortem conducted. In his report, Dr Killeen observed that Martha had received thirty-nine separate stab wounds to various areas of her body, including one to 'the lower part', and apparently there was a great deal of blood between her legs. This three-inch wound was, in all probability, to her genitalia. The lungs were pierced multiple times, as well as her heart, liver, spleen and stomach. Dr Killeen also believed that two different weapons had been used; one was a small pen knife, no bigger than a few inches, which had caused thirty-eight of the wounds, the other weapon was a large knife around six inches long or more, thought to be similar to a bayonet. It was the cause of a single injury which had penetrated the breastbone, and according to Dr Killeen this wound alone was sufficient to kill her.

But there is evidence she may have been strangled before she was slashed, which fits in with the Ripper's pattern. *The*

Illustrated Police News of 18 August 1888 reported that she had received severe injuries to her head, the result of 'being throttled while held down, the face and head so swollen and distorted that her real features are not discernible.' The number of wounds and the savagery of the attack put the case outside the normal run of East End violence, and provoked a growing public alarm.

George Yard Buildings had many residents and it's remarkable that nobody in the tenement heard any cries or commotion during the night, which I believe supports the theory that she was strangled before the stabbing occurred. Significantly, just over an hour before Martha's body was found, a young cab driver named Alfred Crow had climbed the staircase and seen somebody lying on the first-floor landing, but as he was used to seeing people sleeping rough there, he took little notice. The lights inside George Yard Buildings were turned off at 11 p.m., so it was probably not light enough for him to see that Martha Tabram was dead. Earlier, at 2 a.m., she was not there: another couple passed the landing and saw nothing, so the time of her death could be narrowed down to between 2 and 3.30 a.m.

With an obvious murder having been committed, potential witnesses were sought by the police, but the only one who was able to shed any light on the last hours of Martha's life was another 'unfortunate' by the name of Mary Ann Connelly, commonly known as 'Pearly Poll'. After hearing of the murder, she went to Commercial Street Police Station and claimed that she and Martha had spent much of the previous night visiting the pubs of Whitechapel. They had met two soldiers at about 10 p.m., one a corporal and the other a private, in the Two Brewers pub. They continued to drink together in other local pubs including the White Hart, which still thrives today and is a regular point of interest on the Ripper tours.

At approximately 11.45 p.m. the two women and their soldiers split up on Whitechapel High Street. Pearly Poll saw Martha going with the private into George Yard. Pearly Poll went with the corporal into Angel Alley, a few yards away, probably for sex. That is the last she saw of her friend, and is the last confirmed sighting before the murder. Both these passageways were narrow and poorly lit and had mean reputations, making them ideal hiding places for criminals and perfect venues for prostitution. Pearly Poll told the police that she would be able to identify the two soldiers.

Detective Inspector Edmund Reid headed the murder investigation and arranged an identity parade at the Tower of London on the strength of her claims. All the soldiers from the Grenadier Guards regiment who had been on leave that evening were brought for inspection. The parade was attended by PC Barrett, who said that at about 2 a.m. on the morning of the murder he had seen a private of the Grenadier Guards standing at the corner of George Yard and Wentworth Street; when questioned, the soldier said that he was waiting around for his 'chum'. At the parade, Barrett picked out a private before changing his mind and selecting a second man, who, it transpired, had a strong alibi for that fateful night. Pearly Poll failed to turn up.

She was eventually found by Sergeant Eli Caunter staying with a cousin near Drury Lane and so a new parade was arranged for 13 August, which she did finally attend. She failed to pick out the two men that she and Martha were with that evening, but belatedly mentioned that they had had white bands around their caps, meaning they were from the Coldstream Guards, not the Grenadiers.

So another identity parade was arranged, and two days later, Pearly Poll was taken to Wellington Barracks where she picked out two soldiers, known as George and Skipper, whom she said were without doubt the two men that she and Martha had been with. Both the soldiers were interviewed and insisted they were nowhere near the Whitechapel area on the night of the murder. After extensive investigation, the police concluded they were telling the truth. Other soldiers were investigated, having their bayonets checked and their whereabouts on the night of 6/7 August ascertained.

After all reasonable enquiries into the murder of Martha Tabram were exhausted, the investigation appeared to fizzle out. At the inquest, the jury delivered a verdict of 'wilful murder, by person or persons unknown' yet again. The deputy coroner at the inquest said, 'It is one of the most terrible cases that anyone can possibly imagine. The man must have been a perfect savage to have attacked the woman in that way,' and Inspector Reid described the case as 'almost beyond belief'.

The murder of Martha Tabram typified the difficulties that the police at the time faced. Evidence was often built on vague eye-witness statements that could not be confidently corroborated and as a result the police had no further reliable information to go on. Whether the two unidentified soldiers were involved is doubtful, as the murder happened more than two hours after Pearly Poll saw Martha go into George's Yard with one of them. And you have to remember that Pearly Poll, like Martha, had had a great deal to drink that night, which may have compromised her ability to identify them.

The murder of Emma Smith, four months previously,

had obviously stuck in the minds of the local people and the press, and the fact that these two murders were committed within very close proximity, on bank holiday weekends, that they were of the same class and lived in the same disreputable neighbourhood, struck a chord. I am certain that these two murders were not committed by the same person (or persons), but the similarities started the furore that would eventually engulf the East End. Martha's murder, in particular, appeared to be random and savagely brutal and in some ways matched the killings of the later Ripper victims.

Although there was no skilful mutilation as there was in the next five, I believe there were enough common factors for this to have been his first attempt, a 'try-out', probably very hurried as he was testing out how much time he would have to carry out his mission and then escape. Like the others, the death occurred at a secluded spot, in the small hours of the morning, and the victim was an impoverished prostitute. It is probable that among the many wounds inflicted on Martha, at least one was to her genitals. We know today that while serial killers often develop a 'signature' or style of killing as their headcount increases, they do not always display that signature from the word go. So Martha Tabram's murder is definitely more likely to have been one of his than Emma Smith's and, although many experts will disagree, I will stick my neck out and declare that in my opinion she was the first Jack the Ripper victim.

But even if he was not involved, there is a possibility that the publicity surrounding the deaths (and the press coverage was bordering on frenzied) triggered in him a desire to emulate these savage attacks, and launched his grisly career. In the years since I became fascinated by the case, I have acquired various items dating back to 1888, and among these I have the original newspapers covering Martha's death. The *East London Advertiser* reported, 'The virulent savagery of the murder is beyond comprehension.'

Yet in the next five murders, which are definitely accepted as Jack the Ripper's (they are known to experts on the case as 'the canonical five', meaning that they belong together and are the work of one person), this 'virulent savagery' would be a common factor, and the press and the public would find their comprehension stretched even further.

❶ Polly Nichols   ❸ Elizabeth Stride

❷ Annie Chapman   ❹ Catherine Eddowes

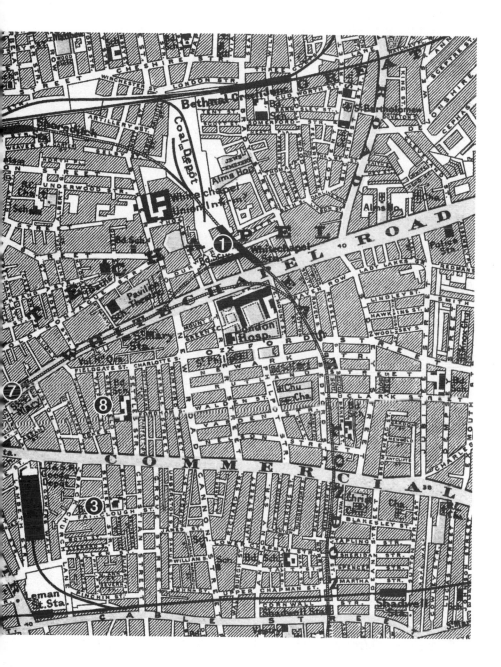

❺ Mary Jane Kelly
❻ Goulston Street, where the
  bloody apron was found

❼ Sion Square
❽ Greenfield Street

CHAPTER THREE

A NAMELESS MIDNIGHT TERROR

*The Deaths of Mary Ann Nichols
and Annie Chapman*

At 3.40 a.m. on the morning of 31 August 1888, Charles Cross walked along Buck's Row, a quiet, dark street behind Whitechapel Underground Station, bordering the Jewish Cemetery. Cross was on his way to work at Pickfords in Broad Street, close to Liverpool Street Station, where he was employed as a carman, transporting goods on the back of a hand-pushed cart. The first glimmers of dawn were lighting up the sky, but Buck's Row, poorly illuminated like many East End streets, was still shrouded in darkness, cut off from the encroaching light by the tall walls of warehouses and terraced dwellings.

As he approached the gates of Brown's Stable Yard, Cross saw what looked like a large piece of tarpaulin on the ground. As he got nearer he realized that it was the body of a woman lying on her back on the pavement. While he was standing near the body, he saw another man walking down Buck's Row, Robert Paul, who was himself on his way to work at Corbett's

Court in Spitalfields and was also a carman. Cross touched Paul on the shoulder as he passed him and asked him to look at what he had found. They both approached the body and saw that the woman's clothes were in disarray and her skirts were pushed up to her middle. Touching her hands they realized that they were not entirely cold, and Paul thought she moved slightly and may be breathing 'but it is very little if she is'.

Not knowing whether she was dead or alive, and worried they were going to be late for work, they made sure her skirts were pulled back down to preserve her modesty and made their way west in the direction of Baker's Row with the intention of alerting the first policeman they found. Charles Cross and Robert Paul walked out of Buck's Row and into the history books, for they had unwittingly discovered the body of Mary Ann Nichols, commonly known as 'Polly', who is widely regarded today as the first victim of Jack the Ripper.

She was born Mary Ann Walker in Fetter Lane, near Fleet Street, in the City of London, in 1845. In 1864 she married a printer, William Nichols, at St Bride's Church. Together they had five children, but the marriage was troubled and in 1880 Mary Ann and William separated for the final time: they had lived apart on five or six previous occasions. He claimed it was due to her drinking, but Mary Ann's father said that William had an affair with the young midwife who attended Mary Ann through the birth of her last child.

Whatever the reason, Mary Ann was left to her own devices while her husband and other close family members looked after the children. William paid her a weekly allowance of five shillings for her subsistence, but after hearing that she had begun earning a living through prostitution around 1882, he stopped the payments. Mary Ann spent the rest of her life in various workhouses and infirmaries – where the 'charitable' regime was brutal, and inmates slept in rat-infested wards and spent the days in cruel manual labour – and in dosshouses, whenever she could afford a bed. She was arrested for vagrancy in Trafalgar Square in 1887, sleeping rough, and went back to the workhouse. In May 1888 things seemed to look up when she spent a brief time in the service of a wealthy family in Wandsworth, but the job ended disastrously when she left unannounced, taking some valuable clothes with her. The couple who employed her were teetotal, and she was an alcoholic: her own father testified at her inquest that she was 'a dissolute character and drunkard whom he knew would come to a bad end'.

Eventually, in the summer of 1888, Mary Ann found her way to the lodging houses of Spitalfields, at first sharing a bed with another prostitute in a dosshouse in Thrawl Street, then moving on to nearby Flower and Dean Street, to a notorious dosshouse called The White House where women were allowed to share beds with men, and then back again to Wilmott's in Thrawl Street, where she was staying on the last day of her life. She was forty-two years old, 5 foot 2 inches tall, with greying brown hair and a number of teeth missing from her upper and lower jaws.

At 11 p.m. on the night of 30 August 1888, a Thursday, she was seen strolling down the Whitechapel Road on her own; at 12.30 a.m. the following morning (31 August), she was seen leaving the Frying Pan public house, at the corner of Thrawl Street and Brick Lane (it's now a restaurant and small hotel). By approximately 1.30 a.m. she had returned to the kitchen of the dosshouse in Thrawl Street somewhat the worse for drink.

Unable to produce four pence for her bed, she was asked to leave, but she confidently told the warden to keep her regular bed for her, as she would soon get her doss money because she was wearing a 'jolly bonnet'. She had on a little black hat that none of the other women there had seen before.

Just under an hour later, she was seen by a friend from the lodging house, Emily Holland, at the corner of Osborn Street and Whitechapel Road; Holland later said that Mary Ann was 'very drunk and staggered against the wall', and that she claimed to have had the money for her bed three times already that day, but had spent it all on drink. Emily tried to persuade her to return to the dosshouse, where they could share a bed, but Mary Ann was confident that one more client would give her the money she needed, and said, 'It won't be long before I'm back.' The couple chatted for several minutes, and Emily remembered the church clock striking 2.30 a.m. before they parted. Mary Ann walked unsteadily eastward along Whitechapel Road. This was the last record of her being seen alive. The route to her death took her from close to the place where Emma Smith was attacked, past the famous Whitechapel Bell Foundry, which started in the reign of Queen Elizabeth I and where the Liberty Bell and Big Ben were both cast, for at least half a mile to Buck's Row, the dingy alley where her body was found.

After discovering Mary Ann's body the two carmen, Cross and Paul found PC Jonas Mizen at the corner of Hanbury Street and Baker's Row and told him about the murder. In the meantime, probably moments after the two carmen had left the scene, PC John Neil was walking along Buck's Row in the direction of Brady Street and he too noticed the body, which had not been there thirty minutes earlier when his beat last took him along the street. He went to investigate, but he could not possibly have prepared himself for what he discovered.

Mary Ann was lying on her back, her head was facing in an easterly direction, and her left hand was near to the stable yard gate. Her eyes were 'wide open and staring', which means she may have died with her killer's face, or at least the outline of his shape, in her sight – a last, terrible vision. Her open hands were palm upwards and her legs were laid out and slightly apart. With the benefit of his policeman's lamp, PC Neil could see that blood was oozing from a gash in the woman's throat. He signalled by flashing his lantern to PC John Thain, a fellow constable he heard passing the end of Buck's Row in the distance, and told him to fetch Dr Rees Ralph Llewellyn who lived nearby at 152 Whitechapel Road.

Having left Charles Cross and Robert Paul, who continued on their way to work, PC Mizen arrived at Buck's Row and was immediately told to fetch the ambulance. Dr Llewellyn quickly arrived at the scene and pronounced Mary Ann dead. Under his orders, her body was taken by ambulance to the mortuary in Old Montague Street for proper inspection and that's when more injuries that had been concealed by her clothing were discovered.

The throat had actually been cut twice, one incision going as deep as the spine. The abdomen had a long, jagged cut which ran from the centre of the bottom of the ribs down to the groin, and there were a number of other cuts and stabs to the lower abdomen. There were two small deep stab wounds to the vagina. There were also two bruises that were noticeable, one on the right lower jaw and the other on the left cheek, like the impression of a thumb print. Dr Llewellyn made the assumption that the murder was carried out by a left-handed person due to the perceived direction of the cut to the throat, but later expressed doubt about this.

Mary Ann's body was soon identified after the words 'Lambeth Workhouse' were found stencilled inside her petticoats. Inquiries at the workhouse brought forward a number of people who could put a name to the murdered woman and eventually William Nichols confirmed the identity of his dead wife. An inquest was convened, observed on behalf of the Metropolitan police by Inspector Joseph Helson, divisional inspector of J Division (Bethnal Green) within whose jurisdiction the body was found. On the second day of the inquest, Helson was joined by a new figure in the story, Inspector Frederick Abberline.

Abberline, who has since become famous for his role in the Ripper case, was brought in because of his great knowledge of the East End. He'd been Inspector of H Division (Stepney) for fourteen years, from 1873 until 1887, when he was transferred to the Commissioner's Office at Scotland Yard, which basically removed him from field-work. He was described as 'portly and gentle speaking', the type of policeman who could easily be mistaken for a bank manager or solicitor. He was very highly regarded, and when somebody with an encyclopaedic knowledge of Whitechapel and the goings-on there was required, Abberline was sent back to his old haunts. Now, he would be in charge of the individual investigations into the murders of the women who would soon be known as the victims of one man.

The day after the murder, 1 September 1888, was also the first day in office for the new Assistant Commissioner of the Metropolitan police, Dr Robert Anderson. Unfortunately,

Anderson, upon starting his new job, immediately left Britain on extended sick leave: it meant that the man who, as head of the CID, would be responsible for overseeing the Whitechapel murder cases was not present as events unfolded through the coming weeks, but he would eventually be privy to all the reports and details of the investigations.

The inquest and press interviews with local residents revealed more about the night of the murder. Mrs Emma Green was a widow who lived at New Cottage with her three children, and even though they lived right next to the murder site, and their bedroom windows were almost directly above where the body of Mary Ann Nichols was found, none of the family were woken in the night by any noise outside. Just opposite was Essex Wharf where Walter Purkiss, the caretaker, was with his wife in the first-floor front bedroom. Again, neither heard any noises from Buck's Row, even though Mrs Purkiss was awake much of the night and was at one point pacing up and down the room suffering with insomnia. The only resident of the street who may have heard anything significant was Harriet Lilley of 7 Buck's Row who had heard a 'painful moan', followed a little later by whispering, which may have been the exchange between the two carmen, Cross and Paul.

All this amounted to very little useful evidence, with potential witnesses generally describing what they did not, rather than what they did, hear. The murder remained a mystery, generating the usual inquest verdict of 'murder against person or persons unknown'. The cause of death was attributed on the death certificate to 'loss of blood from wounds to the neck and abdomen inflicted by some sharp instrument'. But Mary Ann may well have been strangled to the point of unconsciousness, if not death, before she was stabbed: this would explain the lack of noise from her and her bruises. It was clear from the medical evidence of where the blood pooled that she was lying down when her body was slashed.

Mary Ann has earned her place in the annals of crime because she is acknowledged as the first victim of the Ripper, but perhaps a kinder, fairer epitaph would be the comment made at her inquest: that she was very well liked by people she knew, and even her father, who despaired of her drinking, said she had no enemies. It is sometimes hard to remember the victims as human beings, with personalities, friends and relatives, when their lives are subsumed into the greater quest for an answer to this huge mystery. But if they had died like so many women of their class, in the workhouse, their sad lives would be completely forgotten. As it is, because they are Ripper victims, they have achieved a strange immortality.

After Mary Ann's death, links were made between her murder and those of Emma Smith and Martha Tabram. The idea that criminal gangs were responsible for these terrible crimes was diminishing. Even though the police were still looking into the movements of such gangs, the press had other ideas; the *Star*, a popular radical evening newspaper which would later report extensively and sensationally about the Whitechapel murders, claimed quite confidently that this latest murder was 'the third crime of a man who must be a maniac'.

Once again, no culprit was found, but attention began to veer towards the eastern European Jewish immigrants. Not only were they the scapegoat for many of Whitechapel's social problems, they also now became a scapegoat for the murders. Amid this growing suspicion and friction, rumours began to circulate about a Jewish slipper-maker with a reputation for ill-using prostitutes. Known only as 'Leather Apron', because he was supposedly often seen wearing such a garment, his profile began to grow as tale after tale of his sinister behaviour reached the press. The more sensational newspapers, in their turn, began to build him up as something to be feared, a 'noiseless midnight terror' who lurked in the shadows and from whom no woman was safe. Despite the stories, 'Leather Apron' could not be traced.

But fear was beginning to grip the whole area, and when, only nine days later, another body of an unfortunate was found, again with her corpse brutalized, the public, the press and the police all began to speculate about a madman killer on the loose.

It was about 6 a.m. on the morning of Saturday, 8 September 1888, when John Davis, one of seventeen residents of 29 Hanbury Street, Spitalfields, went down the stairs of the house and opened the back door leading to the yard. He noticed that the front door of the house, which led directly to the passageway that went to the yard door, was open, but this was nothing unusual. Nor was it unusual to find drunks sleeping it off in the passageway. He was about to leave for work and was probably going to use the outdoor privy before setting off. As the back door swung open, he was shocked to see the mutilated body of a woman lying at the bottom of the stone steps leading to the back yard. She was lying beside the fence that separated the yards of numbers 27 and 29, with her head almost touching the steps. Her skirts had been pulled right up, revealing a horrendous gash to the abdomen. On one shoulder were pieces of flesh from the belly and over her other shoulder was a pile of intestines. Around her neck was a deep jagged wound that almost severed her head from her body. This latest victim of the Whitechapel horrors was forty-seven-year-old Annie Chapman, known to some as 'Dark Annie', because of her dark hair, or 'Annie Sivvey'.

Annie Chapman was born Annie Eliza Smith in Paddington, London, in 1841. Like the three women who were murdered before her that year (and many of the unfortunates) she had a family – and yet she ended up in the squalid district of Spitalfields where she would ultimately meet her end. Again, like the others, alcohol was a major factor in her descent to the very bottom of the social pile.

Annie married John Chapman, a coachman, in 1869. There is a studio photograph of them, probably at the time of the wedding, looking every inch the respectable, attractive young couple. They had three children, two daughters and a son, who was born a cripple. The elder daughter tragically died from meningitis aged twelve. Owing to John's work, they were provided with simple accommodation by his employers and lived in many affluent parts of west London, as well as Clewer in Windsor; it was while they were here that Annie left the family in around 1885 as a result of her heavy drinking and the behaviour that resulted from it.

It is possible that John was a heavy drinker too, because the ten shillings he paid Annie weekly following their separation stopped when he died of cirrhosis of the liver and dropsy on Christmas Day, 1886. The two surviving children, the boy living in an institution called The Cripples' Home, and a girl who had been well educated (possibly at the expense of John's employer) and was living in France, wanted nothing to do with their mother.

Back in London, Annie was living with a sieve-maker

named John Sivvey, a nickname from his trade, but he left her soon after her husband's death, perhaps because the money dried up. According to one friend, Annie appeared to be very affected by John's death, and 'seemed to have given away all together'.

By the spring of 1888, Annie had begun living at a dosshouse in Dorset Street, Spitalfields, known as Crossingham's, run by a keeper called Tim Donovan. She began a relationship of sorts with a man called Edward Stanley, a bricklayer's mate known as 'The Pensioner', and they often spent weekends together at Crossingham's, their bed paid for by Stanley. He also sometimes paid for her bed there during the week, but told Donovan to kick her out if she ever came back with another man.

Like most of the other unfortunates, Annie tried to make an honest living selling crochet work and flowers, but it rarely paid enough to keep her, and the pub had the first call on any money she made. In the summer of 1888, she bumped into her younger brother, Fountain Smith, and asked for money, but he had given her loans before and now cut her off.

At some time in the first days of September, Annie got into a fight with fellow lodger Eliza Cooper; some accounts say it was over the attentions of Edward Stanley, others say it was over a bar of soap, and the place where the fight took place was variously given as in Crossingham's itself or the Britannia pub at the corner of Dorset Street and Commercial Street. Whatever the case, Annie received several bruises to the chest and a black eye. Her health had been poor all year, and she had been in and out of the infirmary; the injuries would not have made her feel any better. She was clearly unwell when she met a friend, Amelia Palmer, near Christ Church on the evening of 7 September, the night leading up to her death. Annie complained of feeling ill and said she had been to the infirmary where they had given her some pills and a bottle of medicine; she appeared world-weary, but knew what she had to do, saying, 'It's no good my giving way. I must pull myself together and go out and get some money or I shall have no lodgings'. Amelia Palmer gave her the money for a cup of tea, making her promise not to spend it on rum.

Later that evening, Annie was seen in the kitchen at Crossingham's by several people. Some witnesses saw her take out the box of pills which promptly broke and she had to use a scrap of envelope to keep them in. At about 1.35 a.m., the lodging keeper, Donovan, approached Annie for her bed money, but she had nothing to give.

'Don't let the bed, I will be back soon,' she told him.

'You can find money for drink, but not for your bed,' Donovan reproved her.

He watched as she walked up Little Paternoster Row in the direction of Brushfield Street and Spitalfields Market. Annie would never return. The last person to speak to her was the nightwatchman, and she told him she would not be long, and to make sure 'Tim [Donovan] keeps my bed for me.'

For the next three-and-a-half hours, there is no information about Annie. It was cold for the time of year, and the streets were wet with rain, an unpleasant night to be out, especially for someone who was clearly unwell. At 5.30 a.m. a woman was seen talking to a man on the street just a few yards from 29 Hanbury Street, where the body was found, and the witness, Elizabeth Long, was certain the woman was Annie, although she did not know her. She later testified that the couple were talking loudly but seemed to be getting on, and she heard the man ask 'Will you?' and the woman reply 'Yes.'

Mrs Long described the man as of 'shabby-genteel' appearance and said he looked like a 'foreigner', a word that was used in the East End as a euphemism for Jewish. She estimated his age as forty, and said he was wearing a dark overcoat and a deerstalker hat. But he had his back to her, so she got no look at his face.

At about the same time, Albert Cadosch, who lived next door to No. 29, went out to the yard at the back of the house, probably to relieve himself, and heard voices in the adjoining yard. He heard a woman's voice saying 'No!', and then the sound of something falling against the five-foot-high fence which separated the two yards. Like everyone living in the area, Cadosch was used to drunks and prostitutes in the yards, and took little notice. It is more than possible that he heard the murder of Annie Chapman taking place, and had he peered over the fence he may have witnessed it.

Half an hour later, John Davis stumbled on the body. In a state of shock, having glimpsed the horrific injuries, he ran out into Hanbury Street and came across Henry Holland, who was on his way to work. Nearby were two other men, James Green and James Kent, standing outside the Black Swan pub at 23 Hanbury Street, waiting to go to work at the packing case manufacturer's at the rear.

'Men, come here!' Davis shouted. 'Here's a sight, a woman must have been murdered!'

After seeing the body for themselves, the men spread out looking for assistance; at the end of Hanbury Street was Inspector Joseph Chandler who accompanied them back to No. 29. Chandler immediately sealed off the passageway leading from the front of the house to the back yard and sent for police reinforcements and for the divisional surgeon, Dr

George Bagster Phillips, who lived at Spital Square close by.

In his initial examination of Annie's corpse, Dr Phillips noted the obvious injuries to her body, as well as the bruising to her chest and eye from the fight a few days earlier. Removed from, but still attached to her body and placed over her right shoulder, were her small intestines and a flap of her abdomen. Two other portions of the abdomen were placed above her left shoulder in a large quantity of blood. The uterus, the upper part of the vagina and the greater part of the bladder had been removed and were missing.

There were also abrasions on the fingers which indicated that the two brass rings Annie always wore had been forcibly removed. Dr Phillips also noted that despite the massive injuries to her neck and torso, there was not a significant amount of blood loss from the body, and that her tongue was left protruding from her swollen head, indicating that she was strangled before being mutilated.

Dr Phillips said that he himself, a surgeon, could not have carried out such a mutilation in less than a quarter of an hour.

The style of Annie's murder was clearly similar to that of Mary Ann Nichols, eight days before. Dr Phillips did not give too much away at the inquest regarding the injuries to Annie Chapman, but his findings were published in the medical journal the *Lancet* a few weeks later. He stated that the murderer would have had to possess some form of medical or anatomical knowledge: 'Obviously the work was that of an expert – of one, at least, who had such knowledge of anatomical or pathological examinations as to be enabled to secure the pelvic organs with one sweep of a knife.' The autopsy also revealed the reasons for Annie's apparent illness: she was suffering from advanced disease of the lungs which had begun to affect the membranes of the brain; in other words, she was already terminally ill. She would have died soon, just not so gruesomely.

The inquest, as always, generated new information and brought forward more witnesses. A piece of leather apron was found in the back yard, leading to a minor flurry of sensation in that it was somehow linked to the mysterious 'Leather Apron' character. It was soon realized that it had no genuine significance as it was left there by Amelia Richardson, a resident who ran her own packing case business from the house. Testimony from her son, John, was rather more interesting. Being in the habit of checking the security of the cellar doors (in the back yard) following an earlier burglary, John had sat on the steps leading from the back door at 4.45 a.m. that morning and had seen nothing. He also commented that it was already getting light.

One story that appeared in several newspapers claimed that Annie was seen in the Ten Bells pub on Commercial Street between 5 and 5.30 a.m. Some accounts say she was drinking with a man, others that she was alone, and that a man wearing a skull cap and no jacket popped his head in the door and called for her before immediately leaving, at which she followed him out. Apparently the description of the woman tallied with that of Annie Chapman, especially with regard to age, hair and clothing. This story is not reliable, however: there were plenty of other women who fitted the loose description.

At about 7 a.m. that same morning, a Mrs Fiddymont, who ran the Prince Albert Pub on Brushfield Street, said that a man came into the pub and excited quite a bit of suspicion. He was wearing a dark coat and a brown stiff hat which was pulled down over his eyes. He asked for half a pint of 'four ale' and Mrs Fiddymont was immediately struck by the fact that there were blood spots on the back of his right hand, on his collar and below his ear, and that he behaved most suspiciously, as if he didn't want to attract attention to himself. The man drank the beer in one gulp and left in a hurry, at which Mrs Fiddymont's friend, Mary Chappell, followed him into Brushfield Street. She pointed the man out to passer-by Joseph Taylor who followed him in the direction of Bishopsgate before he lost sight of him.

This was the kind of vague testimony the police became used to, as the murders created such a storm of publicity. The killer of Mary Ann Nichols was not caught, and yet another vicious murder involving horrific mutilations created a tidal wave of anger, frustration and sheer panic amongst the East End community. The fact that he had taken Annie through the passageway of a busy house, at a time when at least some of the seventeen lodgers living in the building were likely to be getting up for work, and walked back out the same way, presumably with blood on him and carrying the organs he removed from the body, without being seen, added to the escalating fear and hysteria. Newspaper reports spoke of outbreaks of unrest in the area and innocent men being targeted as 'Leather Apron'. The police had to use precious resources and men just keeping the peace.

Despite their problems, there was a brief glimmer of hope when, on 10 September, Sergeant William Thick went to the Whitechapel home of John Pizer, a Jewish slipper-maker, and arrested him on suspicion of Annie Chapman's murder, and of being 'Leather Apron' himself. Fortunately for Pizer, despite being a person of interest to the police for some time, he could show he was elsewhere when both Mary Ann Nichols and Annie Chapman were murdered. On 31 August, he was in Holloway in north London, staying at a lodging house called Crossman's (just over a century later, in 1989, I moved to Holloway, another of the small ways in which my own story overlaps with the history I have researched). He had even spoken to a policeman regarding the glow from a fire in the London docks that could be seen even from that distance. On 8 September he was at home, kept there by his family who felt, with the rumours flying about that he was 'Leather Apron', it was wise to keep a low profile. With Pizer having cast-iron alibis, there was nothing else of substance for the police to go on, and there was a growing feeling of dissatisfaction with them. The sensational newspapers summed up the situation in outlandish terms, none more so than the *Star*:

> London lies today under the spell of a great terror. A nameless reprobate – half beast, half man – is at large, who is daily gratifying his murderous instincts on the most miserable and defenceless classes of the community . . . Hideous malice, deadly cunning, insatiable thirst for blood – all these are the marks of the mad homicide. The ghoul-like creature who stalks through the streets of London, stalking down his victim like a Pawnee Indian, is simply drunk with blood, and he will have more.

This kind of reporting only created more anger and panic. Accounts of public reaction to Annie Chapman's murder make it sound as if the entire East End of London had taken leave of its senses and was gripped by hysteria. On the morning of the murder, Hanbury Street and the surrounding thorough-fares were crammed with excitable onlookers, some of whom took advantage of the large crowds by selling refreshments.

Perhaps even more macabre was the 'renting' of the windows of those houses which looked down on the back yard of No. 29. Residents made a tidy profit charging one penny a go, so that interested people could look down on the murder site and perhaps catch a glimpse of the bloodstains.

Outbreaks of civil unrest occurred, usually related to sightings of men who appeared suspicious. It did not take much for somebody to be labelled a suspect, and the very word that the murderer had been seen in some part of the district caused lynch mobs to gather to seek out their quarry. One often-quoted story was that a local criminal nicknamed 'Squibby' was being chased by two policemen through Spitalfields on the day of the Annie Chapman murder and, when the gathered masses saw this, they automatically assumed that the officers were chasing the killer and joined in. Apparently 'Squibby' was quite a bullish character and it would often take more than one officer to arrest him, but on this occasion he practically begged them to get him somewhere safe as the mob howled for his blood.

To top it all, a lady called Mary Burridge, living in Blackfriars, after reading one of the typically gruesome newspaper accounts, fell into a fit at her home. She briefly recovered but relapsed and died soon after. It appeared she was effectively frightened to death.

In mid-September, in the absence of Dr Robert Anderson, who was still on sick leave, Chief Inspector Donald Swanson was given the important task of overseeing all information regarding the Whitechapel murders. A well-respected officer, Swanson was authorized by Metropolitan Police Chief Commissioner Charles Warren to be the Commissioner's 'eyes and ears' to be 'acquainted with every detail . . . He must have a room to himself, and every paper, every document, every report, every telegram must pass through his hands. He must be consulted on every source.'

Because of this, the importance of Swanson in this case cannot be overemphasized, and it is fair to say that his knowledge of the crimes exceeded that of any other officer, even though he was not out on the streets involved with fieldwork. Because his was the desk over which crossed the witness statements, the pathology reports and every scrap of suspicion from every officer involved, he was the one to make and veto decisions about all the forensic work. Inspector Abberline, who joined the hunt for the Ripper shortly before, has traditionally been given the honour of being the officer in overall charge of the case; however, that role really fell to Swanson. His experience would lead to his comments about the murders, and even the identity of the killer himself, being taken very seriously in later years. I certainly feel that his words should, and do, carry enormous weight: nobody knew every dimension of the case as well as Swanson.

CHAPTER FOUR

A MURDERER INTERRUPTED

The Death of Elizabeth Stride

The murderer was now developing his ritualistic style: the bodies were being mutilated in specific ways, organs were being taken as souvenirs, there was a heavily sexualized theme to the mutilations. He chose as victims women who were working in the sex trade, and after killing them he viciously lacerated their whole bodies, but particularly their genital and reproductive organs. He struck at night, he struck at seemingly random intervals. It is not surprising that fear and hysteria were escalating – but never enough for some of the unfortunates, the sad women who needed pennies for their bed and to pay for their gin, to stop plying their trade.

Newspapers were full of theories and reports about potential arrests and incidents that were immediately seized upon as being related to the 'Whitechapel monster'. On 27 September 1888, the Central News Agency, a press agency based near Blackfriars Bridge, received a letter, allegedly from the murderer himself and written in red ink.

25 Sept. 1888

Dear Boss

I keep on hearing the police have caught me but they wont fix me just yet. I have laughed when they look so clever and talk about being on the right track. That joke about Leather Apron gave me real fits. I am down on whores and I shant quit ripping them till I do get buckled. Grand work the last job was. I gave the lady no time to squeal. How can they catch me now. I love my work and want to start again. You will soon hear of me with my funny little games. I saved some of the proper red stuff in a ginger beer bottle over the last job to write with but it went thick like glue and I cant use it. Red ink is fit enough I hope ha. ha. The next job I do I shall clip the ladys ears off and send to the police officers just for jolly wouldn't you. Keep this letter back till I do a bit more work, then give it out straight. My knife's so nice and sharp I want to get to work right away if I get a chance. Good Luck.

Yours truly

Jack the Ripper

Dont mind me giving the trade name

Written at right-angles to the main text was a further message, written in pencil:

Wasn't good enough to post this before I got all the red ink off my hands curse it No luck yet. They say I'm a doctor now. ha ha

This was not the first letter claiming to have been written by the murderer, as Commissioner Charles Warren had received one on 24 September from somebody who said he had carried out the attacks, and claiming that he would do some more before giving himself up. It was pretty much ignored, unlike this new letter which Central News sent to the police two days after receiving it, with a covering letter suggesting that it was a hoax. The police, it seems, agreed, but they took some notice of the content, deciding to keep the letter out of the public gaze until the murderer had, as he promised, done 'a bit more work'. That moment was not a long time in coming.

The next murders occurred in the early hours of 30 September 1888, less than three weeks after the brutal death of Annie Chapman. Two prostitutes were killed within an hour of each other and in two different locations; it would later be hailed in Ripper folklore as the 'Double Event'. It is clear, examining the details, that the killer was disturbed at his first attempt to murder, and did not have enough time to ritually mutilate the body and was compelled to strike again: killing alone was not enough. Whatever thrill he got from his handiwork, it did not come at the moment of death, but was associated with what he did to carve up the body.

The first victim that night was Elizabeth Stride, commonly known as 'Long Liz', though how she got her nickname is a mystery as she was not particularly tall. Born Elizabeth Gustafsdottir in 1843 in Stora Tumlehead, on the western coast of Sweden, she had been registered by the police in her home country as a professional prostitute by the age of twenty-two. She was plagued by venereal infections and gave birth to a stillborn daughter in 1865, not long after her mother died. With money she inherited from her mother, she managed to emigrate to London in 1866 and settled in the Whitechapel district. Her troubled life appeared to be on the mend once she married John Stride in 1869 but thanks to her heavy drinking, and her frequent arrests for being drunk and disorderly, the couple separated in 1881. John died three years later of heart disease at the sick asylum in Bromley.

Without the support of her husband, Elizabeth returned to prostitution to support herself. From then on she found it extremely difficult to escape the hard life of an unfortunate, but she was a fantasist who embellished her sad story, probably trying to escape, if only in her boasts, the depths to which she had sunk. She claimed to have worked for a rich family, she said that her husband and two of her nine children had drowned in a famous incident where a ship sank in the River Thames (in fact he died six years later, and they had no children). She lied about her age, saying she was ten years younger than she was, and she was embarrassed about having lost her front teeth, claiming they were knocked out and her palate damaged in the riverboat sinking. The post-mortem showed no damage to her mouth apart from the missing teeth. But I can understand her need to try to build a better past for herself: maybe she even believed some of it herself by the time she had told the lies so often.

Like the other unfortunates, she tried to support herself without patrolling the streets at night looking for clients: she worked as a cleaner and she did some sewing. But, as with so many of the others, there simply wasn't enough work to keep her going, especially with her drink habit. She lived, like almost all of the victims, in the temporary and affordable accommodation of the common lodging houses. She was living in Brick Lane around December 1881, but spent the Christmas and New Year in the Whitechapel Infirmary, suffering with bronchitis. After moving from Brick Lane, Elizabeth lived at a dosshouse at 32 Flower and Dean Street, staying there until 1885, when she met Michael Kidney, a waterside labourer. They moved in together at 38 Devonshire Street, Commercial Road, but their relationship was volatile: they quarrelled often and frequently separated until, on 25 September 1888, Elizabeth left Kidney for the last time and returned to her old lodgings in Flower and Dean Street. In the years 1887 and 1888, she had clocked up eight convictions for drunkenness at Thames Magistrates Court.

On Saturday 29 September 1888, Elizabeth did her regular job of cleaning rooms in the lodging house during the day, earning a small wage. At 6.30 p.m. she was in the Queen's Head pub on the corner of Commercial Street and Fashion Street and shortly afterwards she made her way back to Flower and Dean Street with a friend to get herself ready for the evening ahead. Her subsequent movements were reasonably well documented.

Fellow resident Catherine Lane, a charwoman, stated that she saw Elizabeth between the hours of 7 and 8 p.m. that evening in the lodging house kitchen, wearing a long jacket and black hat and appearing relatively sober. Charles Preston, a barber, stated that he too saw Elizabeth in the kitchen that evening, lending her his clothes brush as she was preparing to go out and wanted to smarten herself up. He described her black jacket as having a fur trim and said there was a coloured, striped silk handkerchief round her neck.

Several hours later, John Gardner and John Best saw Elizabeth leave the Bricklayers Arms in Settles Street shortly before 11 p.m. with a man they described as about 5 foot 5 inches tall, with a black moustache, weak, sandy eyelashes and wearing a morning suit and a billycock (bowler) hat. Gardner and Best, noticing that the couple were sheltering briefly from a sudden downpour, joked to her, 'That's Leather Apron getting round you,' before Elizabeth and the man went off.

Mathew Packer, a fruiterer of 44 Berner Street, said that he sold half a pound of black grapes at about 11 p.m. to a young man about twenty-five to thirty years of age, who was accompanied by a woman dressed in a black frock and a jacket with fur round the bottom and a black crêpe bonnet. She was also wearing a flower in her jacket, resembling a geranium, which was white outside and red inside. The man was about 5 foot 7 inches tall wearing a long black coat which was buttoned up and a soft felt hat described as a kind of 'Yankee' hat. He had broad shoulders and spoke rather quickly in a rough voice. Packer later identified the woman as Elizabeth Stride in St George-in-the-East mortuary, but Packer's evidence was later questioned, and there was no evidence from the contents of her stomach of the dead woman having eaten grapes. All crimes attract 'groupies', people who want to be at the centre of attention, and this is probably all that Packer was. Chief Inspector Swanson wrote in a report that Packer 'made different statements . . . any statement he made would be rendered almost valueless as evidence.'

At 11.45 p.m., William Marshall, a labourer who lived at 64 Berner Street, witnessed a man kissing Elizabeth Stride (he positively identified her in the mortuary) as they were standing near his lodgings. He heard the man say, 'You would say anything but your prayers.' He described the man as middle aged, wearing a round cap with a small peak, about 5 foot 6 inches tall, rather stout in build and decently dressed. As the sighting was an hour before the likely time of the murder, the man he saw is probably an earlier client of Elizabeth's.

At 12.35 a.m. PC William Smith was pounding his beat along Berner Street when he saw a man and a woman standing in the street opposite a narrow passageway known as Dutfield's Yard. The man was about 5 foot 7 inches tall, about twenty-eight years old, with a small dark moustache and a dark complexion. He was wearing a black diagonal cutaway coat, a hard felt hat, a white collar and tie, and was carrying a parcel wrapped up in newspaper about 18 inches long and 6 to 8 inches wide. The woman was wearing a red flower pinned to her jacket, which PC Smith later recognized at the mortuary when he went to view Elizabeth Stride's body.

Another witness, Mrs Fanny Mortimer who lived just a few houses from the murder scene, gave different stories to journalists, but it boiled down to her seeing nothing more than a young couple at the corner of the road, about twenty yards from her.

On the corner of Berner Street and Dutfield's Yard was the International Working Men's Educational Club, a two-storey building which housed a club for Jewish socialists and anarchists, mostly of Russian and Polish origin, and on this evening it had hosted a meeting and lecture about the iniquitous 'sweaters', the sweatshops where the poor were forced to work for very low pay. At the end of the meeting members stayed behind, drinking and singing songs in Russian.

Morris Eagle, a member of the club, walked down Dutfield's Yard at 12.40 a.m., having been away from the premises for just under an hour to take his girlfriend home, and he saw nothing unusual before he went back inside.

Only five minutes later, the most important witness of the night, and in my opinion, the whole case, Israel Schwartz, witnessed what I believe is the only definite sighting of the Ripper. Very little is known about Schwartz other than that he was a Hungarian who spoke hardly any English and who had 'the appearance of being in the theatrical line'. He was certainly married by this time as it was stated that he and his wife had moved from their lodgings in Berner Street to a new address in Helen Street, near Backchurch Lane, on the day of the incident.

Schwartz was on his way to his new home and was walking towards the gateway of Dutfield's Yard at about 12.45 a.m. The report of what he saw was written down in a statement taken by Chief Inspector Donald Swanson, and I'm reproducing it here in full because it is so vital:

12.45 a.m. 30th Israel Schwartz of 22 Helen Street, Backchurch Lane, stated that at this hour, on turning into Berner Street from Commercial Road and having got as far as the gateway where the murder was committed, he saw a man stop and speak to a woman who was standing in the gateway. The man tried to pull the woman into the street, but he turned her round and threw her down on the footway and the woman screamed three times, but not loudly. On crossing to the opposite side of the street he saw a second man standing lighting his pipe. The man who threw the woman down called out, apparently to the man on the opposite side of the road 'Lipski', and then Schwartz walked away, but finding that he was followed by the second man he ran so far as the railway arch, but the man did not follow so far.

Schwartz cannot say whether the two men were together or known to each other. Upon being taken to the mortuary Schwartz identified the body as that of the woman he had seen. He thus describes the first man who threw the woman down :– age, about 30; ht 5ft 5in; comp. [complexion], fair; hair, dark; small brown moustache; full face; broad shouldered; dress, dark jacket and trousers, black cap with peak, and nothing in his hands.

He then went on to describe the second man as 5 foot 11 inches, thirty-five years old, with a fresh complexion, light brown hair and a brown moustache. He wore a dark overcoat and an old black hard felt hat with a wide brim.

According to Inspector Abberline, 'Lipski' had become an abusive term for the Jews in that part of London since the arrest of Israel Lipski the previous year. Lipski, who was of Polish–Jewish descent, had been accused of murdering Miriam Angel in nearby Batty Street, having forced her to drink nitric acid. Lipski was found under her bed with acid burns in his mouth and was arrested, brought to trial, found guilty and hanged, despite his protestations of innocence.

At first the police hoped that 'Lipski' was the name of the second man, so that he could be traced and questioned, but this was fruitless and they accepted that it was an insult, possibly aimed at Schwartz because of his Jewish appearance.

The *Star* was the only newspaper to cover Schwartz's story in any depth, on 1 October. There are discrepancies between the police account and the one the newspaper published, perhaps because of some over-enthusiastic journalism (all newspapers wanted to sensationalize the murders as much as possible) but also possibly because of Schwartz's poor English, which necessitated the use of a translator. Because I believe Schwartz is so important to this case, I think it's important to reproduce the full article:

Information which may be important was given to the Leman Street police yesterday by an Hungarian concerning this murder. The foreigner was well-dressed and had the appearance of being in the theatrical line. He could not speak a word of English, but came to the police station accompanied by a friend, who acted as interpreter. He gave his name and address but the police have not disclosed them. A *Star* man, however, got wind of his call and ran him to earth in Backchurch Lane. The reporter's Hungarian was quite as imperfect as the foreigner's English, but an interpreter was at hand and the man's story was retold just as he had given it to the police. It is, in fact, to the effect that he saw the whole thing.

It seems that he had gone out for the day and his wife had expected to move, during his absence, from their lodgings in Berner Street to others in Backchurch Lane. When he first came homewards about a quarter to one he first walked down Berner Street to see if his wife had moved. As he turned the corner into Commercial Road he noticed some distance in front of him a man walking as if partially intoxicated. He walked on behind him, and presently he noticed a woman standing in the entrance to the alleyway where the body was found. The half-tipsy man halted and spoke to her. The Hungarian saw him put his hand on her shoulder and push her back into the passage, but feeling rather timid of getting involved in quarrels he crossed to the other side of the street. Before he had gone many yards, however, he heard the sound of a quarrel and turned back to learn what was the matter, but just as he stepped from the kerb a second man came out of the doorway of a public house a few doors off, and shouting some sort of warning to the man who was with the woman, rushed forward as if to attack the intruder. The Hungarian states positively that he saw a knife in the second man's hand, but he waited to see no more. He fled incontinently to his new lodgings.

He described the man with the woman as about 30 years of age, rather stoutly built, and wearing a brown moustache. He was dressed respectably in dark clothes and felt hat. The man who came at him with the knife he also describes, but not in detail. He says he was taller than the other but not so stout, and that his moustaches were red. Both men seemed to belong to the same grade of society. The police have arrested one man answering the description the Hungarian furnishes. The prisoner has not been charged, but is held for inquiries to be made. The truth of the man's statement is not wholly accepted.

The substantive differences between the two versions of Schwartz's testimony are the intoxication of the first man; the fact he tries to push Elizabeth Stride into the passage, not pull her into the road; that in the *Star* version it is the second man who calls out the warning; and the second man has a knife not a pipe. As the police presumably took more care to write down their statement than the reporter did, it is their version that is most widely accepted. Whatever the differences, the main story remains the same, and Schwartz was considered then, and now, a very important witness. Sadly, the second man did not come forward as a witness to corroborate, or contradict, Schwartz's version of events.

Elizabeth Stride's body was discovered at 1 a.m., when Louis Diemschutz returned with his horse and cart to the International Working Men's Educational Club, where he lived. He had been working that day at Westow Hill market, in Crystal Palace, where he sold costume jewellery from his barrow. He was also the steward of the club which he ran with his wife. As he turned into the gateway of Dutfield's Yard, his horse shied to the left, causing Diemschutz to glance down at the ground next to the club wall to see what was spooking the horse. Realizing that there was something there, he got off his cart, prodded the shape with his whip and struck a match to give him light to see by. The wind instantly snuffed out the match, so he ran upstairs into the club to fetch a candle, as he had glimpsed what he thought was a drunken woman lying on the ground.

Diemschutz told his wife and a few club members that there was a woman lying in the yard and that he was 'unable to say whether she was drunk or dead'. He grabbed a candle and went back downstairs, with one of the club members. As they approached the body they could see blood, a large pool on the cobbles next to the body, which had a deep wound in the neck. Diemschutz let out a cry which brought more members from the club upstairs, including his wife who screamed when she saw the blood and the woman's 'ghastly face'.

The men ran out shouting 'Police!' as they went. Morris Eagle managed to find two police constables, Henry Lamb and Edward Collins, in Commercial Road. When they got back to Dutfield's Yard they saw a crowd of people already gathering at the gateway into the yard. PC Lamb managed to keep them back, telling them that if they got blood on their clothes then they would only attract trouble for themselves.

He shone his lantern on the body, and touched the woman's face; it was still slightly warm. He could see that the blood by the body was still in a liquid state but when he felt for a pulse he found nothing. PC Collins went for Dr Frederick Blackwell, who lived in Commercial Road, but as Dr Blackwell was not dressed, his assistant Edward Johnston went on ahead of him. He stated that the body was warm when he arrived – except for the hands which were quite cold – and that the blood had stopped flowing from the neck wound.

Dr Blackwell arrived at 1.16 a.m., according to his pocket watch. He reported that:

The deceased was lying on her left side obliquely across the passage, her face looking towards the right wall. Her legs were drawn up, her feet close against the wall of the right side of the passage. Her head was resting beyond the carriage-wheel rut, the neck lying over the rut. Her feet were three yards from the gateway. Her dress was unfastened at the neck. The neck and chest were quite warm, as were also the legs, and the face was slightly warm. The hands were cold. The right hand was open and on the chest, and was smeared with blood. The left hand, lying on the ground, was partially closed, and contained a small packet of cachous wrapped in tissue paper. There were no rings, nor marks of rings, on her hands. The appearance of the face was quite placid. The mouth was slightly open. The deceased had round her neck a check silk scarf, the bow of which was turned to the left and pulled very tight. In the neck there was a long incision which exactly corresponded with the lower border of the scarf. The border was slightly frayed, as if by a sharp knife. The incision in the neck commenced on the left side, 2 ½ inches below the angle of the jaw, and almost in a direct line with it, nearly severing the vessels on that side, cutting the windpipe completely in two, and terminating on the opposite side 1 ½ inches below the angle of the right jaw, but without severing the vessels on that side. I could not ascertain whether the bloody hand had been moved. The blood was running down the gutter into the drain in the opposite direction of the feet. There was about 1lb. of clotted blood close by the body, and a stream all the way from there to the back door of the club.

Dr George Bagster Phillips was also sent for and arrived on the scene at approximately 2 a.m. He agreed with Dr Blackwell's account. At 4.30 a.m., amid growing excitement in the area, the body of Elizabeth Stride was taken to the small St George-in-the-East mortuary. At the time of her death she was described as being about forty-two years old, 5 foot 2 inches in height, with dark-brown curly hair and a pale complexion, with light grey eyes. She was wearing a long black jacket trimmed with black fur which she had on when she left her lodgings, an old skirt, a dark-brown velvet bodice, two light serge petticoats, a white chemise, a pair of white stockings, a pair of side-spring boots and a black crêpe bonnet.

At the inquest the cause of Elizabeth Stride's death was given as 'loss of blood from the left carotid artery and the division of the windpipe'. In other words, she died when the Ripper slashed her throat. Some experts believe that she actually had a heart attack before the throat slashing, because she was, according to Dr Blackwell 'pulled backwards' by her silk scarf, and the pressure on her throat could have caused a reflex cardiac arrest. Whichever version is correct, she died quickly.

Israel Schwartz's account of the attack on the woman he later identified as being Elizabeth Stride, and his description of the man attacking her only fifteen minutes before she was found dead, was an important lead. Coupled with Dr Blackwell's opinion that death occurred between 12.46 a.m. and 12.56 a.m., it is highly probable that Schwartz saw the man who killed her. It was also widely felt that, because Stride's body exhibited none of the abdominal mutilations evident in the previous cases, the murderer may well have been disturbed by the arrival of Louis Diemschutz on his pony and cart and either he left before Diemschutz got close enough to see the entrance or, more likely I believe, he had hidden in the shadows of the yard, escaping during those brief moments when Diemschutz first went into the club. If Diemschutz had locked the gate, the Ripper's reign could have been over.

Another element of Israel Schwartz's statement that is interesting is that he said the would-be attacker called out, 'Lipski!' Israel Schwartz was described in the press as 'Semitic' in appearance, leading to the possibility that the man's outburst was aimed at him. Interestingly, Chief Inspector Donald Swanson, in whose hand Schwartz's statement is written, made a note on the statement to the effect that he believed that the use of this word suggested that Stride's *attacker* was Jewish, although it's hard to see why he would shout out an insult to himself, unless he is referring to himself as a Jewish man, and perhaps appealing to someone he assumed is also Jewish to ignore the attack. It does not seem rational, but 'rational' is hardly a word to apply to a crazed and sadistic killer.

What is unusual about Israel Schwartz as a witness is that he did not appear to have been called to the inquest to give his evidence, possibly because he spoke poor English. Matthew Packer, the fruiterer who claimed to have sold grapes to Stride and a man shortly before the murder, was not called because his evidence was unreliable. Schwartz, however, had an important story to tell and regardless of how it was covered, his claims would have considerable influence on the hunt for the Ripper in years to come, and could have ironed out the differences between the official statement and the newspaper account. It could be that the police did not call him because he was the only witness who appeared to have witnessed an actual attack on a victim. They may have taken his statement privately, to avoid the description of the man he saw being published in all the press reports of the inquest. (The detectives were constantly battling the red herrings the press threw into their investigations.) It is also possible that he refused to testify because he was Jewish, a theory I will come back to later.

Because there are more witnesses, or potential witnesses, to this killing than to any of the other Ripper murders, the fate of Elizabeth Stride has been the most debated part of the whole case over the years: it is one of the few attacks that yields possibly vital clues. Until I found my proof, which is in a different league from the speculation that has been all we have had until now, it was widely believed to be the murder that would most likely be the key to solving the mystery. I believe that, in Israel Schwartz, we come the nearest to a true account of events just before the unfortunate Elizabeth met her death, and we have no comparable evidence from any of the other killings. Israel Schwartz is an important plank in my case, but, thankfully, only a plank: the substance of the structure is incontrovertible science.

But that night, 30 September 1888, would see a second murder, so far the most violent in the series. It seems that the arrival of Louis Diemschutz stopped the Whitechapel murderer in the act and left him frustrated and unfulfilled, having not had the chance to carry out his ritualistic mutilations, driving him to kill again with renewed ferocity within three quarters of an hour.

CHAPTER FIVE

FROM HELL

The Death of Catherine Eddowes

At about the same time that Elizabeth Stride's body was discovered in Berner Street, forty-six-year-old Catherine Eddowes was being released from Bishopsgate Police Station in the City of London. At 8.30 p.m. that night she had been found slumped in front of 29 Aldgate High Street in a very drunken, but still conscious, state. A small crowd had assembled around her which attracted the attention of City PC Louis Robinson. In vain, he tried to prop Catherine up against the front of No. 29, but she immediately slumped back down again. When he asked her name, she replied 'nothing'. PC Robinson was soon joined by PC George Simmons and together they lifted Catherine and escorted her, perhaps with some difficulty, to Bishopsgate Police Station.

At the station, Sergeant James Byfield, who was on desk duty that night, booked Catherine in and she was taken to a cell to sleep off her drunken stupor. Throughout the evening PC George Hutt made regular checks on the cell and at 12.55 a.m., after hearing Catherine singing quietly to herself, he checked one last time. He felt that she was now sober enough to be released. Before leaving, she was asked her name and said that she was 'Mary Ann Kelly' and that she lived at 6 Fashion Street. It is strange that she chose as her alias a name so similar to two of the other victims, Mary Jane Kelly and Mary Ann Nichols. She also asked the time, at which PC Hutt told her that it was too late to get any more drink. Catherine muttered that she would get 'a damn fine hiding' when she got home and PC Hutt responded with something resembling a reprimand: 'And serve you right, you have no right to get drunk.'

By the time she was released into the street it was 1 a.m.; PC Hutt asked Catherine to pull the door to on her way out. As she did so she said, 'Good night, old cock,' and he saw her turn in the direction of Houndsditch. Forty-five minutes later, she was dead, the next victim of Jack the Ripper.

The murder of Catherine Eddowes, the most violent yet in the series, provides the key to the entire story set out in this book, so I'm going to look at her life and the events leading to her death in detail.

She was born on 14 April 1842 in Graisely Green, Wolverhampton, to George Eddowes, a tin-plate worker, and his wife Catherine, the sixth child of twelve. By the time she was two years old, the family had made the big decision to move to London, probably walking all the way, and settled in Bermondsey, one of several impoverished neighbourhoods south of the river Thames. Catherine was educated at St John's Charity School but tragedy soon struck when her mother died in 1855, when she was thirteen, followed by her father two years later. The children, now orphans, went their separate ways, many going to the Bermondsey Workhouse, but Catherine returned to Wolverhampton and stayed with an aunt, finding employment as a tin-plate stamper, a job she may have obtained through family connections.

By the early 1860s, she began a relationship with a man named Thomas Conway who drew a pension from the 18th Royal Irish Regiment. Together they eked out a living around the Midlands, often selling cheap 'chap-books' written by Conway, the content of which usually consisted of little histories, nursery rhymes or accounts of current events. One of their books was a ballad commemorating the execution of Catherine's cousin, Christopher Robinson, which was sold among the crowds gathered for his hanging for murder.

In 1863, Thomas and Catherine's first child, Catherine Anne (or 'Annie') Conway was born in Norfolk where Thomas was employed as a labourer. By 1868, the family had moved to London, taking lodgings in Westminster. By this time Catherine was using the surname Conway, a common enough thing to do when a couple were living as man and wife – she even had Thomas's initials crudely tattooed on her arm – but there is no record that they ever married. It was at Westminster that their second child, Thomas, was born. Continually on the move, the Conways moved to Southwark where their last child, Alfred, was born in 1873.

By now, things were not going too well and Catherine's growing taste for alcohol had become an issue, as had Thomas's occasionally violent behaviour towards her. At Christmas 1877, Catherine's older sister Emma met her for the last time and noted that she was sporting a black eye. With domestic problems mounting, the inevitable happened and Catherine separated from Thomas in 1881. Her daughter Annie had already left home, and the two boys stayed with their father.

Another older sister of Catherine's, Eliza, lived in Spitalfields and Catherine followed her there, settling in the common lodging house at 55 Flower and Dean Street, where she began a relationship with a labourer named John Kelly. They were to remain as a couple at the lodging house for the rest of her life. Soon after, Catherine became a grandmother when her daughter Annie gave birth to a son, Louis. But although she lived not too far away in Bermondsey, Annie's relationship with her parents was fraught. Thomas had come to stay with her at one time and had left on bad terms, and Catherine's regular visits to borrow money resulted in Annie and her family moving house without telling her mother of the new address.

During September 1888, Catherine and John Kelly, now an established couple, decided to go 'hopping', a popular escape from the grime of the city. Every year many families from the poorer districts of London would go to Kent to pick hops, earning some money with the seasonal work and at the same time benefitting from the cleaner air of the countryside. Unfortunately, bad weather that summer resulted in a poor crop and soon the couple, along with many others in the same situation, were forced to make the long walk back from Kent to London, penniless. As Catherine and John did so, they struck up a friendship with a Mrs Emily Burrell and her partner, who were on their way to Cheltenham. Mrs Burrell gave Catherine a pawn ticket for a man's shirt which was no use to them as they were not going to London.

When they reached the city on 27 September, weary and footsore, Catherine and John went their separate ways for the night: John stayed at 52 Flower and Dean Street and Catherine went to Shoe Lane, in the City of London, to stay at the casual ward there, where the homeless were allowed brief accommodation, usually for one night only. They only had four pence between them, and that paid for John's bed. When she left the ward the following morning, she told others there that she had returned to London 'to earn the reward offered for the apprehension of the Whitechapel Murderer. I think I know him.' The superintendent of the ward warned her not to get herself killed, to which she replied: 'Oh, no fear of that.'

On the morning of 29 September, Catherine and John reunited and went to Jones's pawnbrokers near Christ Church Spitalfields to pawn a pair of John's boots; with the two shillings and six pence they received, they bought some provisions and had breakfast in the kitchen at 55 Flower and Dean Street. The last time the couple were together was at about 2 p.m. in Houndsditch, by which time they appeared to be penniless again. John said he would find some casual work somewhere and Catherine said she would cross the river to see her daughter at an address in Bermondsey (which she did not know her daughter had left) and get some money from her. She never made it to Annie's, but by 8.30 p.m. she had managed to get herself extremely drunk – where the money came from to pay for this is not clear, but prostitution could well have been one option, despite John Kelly later saying that he was not aware of Catherine ever having earned money through 'immoral purposes'. And so Catherine Eddowes was found slumped, drunk, in a doorway in Aldgate High Street, arrested and placed in the cells at Bishopsgate Police Station.

Her release at 1 a.m. the following morning was charged with a tragic serendipity: being in the custody of the City police, she was allowed to go once she was deemed sober enough to look after herself, which was the City police policy. Had she been found drunk a short distance further east, she would probably have been spotted by a Metropolitan police officer and taken to Leman Street or Commercial Street police stations. It was Metropolitan police policy to hold drunks until the following morning – in which case Catherine would not have encountered the Whitechapel murderer.

It is an historical anomaly that the City of London has its own force within the boundaries of the Met police. It goes back centuries, when the city, the heart of London, had the first paid law men. When the Met was founded in 1829 Sir Robert Peel tried to take over the city area, but the City Corporation resisted, and despite another attempt ten years later, the City police was given statutory power to remain an independent force, as it is to this day.

It was Catherine's bad luck that she was found drunk in the city area, and forty-five minutes after her release, her brutally mutilated body was found in Mitre Square by City PC Edward Watkins. Mitre Square was a small enclosure mostly surrounded by warehouses, except for two houses (one occupied, one empty) and the backs of properties on Mitre Street. There were three entrances, one from Mitre Street, another from St James's Place (now called Mitre Court) and Church Passage, which ran from Duke Street. PC Watkins's beat usually took fifteen minutes to cover and that night he was working 'left handed', which means he was walking his beat in reverse, a common enough ploy used by patrolling officers to confuse any potential wrongdoer who had become accustomed to the route of the beat. When he passed through Mitre Square at 1.30 a.m. there was nothing out of the ordinary to be seen and he continued on his way. Yet at 1.44 a.m. he returned to the square and, turning to the dark, south-west corner, he saw a body lying on the pavement. As he shone his lantern across the body, he could see that the woman had been killed and her body mutilated. He later told a reporter from the *Daily News* that:

> . . . her clothes were right up to her breast and the stomach was laid bare, with a dreadful gash from the pit of the stomach to the breast. On examining the body, I found the entrails cut out and laid round the throat, which had an awful gash in it, extending from ear to ear. In fact, the head was nearly severed from the body. Blood was everywhere to be seen. It was difficult to discern the injuries to the face for the quantity of blood which covered it. The murderer had inserted the knife just under the nose, cut the nose completely from the face, at the same time inflicting a dreadful gash down the right cheek to the angle of the jawbone. The nose was laid over on the cheek. A more dreadful sight I never saw; it quite knocked me over.

Watkins immediately ran the eighty yards or so across the square to the large Kearley and Tonge warehouse to seek help from the nightwatchman there, George Morris, who happened to be a retired Metropolitan policeman. After seeing for himself the gruesome sight splayed across the pavement, Morris left Watkins with the body, raced out of the square, through Mitre Street and into Aldgate, all the while blowing his old policeman's whistle: City police officers were not issued with whistles at that time.

He managed to find PCs James Harvey and James Holland and they all ran back to Mitre Square. PC Holland was promptly dispatched to nearby Jewry Street to fetch Dr George Sequeira, who arrived at the scene at 1.55 a.m. At the same time,

Inspector Edward Collard at Bishopsgate Police Station heard news of the murder and left for Mitre Square, after sending a constable to fetch Dr Frederick Gordon Brown, the City police surgeon, who lived at Finsbury Circus. Arriving at the scene at approximately 2.18 a.m., Dr Brown noted that several policemen were there along with Dr Sequeira, but nobody had yet touched the body.

According to Dr Brown's report:

The body was on its back, the head turned towards the left shoulder, the arms were by the side of the body, as if they had fallen there. Both palms were upwards and the fingers were slightly bent. A thimble was lying in the ground near the right hand, the clothes were drawn up above the abdomen, the left leg was extended straight down, in a line with the body, and the right leg was bent at the thigh and knee, there was great disfigurement to the face, the throat cut across, below the cut was a neckerchief, the upper part of the dress was pulled open a little way, the abdomen was all exposed, the intestines were drawn out to a large extent and placed over the right shoulder, they were smeared over with some feculent matter, a piece of about 2 feet was quite detached from the body and placed between the body and the left arm, apparently by design, the lobe and the auricle of the right ear was cut obliquely through, there was a quantity of clotted blood on the pavement on the left side of the neck, round the shoulder and upper part of the arm, and fluid blood coloured serum which had flowed under the neck to the right shoulder, the pavement sloping in that direction, the body was quite warm, no death stiffening had taken place, she must have been dead most likely within the half hour, we looked for superficial bruises and saw none, no blood on the skin of the abdomen or secretion of any kind on the thighs, no spurting of blood on the bricks or pavement around, no marks of blood below the middle of the body, several buttons were found in the clotted blood after the body was removed, there was no blood on the front of the clothes, there were no traces of recent connection [meaning sexual intercourse].

Dr Brown stated that the cause of death was 'haemorrhage from the left carotid artery. Death was immediate and the mutilations were inflicted after death.' It is the same cause of death as given for Elizabeth Stride, so soon before, which confirms that the Ripper was about to start mutilating Elizabeth when he was disturbed, then felt compelled to strike again.

A pencil sketch of the crime scene, with the body *in situ*, was also made before Catherine Eddowes was taken to the mortuary in Golden Lane. The face had been horrifically mutilated; a piece of her ear dropped from her clothing when she was undressed at the mortuary, her nose had been cut off and two inverted 'V' cuts were evident under each eye. As if this was not enough, it was found that her left kidney and her womb were missing. Dr Brown later commented that someone who knew the position of the kidney must have done it. He stated that the killer must have possessed 'a good deal of knowledge as to the position of the organs in the abdominal cavity and the way of removing them'.

A comprehensive list of Catherine's clothing and belongings found on her person was made at the mortuary by a police inspector. Because she was homeless, she was wearing everything she owned and carrying all her belongings. As well as everything listed here, Dr Brown also noted in his report on her body that nearby was a mustard tin containing two pawn tickets: one for John Kelly's shoes, the other the one she had been given as they walked back from hop picking. This is the list:

- Black Straw Bonnet trimmed with green & black Velvet and black beads, black strings. The bonnet was loosely tied, and had partially fallen from the back of the head, no blood on front, but the back was lying in a pool of blood, which had run from the neck.
- Black Cloth Jacket, imitation fur edging round collar, fur round sleeves, no blood on front outside, large quantity of blood inside and outside back, outside back very dirty with blood and dirt, 2 outside pockets, trimmed black silk braid & imitation fur.
- Chintz Skirt, 3 flounces, brown button on waistband. Jagged cut 6 ½ inches long from waistband, left side of front. Edges slightly Bloodstained, also Blood on bottom, back & front of skirt.
- Brown Linsey Dress Bodice, black velvet collar, brown metal buttons down front, blood inside & outside back of neck & shoulders, clean cut bottom of left side, 5 inches long from right to left.
- Grey Stuff Petticoat, white waist band, cut 1 ½ inches long, thereon in front. Edges blood stained, blood stains on front at bottom of petticoat.
- Very Old Green Alpaca Skirt. Jagged cut 10 ½ inches long in front of waistband downwards, blood stained inside, front under cut.
- Very Old ragged Blue Skirt, red flounce, light twill lining, jagged cut 10 ½ inches long, through waist band, down-ward, blood stained, inside and outside, back and front.

- White Calico Chemise, very much blood stained all over, apparently torn thus in middle of front.
- Mans White Vest, button to match down front, 2 outside pockets, torn at back, very much blood stained at back, Blood & other stains on front.
- No Drawers or Stays.
- Pair of Mens lace up Boots, mohair laces. Right boot has been repaired with red thread, 6 blood marks on right boot.
- 1 piece of red gauze Silk, various cuts thereon found on neck.
- 1 large White Handkerchief, blood stained.
- 2 Unbleached Calico Pockets, tape strings, cut through also top left hand corners, cut off one.
- 1 Blue Stripe Bed ticking Pocket, waist band, and strings cut through, (all 3 pockets) blood stained.
- 1 White Cotton Pocket Handkerchief, red and white birds eye border.
- 1 pr. Brown ribbed Stockings, feet mended with white.
- 12 pieces of white Rag, some slightly bloodstained.
- 1 piece of white Coarse Linen.
- 1 piece of Blue & White Shining (3 cornered).
- 2 Small Blue Bed ticking Bags.
- 2 Short Clay Pipes (black).
- 1 Tin Box containing Tea.
- 1 do. do. do. [ditto] Sugar.
- 1 Piece of Flannel & 6 pieces of soap.
- 1 Small Tooth Comb.
- 1 White Handle Table Knife & 1 metal Tea Spoon.
- 1 Red Leather Cigarette Case, white metal fittings.
- 1 Tin Match Box, empty.
- 1 piece of Red Flannel containing Pins & Needles.
- 1 Ball of Hemp.
- 1 piece of old White Apron.

Unlike the police list, a press report in the *East London Observer* said, 'Her dress was made of green chintz, the pattern consisting of Michaelmas daisies.' This description was repeated by other periodicals and newspapers at the time. This is a vital piece of information, and it is on this item of clothing that my whole investigation into the identity of Jack the Ripper rests. So why was it not on the police list of her belongings? As I found out, and as I am going to show you later, while the body was being transported to the mortuary, Acting Sergeant Amos Simpson who was accompanying it, asked another, more senior officer if he could have this piece of clothing, which was in fact a shawl not a skirt. He wanted it for his wife, because the silk was clearly of good quality, and he thought she might be able to use it for her dressmaking.

By today's standards of policing, it was shoddy to remove a possible piece of evidence. But in those days, there was no importance attached to the belongings of a victim because without the benefit of the modern forensic tests we can carry out today, they added nothing to the investigation. In terms of solving these crimes, well over a century later, it was the best possible thing to happen. If the shawl had gone with the rest of Catherine's possessions, it would have been destroyed with so much other evidence. I will always be hugely grateful to PC Simpson for taking it, and to his descendants for keeping it safe. My investigation has taken a great deal of hard work and patience, but it has also been blessed by some luck: this single fact, the careful preservation of a shawl that was at the scene of one of the killings, must rank as the greatest luck of all.

We can only assume the press included this description of the chintz dress or skirt with the border of Michaelmas daisies in their reports because a journalist was either present at the scene and glimpsed the material (and despite the best efforts of the police, crime scenes were not kept secure as they are today), or that they talked to policemen who were there and who again mistook the distinctively patterned shawl for a skirt or dress.

The 'old white apron' was also described as being extremely dirty and a section of it was missing. This missing piece was found at 2.55 a.m., by PC Alfred Long, lying in the open doorway leading to the staircase of 108–19 Wentworth Model Dwellings, less than a quarter of a mile away in Goulston Street, back over in Whitechapel. The piece of apron was bloodstained. As PC Long checked for any other signs of blood in the immediate area, he saw writing in chalk on the wall directly above where the apron piece had lain. It read: 'The Juwes are the men that will not be blamed for nothing'.

After searching the staircase and finding nothing else of any significance, he found another officer to guard the writing and headed, with the bloodied piece of apron, for Commercial Street Police Station, arriving there at approximately 3.10 a.m. Shortly after this discovery, officers from both the Metropolitan and City police went to the site at Goulston Street. City detectives Daniel Halse and Baxter Hunt were first. Halse, along with DS Robert Outram and DC Edward Marriott, had been standing near Mitre Square when the alarm had been raised and were at that time part of a sweep of the area following the reports of Elizabeth Stride's murder.

Halse took charge of guarding the graffiti and Hunt returned to Mitre Square. As other constables arrived in Goulston Street, it was generally felt by members of the City police that the writing should be photographed. However, their Metropolitan counterparts were already beginning to feel uneasy about leaving the message on view. It was a Sunday morning and the thriving Petticoat Lane Market, of which Goulston Street was an offshoot, would soon be busy with both Jewish and Gentile traders and visitors. Metropolitan Superintendent Thomas Arnold was concerned that the message was inflammatory enough to spark a disturbance, particularly after the mass-panic associated with 'Leather Apron', and he thought it might be necessary to erase it. City officers pushed for the erasure of the word 'Juwes' only, but as Goulston Street was not within their jurisdiction, it was not their decision to make.

When, at 5.30 a.m., Chief Commissioner Charles Warren arrived at the scene he agreed with Arnold's concerns and had the writing erased in its entirety.

It was a controversial decision at the time, and it still is for students of the case today. It is possible that the message could have resulted in a disturbance that could escalate into damage to property and even the death of innocent Jews, and in that case the right decision was taken. We will never know. I believe it could have been well guarded until at least the photograph was taken. There has, inevitably, been a great deal of debate over the significance of what has become known as the 'Goulston Street Graffito', with some believing the Ripper himself wrote it and others feeling that, in an area populated by so many Jewish immigrants, derogatory graffiti would have been commonplace. I think he *did* write it, because it was not in a prominent site where an agitator would have chosen to splash their incendiary message, and the apron piece abandoned with it would seem to be a pointer to its significance. But what did it mean? The double negative means it could be a defence of the Jews, or an attack on them. It could be an attempt to throw the police off the scent.

*

Ultimately it was only one more sensational event on a night full of shocks, and even without the message on the wall, the piece of apron being left there tells us which way the Ripper was heading when he left Catherine's mutilated body, a direction which could take the man I believe to be the Ripper home in about ten minutes.

But for the police investigators at the time, and hundreds of researchers ever since, the question remains: how did the Ripper manage to murder and mutilate Catherine Eddowes in such a short time frame, and so soon after killing Elizabeth Stride? As testimony from various witnesses came forward, the sheer daring of the Whitechapel murderer came into sharp focus.

As PC Watkins checked Mitre Square at 1.30 a.m. that morning, finding nothing out of the ordinary, three men, Joseph Lawende (pronounced Lavender, and sometimes spelt that way), Harry Harris and Joseph Hyam Levy, were preparing to leave the Imperial Club on Duke Street, close by Mitre Square. Having waited for a shower of rain to pass, they left a few minutes after 1.30 a.m. and began to walk along Duke Street towards Aldgate. As they passed the narrow entrance to Church Passage on the opposite side of the road (which led directly into Mitre Square), they noticed a man and a woman standing there. Levy, referring to the couple, said to Harris, 'Look there, I don't like going home by myself when I see those characters about.' Later he said that he assumed 'persons standing at that time of night in a dark passage were not up to much good.'

Neither Harris nor Levy gave the couple much consideration, but Lawende, a Polish cigarette salesman who had come to Britain in 1871, appears to have taken more notice. He described the man to the police as 'of shabby appearance, about 30 years of age and 5ft. 9in. in height, of fair complexion, having a small fair moustache, and wearing a red neckerchief and a cap with a peak.' He also said that the man had the appearance of a 'sailor'. The woman was standing with her back to the three men and was wearing a black jacket and black bonnet. Lawende's detailed description was not given to the press, nor was it repeated in detail at the inquest, where he gave brief evidence. But the police statement with the description was later published in the *Police Gazette*. It was probable the police deliberately withheld it at first, in the same way that they possibly kept Schwartz's evidence away from the public and the media by not including him at the inquest.

The police showed Catherine Eddowes' clothing to Lawende and he believed it was the same he had seen worn by the woman. He said she appeared to be a little shorter than the man and she had her hand on his chest. The couple did not appear to be quarrelling or drunk. Lawende's probable sighting of Catherine Eddowes with a man shortly before her death became the second potential sighting of the murderer (after Israel Schwartz) that night. Sadly, Lawende also went on to say at the inquest that he did not feel he could recognize the man again if he were confronted with him.

There are discrepancies between the descriptions of the man seen that night by Schwartz, Lawende and PC Smith, but there are also many points in common, and from what we now know about the (unintentional) inaccuracy of eye-witness accounts, it seems probable that all three saw the same man.

The sighting by Lawende and his two friends took place at

approximately 1.35 a.m. Five minutes later, PC James Harvey, the only other officer whose beat took him close to Mitre Square that night, passed along Church Passage from Duke Street. He did not see anybody at that time and, as his beat did not take in Mitre Square, he stopped briefly at the entrance to the square. Having noticed nothing out of the ordinary, he turned round and went back the way he had come. It is very likely that as he did so, the murder of Catherine Eddowes was taking place in the dark corner of Mitre Square opposite. Four minutes later, PC Watkins found the body.

But it was not just PCs Watkins and Harvey who came into close proximity to the murderer. George Morris, the watchman at the Kearley and Tonge warehouse, on the opposite side of the square to where the body was found, claimed that he had left the front door of the building open while he cleaned the stairs inside. Off-duty City policeman Richard Pearce, who lived in one of two houses in Mitre Square, was sleeping in the bedroom with his family, none of whom heard any disturbance during the night. Similarly, George Clapp, sharing his home at 5 Mitre Street with his wife and a nurse who looked after Mrs Clapp, heard nothing unusual, even though the bedroom windows were just above the spot where the murder took place. And finally, James Blenkinsop, a nightwatchman looking after some roadworks in St James's Place (connected to Mitre Square by a small passage) had nothing to report other than a well-dressed man apparently passing by at 1.30 a.m. and asking him if he had seen a man and a woman pass through.

It was as if the Ripper was a ghost. He managed to entice his victim into the square, perform a brutal murder, position the body and viscera in a specific manner, steal parts of her body and slip away invisibly into the night within a timescale of eight or nine minutes.

By coincidence, the sites of both the double murders are now schools. I have followed the two possible routes he took between the two scenes. I did the journeys at slow pace, loitering in doorways, as he must have done, to avoid passersby, and both routes took about six minutes, well within the time available to him. At a normal, strolling place it was three minutes, and moving rapidly took only two minutes.

I've tried to imagine what it must have been like for Catherine Eddowes, meeting the Ripper. Was he in a state of great excitement, having failed to carry out his rituals at the first murder? Was he covered in blood? How did he escape all the police out in the area? Not just because of the first murder but because on that night extra men had been drafted in due to fears of unrest caused by Fenian demonstrations in support of a free Ireland? Although she had been released from the police station because she had sobered up, Catherine was still probably the worse for drink, and perhaps she didn't notice anything odd about the man who took her into Mitre Square. It seems, from all the murders, that he was adept at killing his victims quickly, before he started his mutilations – there are very few reports of sounds from the victims.

Catherine's case is the most interesting to me, as it is the shawl taken from the scene of her murder which has finally unlocked the case. I hope, for her sake, that death came immediately and that she did not suffer after the first slash to her neck that killed her.

The night of the 'double event' caused, as you can imagine, a massive storm of press and public interest, with crowds of visitors attracted to the murder spots the next day, despite the police preventing them getting near.

The day after the double murder a postcard, again signed from 'Jack the Ripper', arrived at Central News:

> *I was not codding dear old Boss when I gave you the tip, you'll hear about Saucy Jacky's work tomorrow double event this time number one squealed a bit couldn't finish straight off. Had not got time to get ears off for police thanks for keeping last letter back till I got to work again.*
>
> *Jack the Ripper*

It was obviously written by the same author as the earlier 'Dear Boss' letter, which had never been published, as it referred to its content. It was the arrival of this postcard which prompted the publication of the earlier letter, and for the first time the public heard the name 'Jack the Ripper'. It is tempting to assume that because the postcard arrived the day after the double event, it must have been posted before and thus was written by the murderer who is telling the press about his latest atrocity before it hits the news. But the postal service then was much more frequent than today and included services on Sundays; the author of the postcard could easily have heard of the murders through word-of-mouth by Sunday afternoon, written his missive and had it delivered the following day.

Posters were produced and facsimiles of the letter and postcard were printed in the press, with the intention of prompting anybody who recognized the handwriting to come forward with information. The name 'Jack the Ripper' was seized upon almost immediately as a suitable replacement for 'Leather Apron'. There was one problem however: it inspired a great many copycat letters which began arriving at various institutions in their hundreds over the next few weeks. The Metropolitan police certainly got their share and, after the murder of Catherine Eddowes on their territory, the City police were targeted too. Many letters used the arrogant, mocking tone of the original letter and postcard and one even made a direct threat to somebody, presumably one of the witnesses relating to the double event who had spoken to the authorities:

You though your-self very clever I reckon when you informed the police. But you made a mistake if you though I dident [sic] see you. Now I known you know me and I see your little game, and I mean to finish you and send your ears to your wife if you show this to the police or help them if you do I will finish you. It no use your trying to get out of my way. Because I have you when you dont expect it and I keep my word as you soon see and rip you up.
  Yours truly Jack the Ripper.

One letter, sent to Central News and apparently in the same hand as the 'Dear Boss' letter, explained a rather disturbing motive for the murders and also promised to increase the carnage:

Dear Friend
  In the name of God hear me I swear I did not kill the female whose body was found at Whitehall [probably a reference to one of the Thames Torso murders in 1888]. If she was an honest woman I will hunt down and destroy her murderer. If she was a whore God will bless the hand that slew her, for the women of Moab and Midian shall die and their blood shall mingle with the dust. I never harm any others or the Divine power that protects and helps

me in my grand work would quit for ever. Do as I do and the light of glory shall shine upon you. I must get to work tomorrow treble event this time yes yes three must be ripped. will send you a bit of face by post I promise this dear old Boss. The police now reckon my work a practical joke well well Jacky's a very practical joker ha ha ha Keep this back till three are wiped out and you can show the cold meat.

    Yours truly

    Jack the Ripper

Even at the time, and more so over the years, the letters were assumed by the police to be hoaxes. Today most historians and researchers are agreed that the first were, in all probability, written by an eager journalist, spicing up an already dramatic story. He may have sent everyone on a wild goose chase, but nevertheless he came up with the name, Jack the Ripper, that has followed the case down the years.

The police investigation was intense. Eighty thousand leaflets requesting information were distributed:

POLICE NOTICE
TO THE OCCUPIER

On the morning of Friday, 31st August, Saturday 8th, and Sunday, 30th September, 1888, Women were murdered in or near Whitechapel, supposed by someone residing in the immediate neighbourhood. Should you know of any person to whom suspicion is attached, you are earnestly requested to communicate at once with the nearest Police Station.

Because of the suggestion that the Ripper knew the internal organs of the body well enough to carry out his ritualistic mutilations, butchers and slaughterers were singled out and interrogated, and so were sailors working on the Thames boats. For two or three weeks bloodhounds were deployed, until the experiment of using them was called off. Two thousand lodgers from the local dosshouses were interviewed.

In the days immediately after the murders many of the unfortunates stayed away from the streets, and the East End was virtually deserted after dark. Shops and businesses suffered, as customers stayed away from the area. Almost the only activity on the streets after dark was the police patrols, which were stepped up, and there were even reports of policemen dressing as prostitutes, in a bid to lure the Ripper back to his patch, although their hobnail boots apparently gave them away.

The streets were still busy during the day, however, and when poor Catherine Eddowes' body was taken to its final resting place, eight days after her death, it was a huge occasion. *The Times* described 'a multitude of persons' assembled to see the simple cortege leave the police mortuary. Although Catherine was eventually placed in an unmarked grave at Ilford Cemetery, her procession through the streets was as if she had been a famous dignitary, with a carriage load of press reporters following the mourners. Progress through Whitechapel was very slow, as thousands of people were on the streets to see it, including whole families, with children being held up by their parents. Catherine's four sisters, two nieces and John Kelly, the man she lived with, were at the graveside. By contrast, Elizabeth Stride was given a pauper's funeral two days earlier, with very few people there.

Frustrated by the police's lack of success, and feeling that the murders were beginning to affect their livelihoods, groups of local businessmen got together to create 'vigilance committees'.

Not only did they start a campaign to get the Metropolitan police to offer rewards for the capture of the Ripper, but they also paid men, armed with whistles and stout sticks, to be a visible presence on the streets after dark, essentially attempting to become extra eyes and ears for the beleaguered police.

The most prominent of these organizations was the Mile End Vigilance Committee, whose president was Mile End painter and decorator George Lusk. With his name appearing in the newspapers often, Lusk became the target of some strange incidents, including the receipt of alleged letters from the murderer. The most famous of these and certainly the most notorious ever received by anybody at the time, arrived at his home on the evening of 16 October. The letter came with a parcel containing half a human kidney.

From hell

Mr Lusk,
Sir
   I send you half the Kidne I took from one woman and prasarved it for you tother piece I fried and ate it was very nise.
I may send you the bloody knif that took it out if you only wate a whil longer
   signed Catch me when you can Mishter Lusk

In light of the removal of a kidney from Catherine Eddowes only two weeks previously, it made the whole package highly contentious. Apart from being definitely human, medical experts at the time could not ascertain whether the kidney had even belonged to a woman, let alone Eddowes, and there is a possibility that it came from a dissecting-room corpse. Many rumours have since circulated about the piece of kidney, including the popular suggestion, put forward in memoirs, that it had traces of Bright's disease, a condition that afflicted alcoholics, as did the organ remaining in Catherine Eddowes' body. Although the kidney was analysed several times, sadly the official reports or notes have long been lost. In my opinion, this is the only one of the letters that could be genuine, especially because of the reference to the kidney, and because the writer does not use the Jack the Ripper name. But I have no proof, and it could well be another hoax.

October was a busy month for the police, but a quiet time for the Ripper himself, with no further murders until 9 November 1888. Experts have come up with different theories for what was, for him, a long break. It has been suggested that serial killers often take longer spells away from their 'work' at times.

But I believe I have now solved the mystery of the five-and-a-half-week lull in his activities. Before I explain, here are the details of his final killing, which outstrips everything that came before in its sheer brutality. This time the Ripper returned to Spitalfields, at the heart of the East End's most impoverished district.

CHAPTER SIX

MURDER MOST GHASTLY

The Death of Mary Jane Kelly

The fifth and final Ripper murder is the one I call his *Mona Lisa*. It is the one where he had the time to completely fulfil his warped, sadistic urges, the culmination of all the fantasies he had developed in the escalating complexity of the previous mutilations. He could indulge himself, free from the risk of discovery, and he did.

Again, thank God, the victim was dead swiftly. It is hard to imagine the terror she must have felt when she realized the man she had taken back to her room was not there for straightforward sexual gratification, but at least he murdered her before he began to dismember and mutilate her.

Mary Jane Kelly's body was found in her lodgings at 13 Miller's Court, Dorset Street, on the morning of Friday, 9 November 1888. It was a morning of great police activity in London as it was the day of the Lord Mayor's Parade, when crowds would be out to cheer the new mayor and then 2,000 poor people would be given a free 'substantial meat tea', followed by entertainment. Many of the unfortunates of the area were looking forward to earning money from the men enjoying the holiday mood. But the festivities were eclipsed as the news of another murder spread through the East End.

Mary was a twenty-five-year-old prostitute described as 5 foot 7 inches tall, with a fair complexion, a rather stout build, blue eyes and a very fine head of hair. From descriptions given of her she was good-looking: 'attractive' is the word most used, and a 'pretty, buxom girl' is another description of her.

What we know about Mary's background is contentious as it originates from Mary herself, and is what she told to friends and acquaintances. Even today, with so much access to genealogical databases, confirmation of the facts proves elusive. She had a very common name, and it may not have been the name she was born with: many of the unfortunates were fleeing from their past when they gravitated to the streets of the East End. What follows is her own story of her life, none of which has ever been proven to be true or false.

She was born in Limerick, Ireland, and moved with her family to Carmarthenshire in Wales when she was very young. At the age of sixteen she married a collier by the name of Davies, but, tragically, her husband died in a mining accident within two years of their marriage. Mary apparently moved to Cardiff where, under the influence of a cousin, she became involved in prostitution. From there onwards her life took an unusual turn. Moving to London by 1884, she worked at an exclusive West End brothel which, given her looks, could certainly have been true.

She told friends that she travelled to France with a 'gentleman'. Deciding that this was not the life for her, she returned to England after two or three weeks. The trip to France may have inspired Mary to occasionally call herself 'Marie Jeannette'. Around 1884, Mary settled in the East End, near the London docks, lodging with a Mrs Buki until her growing fondness for alcohol meant that she had to leave. She then stayed at the home of a Mrs Carthy until 1886 when Mary left to live with at least two different men in Stepney for short times, before ending up in the dosshouses of Spitalfields, where she stayed at Cooney's lodging house in Thrawl Street. Her descent, as with so many of the unfortunates, seems to have been rooted in alcohol. She was according to those who knew her a quiet, pleasant girl when sober, but noisy and bawdy when drunk.

On Good Friday 1887, she met Joseph Barnett, a twenty-nine-year-old Billingsgate fish porter, and after only one day they made the decision to live together, which they subsequently did in rooms in various houses in George Street, Brick Lane and Little Paternoster Row before finding a room in Dorset Street, Spitalfields. Dorset Street had a notorious reputation for crime and vice; the philanthropist and social reformer Charles Booth, who campaigned for more government help for the poor, described it in his 1888 survey notebooks as 'the worst street I have seen so far – thieves, prostitutes, bullies, all common lodging houses.' Room 13, Miller's Court, was at the end of a small passageway between 26 and 27 Dorset Street. It was actually the back room of No. 26 which had been separated from the rest of the property with a false partition by the landlord, John McCarthy, who ran a chandlers shop from No. 27. Miller's Court was known as 'McCarthy's Rooms' because he was the landlord for so much of the court. Mary and Joe moved there in early 1888, paying four shillings and six pence a week for the partly furnished, squalid little room.

Joe Barnett supported the couple financially but lost his

job as a fish porter in early August, and gradually the couple fell behind with the rent. What Joe made selling oranges did not provide enough for them, so Mary felt she had no option but to go back to prostitution. This, along with her habit of allowing other prostitutes to sleep in the room on cold nights, caused Joe to walk out on 30 October and move into a lodging house in New Street, Bishopsgate.

Mary was apparently fascinated by the Ripper murders, as were so many of the working women of the East End. She used to ask Joe Barnett to read all the newspaper stories to her, and her fears may account for her inviting other girls to share her room, both for her protection and theirs.

Despite the separation, Mary and Joe were obviously still on good terms and Barnett would regularly stop by to give her some money if he had managed to earn any from casual work. He last visited Mary between 7 and 8 p.m. on the evening of 8 November, this time to apologize for not having any money to give her. That was the last time he saw her alive.

After her death, neighbours in Miller's Court gave evidence about what they had seen and heard on the last night of Mary's life. Mrs Mary Ann Cox, a widow who also earned her subsistence from prostitution, lived at Room 5, Miller's Court and had known Mary Kelly for about eight months. She followed Mary, who was with a man, into Miller's Court at about 11.45 p.m. on that Thursday night. The couple entered Room 13 and as Mary was walking through her door, Mrs Cox said goodnight to her; Mary was very drunk and could scarcely answer, but managed to utter a slurred 'Goodnight'. The man who accompanied her was carrying a quart pail of beer and was described as about thirty-six years old, about 5 foot 5 inches tall, with blotches on his face, small side whiskers and a thick carroty moustache, dressed in shabby dark clothes, a dark overcoat and a dark felt hat. She went on to say that she soon heard Mary singing, 'Only a violet I plucked from my mother's grave'. Mrs Cox was in and out of her room several times that evening and, when she finally returned at 3 a.m., all was dark in Room 13 and she didn't hear any noise for the rest of the night.

Elizabeth Prater lived at Room 20, Miller's Court, the room above Mary's. At about 3.30 or 4 a.m. she was awoken by her kitten and heard a cry of 'murder' in a female voice about two or three times. As Dorset Street was considered the roughest in the area at the time, she was used to such cries and so she ignored them and went back to sleep, not waking until 11 a.m. Sarah Lewis, staying with friends at Room 2, Miller's Court, may have heard the same cries at around the same time. Lewis, however, had more to report. When she got home to Miller's Court, at around 2.30 a.m., she saw a man standing over against the lodging house on the opposite side of the street to Miller's Court. He was described as not tall but stout and had on a wide-awake black hat (a hat with a low crown and wide brim.) The man Sarah Lewis described was probably George Hutchinson, a friend of Mary Kelly. He did not present himself as a witness until after the inquest, when he appeared at Commercial Street Police Station at 6 p.m. on 12 November 1888. He had an interesting story to tell.

He said that he was walking along Commercial Street, between Thrawl Street and Flower and Dean Street, at about 2 a.m. that morning. He was approached by Mary, who said, 'Hutchinson, will you lend me sixpence?' He said that he didn't have it to give her as he had spent it all going to Romford, and Mary went on her way. She was heading back in the direction of Thrawl Street when a man coming in the opposite direction tapped her on the shoulder and said something to her, at which they both burst out laughing. Hutchinson said that he heard her say 'Alright' to him and the man replied, 'You will be alright for what I have told you'. He then placed his right arm around her shoulders. Hutchinson stood against the lamp of the Queen's Head public house at the corner of Fashion Street and watched as the couple came past him. The man dropped his head with his hat over his eyes, so Hutchinson stooped down to look him in the face, at which the man gave him a stern look.

The couple headed into Dorset Street and Hutchinson followed. Mary and her new acquaintance stood at the entrance to Miller's Court for a few minutes and the man said something to her to which Mary replied, 'Alright my dear, come along, you will be comfortable.' The man then placed his arm around her shoulder and gave her a kiss and they both disappeared into the gloomy court together. Hutchinson stood on the other side of the road for about three quarters of an hour, during which time he was seen by Sarah Lewis. When he realized that neither Mary nor her companion were coming out soon, he went away to find lodgings of his own.

Hutchinson gave a description of the man as aged about thirty-four or thirty-five, height 5 foot 6 inches, with a pale complexion, dark eyes and eyelashes and a slight moustache, curled at the ends. He was wearing a long coat trimmed with astrakhan, with a dark jacket underneath, a light waistcoat, dark trousers, a dark felt hat turned down in the middle, button boots and gaiters with white buttons. He apparently wore a thick gold chain, a white linen collar and a black tie with a horseshoe pin, an appearance which suggested affluence. He was Jewish in appearance and walked 'very sharp'. Hutchinson also noticed that he was carrying a parcel. It was an unusual description, but Inspector Abberline personally questioned Hutchinson and felt that he was telling the truth.

Two further sightings of Mary Kelly took place in Dorset Street that morning, but they are extremely problematical. Caroline Maxwell saw her at the corner of Miller's Court between 8 a.m. and 8.30 a.m. They spoke, and Mary said that she 'had the horrors of drink upon her', probably meaning a huge hangover. Mrs Maxwell suggested that she go and have a drink, but Mary replied that she had already done so and had thrown it up in the road, pointing to a small pool of vomit by the kerb. Maxwell saw Kelly again at between 8.45 and 9 a.m. on the corner of Dorset Street, talking to a man who was aged about thirty and had the appearance of a market porter. The other sighting of interest was from Maurice Lewis who believed he saw Mary Kelly leave her room at about 8 a.m. and then saw her again in the Britannia pub at the corner of Dorset Street and Commercial Street. The big problem with both these sightings is, according to later evidence given by medical men, Mary Kelly would have already been dead for a while by the time Maxwell and Lewis saw her. It's possible that, not knowing her well, she was confused with another woman, or that the witnesses simply had the day wrong.

At 10.45 a.m. that morning, the landlord John McCarthy sent his assistant, an elderly man named Thomas Bowyer, to try and collect some of the six weeks overdue rent from Mary. Bowyer went through the passageway to Room 13 and knocked on the door, but there was no answer. He tried opening the door but it would not budge, as though it was locked from the inside, so rather than walk away empty-handed, he went round to the side window, which had a broken pane, put his hand through the hole in the frame and pulled back the muslin curtain that was obscuring his view of the interior. In the gloom of that little room he could make out the corpse of Mary Jane Kelly: she was lying on the bed and she had been literally ripped to pieces. In shock, he immediately ran to fetch John McCarthy who, with Bowyer, swiftly ran to Commercial Street Police Station where they alerted Inspector Walter Beck and Sergeant Edward Badham. After arriving at Miller's Court and seeing for himself the bloody scene, Inspector Beck sent for assistance from Divisional Superintendent Thomas Arnold and the divisional surgeon Dr George Bagster Phillips. Inspector Abberline also visited Miller's Court, as did Assistant Commissioner Robert Anderson, the first time he had been able to visit any of the crime scenes since his return from sick leave in early October.

Miller's Court was sealed off to the public by 11 a.m. On his arrival, Dr Phillips viewed the scene through the window and satisfied himself that the woman in the room was long past needing immediate assistance. A decision was made to use bloodhounds in an attempt to sniff out the killer and so a long wait ensued before the room could be opened; by 1 p.m. no bloodhounds had arrived and so, in the absence of a key, John McCarthy was ordered to break down the door of Mary's room with a pickaxe. The scene that greeted those who entered that tiny room was shocking even to hardened policemen and medical men, as the highly experienced Dr Thomas Bond, the divisional police surgeon for A Division (Westminster), made clear in his post-mortem report:

The body was lying naked in the middle of the bed, the shoulders flat, but the axis of the body inclined to the left side of the bed. The head was turned on the left cheek. The left arm was close to the body with the forearm flexed at a right angle and lying across the abdomen, the right arm was slightly abducted from the body and rested on the mattress, the elbow bent the forearm supine with the fingers clenched. The legs were wide apart, the left thigh at right angles to the trunk and the right forming an obtuse angle with the pubes.

The whole surface of the abdomen and thighs was removed and the abdominal cavity emptied of its viscera. The breasts were cut off, the arms mutilated by several jagged wounds and the face hacked beyond recognition of the features. The tissues of the neck were severed all round down to the bone.

The viscera were found in various parts viz: the uterus and kidneys with one breast under the head, the other breast by the right foot, the liver between the feet, the intestines by the right side and the spleen by the left side of the body.

The flaps removed from the abdomen and thighs were on a table.

The bed clothing at the right corner was saturated with blood, and on the floor beneath was a pool of blood covering about 2 feet square. The wall by the right side of the bed and in a line with the neck was marked by blood which had struck it in a number of separate splashes.

Dr Bond went into further detail:

The face was gashed in all directions the nose, cheeks, eyebrows and ears being partly removed. The lips were blanched and cut by several incisions running obliquely down to the chin. There were also numerous cuts extending irregularly across all the features.

The neck was cut through the skin and other tissues right down to the vertebrae the 5th and 6th being deeply notched. The skin cuts in the front of the neck showed distinct ecchymosis.

The air passage was cut at the lower part of the larynx through the cricoid cartilage.

Both breasts were removed by more or less circular incisions, the muscles down to the ribs being attached to the breasts. The intercostals between the 4th, 5th, and 6th ribs were cut through and the contents of the thorax visible through the openings.

The skin and tissues of the abdomen from the costal arch to the pubes were removed in three large flaps. The right thigh was denuded in front to the bone, the flap of skin, including the external organs of generation and part of the right buttock. The left thigh was stripped of skin, fascia and muscles as far as the knee.

The left calf showed a long gash through the skin and tissues to the deep muscles and reaching from the knee to 5 ins above the ankle.

Both arms and forearms had extensive and jagged wounds. The right thumb showed a small superficial incision about 1 in long, with the extravasation of blood in the skin and there were several abrasions on the back of the hand moreover showing the same condition.

On opening the thorax it was found that the right lung was minimally adherent by old firm adhesions. The lower part of the lung was broken and torn away.

The left lung was intact: it was adherent at the apex and

there were a few adhesions over the side. In the substances of the lung were several nodules of consolidation.

The Pericardium was open below and the Heart absent.

In the abdominal cavity was some partially digested food of fish and potatoes and similar food was found in the remains of the stomach attached to the intestines.

Having made his post-mortem report on Mary Kelly, Dr Bond was shown those written about the previous victims and produced a résumé of the kind of person he felt the Ripper must have been, which is often considered to be the first criminal offender profile. Dr Bond had been a police surgeon for over twenty years at this time, and was also a distinguished lecturer in forensic medicine. He committed suicide at the age of sixty, in 1901, when he was suffering from an untreatable and very painful bladder condition.

He stated that the injuries to Mary Kelly were so severe as to make it impossible to assume any anatomical knowledge on the part of the person who killed her: 'in my opinion he does not even possess the technical knowledge of a butcher or horse slaughterer or any person accustomed to cut up dead animals.' He stated:

The murderer must have been a man of physical strength and of great coolness and daring. There is no evidence that he had an accomplice. He must in my opinion be a man subject to periodical attacks of Homicidal and erotic mania. The character of the mutilations indicate that the man may be in a condition sexually that may be called satyriasis. It is of course possible that the Homicidal impulse may have developed from a revengeful or brooding condition of the mind, or that Religious Mania may have been the original disease, but I do not think either hypothesis is likely. The murderer in external appearance is quite likely to be a quiet inoffensive looking man probably middle aged and neatly and respectably dressed. I think he must be in the habit of wearing a cloak or an overcoat or he could hardly have escaped notice in the streets if the blood on his hands or clothes were visible.

Assuming the murderer to be such a person as I have described he would probably be solitary and eccentric in his habits, also he is most likely to be a man without regular occupation, but with some small income or pension. He is possibly living among respectable persons who have some knowledge of his character and habits and who may have grounds for suspicion that he is not quite right in his mind at times. Such persons would probably be unwilling to communicate suspicions to the Police for fear of trouble or notoriety, whereas if there were a prospect of reward it might overcome their scruples.

Before being moved to Shoreditch mortuary, the body of Mary Kelly was photographed twice, one view taken in full from the side, the other from the foot of the bed. These images, perhaps the earliest examples of murder crime scene photography by the British police, show the full horror of what happened that day and allow us, over a century later, to understand the shock that these killings generated. It is hard to imagine that the murderer could have done any worse.

At the inquest Dr Phillips attributed the cause of death to 'the severance of the carotid artery'.

Mary Jane Kelly's funeral was a massive occasion, with

thousands united in a great outpouring of sympathy and grief along the procession route to St Patrick's Roman Catholic Cemetery in Leytonstone. In just a short space of time, the Whitechapel murders had revealed the dark heart of London's East End, turning forgotten unfortunates into tragic victims and paralyzing the whole district with fear. In November 1888, no one knew that the Miller's Court murder would be the Ripper's last atrocity (according to most experts, and certainly in my opinion). Instead, it was deemed just a further escalation in the series; Queen Victoria herself had apparently been keeping an eye on the events unfolding in the East End and following the Kelly murder felt compelled to fire off a telegram to her ministers, showing great concern:

> This new most ghastly murder shows the absolute necessity for some very decided action. All these courts must be lit, & our detectives improved. They are not what they should be. You promised, when the 1st murders took place to consult with your colleagues about it.

Mary Kelly was not the only victim on 9 November. As news of her murder spread around London, reports that Sir Charles Warren, the Metropolitan Police Commissioner, had resigned were also doing the rounds. Warren had been given a tough time by the radical newspapers throughout the Whitechapel murders and was constantly at loggerheads with Henry Matthews, the Home Secretary. After he had written a forthright article about the police in *Murray's Magazine*, Warren was hauled over the coals by Matthews, at which point he felt that enough was enough and he tendered his resignation, which was duly accepted. Although Warren's resignation had little to do with the Metropolitan police's failure to capture the Ripper, popular legend has continued to promote the idea that Jack the Ripper's crimes had disastrously affected the very highest echelons of authority.

We now know that Jack the Ripper had ended his bloody work with the murder of Mary Jane Kelly, but the hysteria at the time meant any act of violence against women was, for a couple of years at least, ascribed to the Ripper. Two murders in particular were thought to be his handiwork, those of Alice Mackenzie, which did bear some similarities, and Frances Coles, which clearly was completely different. Both happened some time after the Ripper stopped his spree. Alice Mackenzie died the following summer, July 1889, with two stab wounds to her throat. Like the Ripper's victims, she was a prostitute living hand-to-mouth in the dosshouses of the East End, and her body was found in a squalid alleyway off Whitechapel High Street. The murderer had tried to rip her clothing off, but had only pulled it away enough to inflict superficial cuts on her stomach and genital area. Opinion at the time was divided about whether she was a Ripper victim, with Sir Robert Anderson, Inspector Abberline and one of the police surgeons, Dr George Bagster Phillips, all saying that this was the handiwork of a different killer, and Dr Thomas Bond and Police Commissioner James Monro asserting that Alice was another Ripper victim. Opinion has remained divided ever since.

Frances Coles was murdered in January 1891, more than two years after the last Ripper murder. Like the other victims, she was a prostitute. Her body was found under a railway arch between Chamber Street and Royal Mint Street in

Whitechapel, and her throat had been slashed. But unlike the others, the wound had been inflicted with a blunt knife, and there were no other mutilations. There was a suspect, a ship's fireman called James Sadler, who had spent much of the evening and night with her, and both of them were, apparently, very drunk. They had parted company after an argument, and Sadler tried to rejoin his ship at London docks but was turned away because he was so drunk. Sadler was arrested, and briefly came under suspicion as the Ripper. But he was at sea when the other killings were committed, and there was not enough evidence to try him for the murder of Frances Coles.

Why did the Ripper stop? I have my own theory, which I will expound later in this book. But it is also worth noting that the streets were genuinely safer for the unfortunates, because of the heightened public awareness, and the existence of the Vigilance Committees.

Then, as now, different experts and authorities had their own, differing ideas as to who Jack the Ripper really killed – and who he was. In February 1894, the *Sun* newspaper claimed it knew who Jack the Ripper was, but stopped short of giving his name. In response Sir Melville Macnaghten, who was appointed Assistant Chief Constable of the Metropolitan police in 1889, swiftly wrote a memorandum, for whom specifically is uncertain, exonerating the man in question, who he named as Thomas Cutbush. In this lengthy report, he went over the crimes and made a definite statement, that 'the Whitechapel Murderer had 5 victims and 5 victims only ...' These were Nichols, Chapman, Stride, Eddowes and Kelly and although others were mentioned, they were dismissed out of hand. It was the discovery and publication of these notes in the early 1960s which set out what is now called the 'canonical five' victims. Martha Tabram *may* be the Ripper's first foray into the world of brutal murder, and in my opinion she was, but I cannot assert it with complete certainty: however I feel more than certain that Macnaghten's five are true victims of Jack the Ripper.

But there is a more important significance to Macnaghten's memorandum. He named three suspects who he felt were more likely to be the murderer than Cutbush: they were Montague Druitt, Michael Ostrog and 'Kosminski'. Was one of *them* Jack the Ripper?

CHAPTER SEVEN

THE HISTORY OF
THE SHAWL

Knowing the stories of the victims and looking at the line-up of suspects only increased my fascination with the case. Why had it never been solved? How had this man Jack the Ripper perpetrated the crimes which made him the most famous murderer in the world, with so much attention focussed on him, and still been able to defy detection, not just at the time but ever since? The questions went round in my head. I had a busy life, with a difficult business to run and now a toddler son who kept Sally and me at full stretch, as children do. But there was always some free time, after Alexander was asleep, to dig into the books and trawl around on the internet, looking for something that had been missed. I had this niggling, persistent feeling that there was a loose thread somewhere, and if I found it and pulled it the whole mystery would unravel.

Whenever I was in London on business I went to the East End to eat, walking the same streets I'd walked as a student, but now with a different perspective. Yes, I still loved the buzz of the area for its own sake, but now it was overlaid with pictures in my head of how these streets had looked in Victorian times, how the cars I dodged as I crossed Commercial Road had once been horses and carts, how the prostitutes I saw now, with their miniskirts and cigarettes, had once been unfortunates who, like Catherine Eddowes, wore all the clothes they possessed as they looked for a man to pay them the money for a night's sleep.

At weekends, when we went as a family to Cambridge, I'd tour the bookshops, looking for accounts I hadn't read before, getting exasperated with some of the wilder theories, noting anomalies in evidence and always being fascinated by attempts to get inside the head of the killer. This was where I felt the clue would lie: if I could begin to understand him I'd find my way to him. It was a lonely quest: I was never drawn to joining the Ripper community, the experts and enthusiasts who trade their opinions and theories on the internet, who attend conferences and swap snippets of information, although I would read their dissertations and theses if they published them.

At the time there was one suspect who interested me more than the others, for no other reason than that he had a connection with Birkenhead, my home town, and had lived two roads away from where my grandmother lived. Frederick Deeming was hanged in Australia in 1892 for the murder of his second wife. The bodies of his first wife and four children were then found under the floor of a house he had rented on Merseyside, all of them with their throats slashed. Although Deeming had lived in South Africa and Australia, there was a possibility that he had been in England in 1888. Enjoying the notoriety, he told other prisoners as he waited for the death sentence to be carried out that he was Jack the Ripper.

I believe in the power of coincidences and chance, and the

fact that I knew the area where he killed his family made him interesting. The savage murders, with throats slashed, had echoes of the Ripper's modus operandi, even though the bodies were not mutilated. He was an evil man, with no redeeming features: he was a conman, a thief, a braggard, a bigamist. It all sounded to me, at the time, as if he could be a suitable candidate.

But after six years of trawling through books and records, I was unable to find anything to take the Ripper story forward, and I was determined not to be just another Ripper geek, following all the twists and turns but never adding anything. I had just about reached the conclusion that the case was unsolvable.

'Nobody is ever going to know the identity of this man,' I told myself. I decided to put the matter to rest, to move on. I'd had a good stab at it, but in the end, perhaps there genuinely was nothing new to find.

It was at this stage in 2007 that a friend who knew of my interest sent me a text, telling me that in that day's *Daily Mirror* there was a small item about a piece of memorabilia coming up for auction: a shawl that was believed to have been the property of Catherine Eddowes.

It was 9 p.m., too late to dash out and get a copy of the paper, so I looked the news report up, and the next day bought the local papers which also mentioned the auction. I realized that the auction was only a few days away. Initially I wasn't interested: a quick trawl through the usual sources revealed very little about the shawl, and I wasn't convinced that it was genuine. Occasional mentions of it on internet message boards glossed over it rather quickly, as if there was very little available information to discuss. Some commentators denounced it as a fake without saying much else. Yet something made me want to find out more. As I have said, despite the fact that I'm hard-headed in business, I believe in hunches and following my feelings: my instincts are not always right, but they are far more often right than wrong, and I've had occasion to be grateful to them many times, never more so than in the quest for Jack the Ripper.

In the next few days, I logged on to the internet to go over all the information on the Catherine Eddowes murder, for anything that would make me believe that the shawl had something going for it and would be a worthwhile investment. Then I noticed the pattern on the shawl, a deep border of Michaelmas daisies.

I looked again at the police inventory of Catherine Eddowes' clothing and possessions, which included the skirts she was wearing:

Chintz Skirt, 3 flounces, brown button on waistband. Jagged cut 6 ½ inches long from waistband, left side of front. Edges slightly Bloodstained, also Blood on bottom, back & front of skirt.

But the press reports in many newspapers reporting the Eddowes inquest consistently mentioned that 'her dress was made of green chintz, the pattern consisting of Michaelmas daisies'. Did this mean something? I'm a keen gardener, but surprisingly I had no idea what a Michaelmas daisy was until I looked them up on the internet and saw a picture, when I recognized them immediately. I simply hadn't known the name. They are a favourite with gardeners wanting a splash of colour in their borders when other plants are fading, because they come into bloom in late summer and early autumn, and that's how they get their name, because they are in bloom at Michaelmas.

I didn't even know when Michaelmas was, or what it was. I looked it up in the *Encyclopaedia Britannica*, and found that it is the Christian feast of St Michael the Archangel, celebrated in Western and Eastern (Orthodox) Churches. In the Roman Catholic faith it is known as the Feast of Saints Michael, Gabriel and Raphael, the archangels, and in the Anglican Church it is the Feast of St Michael and All Angels. In Western churches, Michaelmas is celebrated on 29 September, whereas in the Eastern (Orthodox) churches it is celebrated on 8 November.

In years gone by, a businessman like me would have been well aware of Michaelmas: it was one of the four quarter days of the year, when legally all rents and debts had to be paid, lawsuits had to be settled, servants could be hired on contracts. This practice dates back to the Middle Ages but fell out of use in the last hundred years or so, although there are still some very traditional leases that refer to it, and the name is enshrined in traditional university terms, and the terms of the Inns of Court. Significantly, it would have been a well-known and important date back at the end of the nineteenth century.

It was while I was reading up about it that something hit me, hard. It was like being knocked over. It was one of my massive moments on this journey, something that made me reel back in surprise. I checked it, checked it again, and then checked it once more. How could I have seen this, when nobody else had?

It was the two dates of Michaelmas that hit me. They were the nights of the last three murders, first the double event on the traditional Michaelmas celebrated in this country, second the final murder of Mary Jane Kelly on the night of the Orthodox Church Michaelmas. The double event deaths happened after midnight, so they were technically on 30 September, but what if Jack the Ripper set out on his mission on the evening of Michaelmas Day? We know that Elizabeth Stride was killed around 12.45 a.m., not long after the date change, and he presumably allowed himself time to find a suitable victim.

I have a natural ability to remember dates: my friends and family tease me that I have the memory of an elephant when it comes to them. As I talk, I pepper my conversation with references to dates: for some reason they have always been important to me. I think this perhaps explains why I, and not any of the researchers who went before me, spotted this connection.

It was the Michaelmas daisies on the shawl that had set me off researching Michaelmas, and now the shawl assumed a much bigger significance than before. Could there be a connection?

It seemed as if I knew something that nobody else did. I was very excited, but as usual there was nobody close to share the information with. Sally would listen, but she didn't share my interest and she made it clear it was my hobby, not hers. She wasn't convinced by my Michaelmas theory.

But now I really wanted the shawl. It was important to me. I was still operating on my hunch alone, and that was enough to make me want to own the shawl, but I wanted to find out if there was any corroborating evidence. I knew, from the auction catalogue, that the shawl had at one stage been housed at Scotland Yard's 'Black Museum', the popular name for the Metropolitan Police Crime Museum, where a fascinating collection of exhibits and items of evidence from notorious criminal cases stretching back into the nineteenth century are kept.

The title Black Museum, apparently coined in 1877, is appropriate, as the collection includes weapons used in actual murders, pieces of crucial evidence from hijackings, sieges, robberies and, most creepily, the death masks of various prisoners hanged at Newgate prison, as well as a plethora of other true-crime ephemera. Some of the more well-known criminal cases represented by the collection include those of John Christie, Ruth Ellis, the Great Train Robbery, Dr Crippen, Dennis Nilsen, the Kray Twins and – not surprisingly – Jack the Ripper.

With the date of the auction fast approaching, I decided to contact the Black Museum to see if I could find out any more about the history of the shawl, and the likelihood of it being genuine (although I was increasingly sure that it was). I rang Scotland Yard and was put through to Alan McCormack, the curator of the Crime Museum. I realized immediately that he was friendly and down-to-earth, so I explained that I was thinking of buying the shawl, and asked if he could tell me anything about it.

I cannot recall the *exact* conversation, but paraphrased, it went something like this:

RE: I wonder if you can tell me any information you have regarding the Jack the Ripper shawl that was taken from Catherine Eddowes' body on the night of the murder?

AM: Well it was never proven to be linked to the case because we've never done any DNA testing on it. In fact, we had it over the years as part of our training museum. Most people call this the Black Museum, but it isn't. It's the Scotland Yard training museum.

RE: Would you say it is genuine?

AM: I can't say one way or the other; it was on loan to us from the descendant of one of our policemen at the time of the murders. If it was ever shown to the public, it would have to say that it was *alleged* so there would be no comeback.

RE: OK, what if I was to say I had found something about the pattern on the shawl which relates significantly to the dates of three of the murders?

AM: Well that would be fresh news that we haven't got and we would be very interested.

RE: When I knew that the shawl was up for sale, I had a look on the internet and saw that the *East London Observer* printed on Saturday, 6 October 1888, that the victim was wearing a dark green chintz dress with Michaelmas daisies, with a golden lily pattern. I noticed that many newspapers had printed the same, so I concentrated on the pattern and tried to find a clue in the significance of the pattern.

AM: Did you find anything?

I told him about the relevance of the celebration dates of Michaelmas to the murders of Elizabeth Stride, Catherine Eddowes and Mary Kelly and he said: 'We never knew that, that's new.'

I felt really pleased: it was the first confirmation I'd had that I was onto something from someone who knew about the case. Now I *knew* I had to buy the shawl.

But before I had long to savour my success, Alan threw something else of vital importance into the ring. He said he could not understand why people still continued to talk about who the Ripper was, because – he claimed – Scotland Yard had always known who he was, and that they had documentation to prove it. I asked if he minded telling me the name:

AM: Well I can tell you the name but you have to go and do the work. Considering you've told me the first bit of news that I didn't know in years, I'll tell you: the murderer was and always has been Aaron Kosminski.

RE: Really? He's always been one of the three publicized suspects.

AM: Yes, but they make too much money on programmes and books to actually give the real culprit!

RE: What do you think about the shawl now?

AM: Well, I don't know now, it is very old. I know Sotheby's examined it and found it could be very early twentieth century, but it could be older. If you feel you want to buy it let me know how you get on. You never know, it could be real after all.

RE: I will keep you posted. So Aaron Kosminski was Jack the Ripper?

AM: Yes, we've got all the information right here, but the museum isn't open to the public. Tell you what, if you buy the shawl, we would be interested in having it back. I'll let you come and see the documents if you ever write a book on it and give me a signed copy.

RE: That would be amazing. Thank you ever so much, I'll let you know how I get on.

So now, in an astonishing couple of days, I had found out the significance of the shawl and, incredibly, the true identity of Jack the Ripper – at least according to Alan McCormack's understanding of the police evidence.

And that is how I came to be at the auction in Bury St Edmunds in March 2007 and a couple of days later agreed to buy the shawl.

When I got it home I spread it across a large footstool covered in pale cream velvet in our drawing room to look at it properly. It was surprisingly large and existed in two sections, the bigger one being 73.5 inches in length and 25.5 inches wide. The smaller piece had been cut more and was 24 inches long and 19 inches wide. The predominant colour was dark brown, with a more golden brown on the reverse. At both ends were blue sections measuring about 2 foot long, patterned with a design of Michaelmas daisies and golden lilies in hues of red, ochre and gold. This pattern also ran along the edges of the main brown central section in the form of a border. Pieces had been cut from the shawl at some time, leaving jagged edges at one end of each piece. The other edges of both sections had a fringe of small tassels.

There were a number of stains on both sections; on the larger, a multitude of small dots could be seen near the fringe and a larger dark stain slightly further in. In the middle brown section, similar dark stains were present as well as some smaller white dots where the colour had leached out. The smaller piece had some minor dark stains and again, near the fringe, more little markings. I was fascinated by the stains. I could clearly see what looked as if it was blood, but I was surprised there wasn't more blood, and I dismissed the white marks as probably nothing more significant than the ageing process. Another pale stain I thought had been caused by bleach. Little did I know.

I stored the shawl in an antique glass-fronted cabinet I bought specifically for the purpose at an antiques shop in The Lanes in Brighton, then carefully concealed the shawl beneath a display of silver which Sally and I also chose: I thought that if we were burgled, the burglars would get away with the silver and would not bother with a couple of old pieces of cardboard and some tatty fabric that were lining the bottom of the cabinet. Storing the shawl there also kept it out of sunlight and contamination.

I read and re-read the letter of provenance from the previous owner:

> *To Whom it May Concern*
>
> *I would confirm that I David Melville-Hayes am the Great Great Nephew of Acting Sergeant Amos Simpson who became the owner of the said Catherine Eddowes shawl after it was taken from her body.*
>
> *The shawl was then given to my Great Grandmother who was Mary Simpson who died about 1927. The ownership of the Shawl then passed to my Grandmother Eliza Mary Smith (1875 to 1966). On her death the shawl was left to my Mother Eliza Elise (Mills) later Hayes (1902 to 1997). The shawl was given to me at the time my Mother went to live in Australia in 1986. However my Mother returned to England in about 1989. Full information on this background is available on my Family Tree, which I will make available to, these details cover approx. Seventeen Pages of Foolscap.*
>
> *For further information I would suggest contacting Andrew Parlour on (telephone number) who has much information on the Metropolitan Police Records.*
>
> *I am, Yours faithfully,*
> *David Melville-Hayes.*

2 4/3/07

To Whom it may Concern

I would ▄ confirm that I David Melville-Hayes am the Great Great Nephew of Acting Sergeant AMOS SIMPSON.who became the owner of the said Catherine Eddowes Shawl after it was taken from her body.

The shawl was then given to my Great Grandmother who was Mary Simpson who died about 1927. The ownership of the Shawl then passed to my Grandmother Eliza Mary Smith(1875 to 1966) On her death the shawl was left to my Mother Eliza Elise (Mills) later Hayes(1902 to 1997) The shawl was given to me at the time my Mother went to live in Australia in 1986. However my Mother returned to England in about 1989.

Full information on this background is available on my Family Tree which I will make available to,these details cover approx Seventeen Pages of Foolscap

For further information I ~~would~~ WOULD suggest contacting: Andrew Parlour on ░░░░ ░░░░ who has much information on the Metropollitan Police Records

I am,

Yoursfaithfully,

David Melville-Hayes.

The letter included his address and phone number.

I had already met Andy Parlour at the auction, and I knew from that encounter that he and Sue knew more about the history of the shawl than anyone else. They only had one copy of their book at the auction, and, besides, I had not wanted to show my hand by being too eager for it at the time. But now I had their telephone number, and within a couple of days I gave them a ring, told them I had the shawl, and arranged for them to come to my house.

Andy and Sue have been helpful and kind friends throughout this journey of mine. They have not betrayed to others who owns the shawl, and they have acted as a buffer between me and various people wanting access to it: lots of people assume it is in their possession. I am, and have always been, very grateful to them.

It was from them, and their book, that I discovered the full history of the shawl.

In December 1993, the curator of the Crime Museum at the time, Bill Waddell, published *The Black Museum: New Scotland Yard*, in which he wrote:

> Recently I acquired a silk screen printed shawl. It had been in the donor's possession for many years and a large section had been cut out by his mother, because she did not like the blood stains on it. I am told that it was the shawl worn by Catherine Eddowes when she was killed. Who knows what will come to light next?

Waddell was not the first person to mention the existence of the shawl in print. That honour went to Paul Harrison in his 1991 book *Jack the Ripper: The Mystery Solved* in which he set out his case for Mary Kelly's former lover, Joseph Barnett, being the Ripper. During his research for the book, Harrison, who at that time was a serving sergeant in the Nottinghamshire Constabulary, received a telephone call out of the blue from London-based Chief Inspector Mick Wyatt, who had heard of Harrison's Ripper research and felt that he would like to know about a possible genuine artefact from the murders. Harrison was fully expecting the item to be a knife and was surprised when Wyatt said that it was a shawl belonging to one of the Ripper's victims, though he could not be sure which one. He gave Harrison the address, in Clacton-on-Sea in Essex, where the shawl was kept.

In late November 1989, about a year after he spoke to Wyatt, Harrison followed up this lead, and found that the address given to him was a video shop owned by John and Janice Dowler. Eventually, Harrison met the Dowlers at their shop in St Osyth Road and found them very helpful, but also very cynical about the genuineness of the shawl, which by then they had returned to its original owner. The story the Dowlers had been told was that the shawl had been taken from the body of Catherine Eddowes. Either the shawl had been acquired at the scene, or *en route* to the mortuary. A friend in the antiques business offered it to the Dowlers a few years earlier, knowing they were from London and thinking that they might be interested in a piece of London history.

The alleged background to the shawl made them feel a little uncomfortable, but they accepted the gift. They were told that the missing section had been removed because of bloodstains, but there were still stains visible on the remaining fabric, which disturbed them enough to ask their friend to take it back. They were presented instead with two cuttings from the shawl which had been placed in a mount and framed, and which they displayed in their shop. On the back of the frame was the inscription:

Two silk samples, taken from Catherine Eddowes' shawl at the time of the discovery of her body by Amos SIMPSON in 1888. (End of September). Victim of Jack the Ripper.

> Arabella Vincent (Fine Art)
> Hand-made Illustrated Mounts
> UK Studio, Tel. Clacton —
> Surface printed silk
> Circa 1886
> Framed 100 years to the day.
> (A. Vincent)

The friend in question was David Melville-Hayes who actually worked for Arabella Vincent Fine Art and who specialized in hand-colouring prints. It is a family tradition: both David's father and grandfather were colourists, and he believes the line of colourists goes back to 1764. David himself has done work for the Queen Mother. He is the great-great-nephew of the police officer Amos Simpson who had acquired the shawl, and the history of the shawl had been passed down over generations. What follows is what David had learnt from his family, and what he, in turn, passed on to me. It is important to put this specific version of events across, as the story of the origins of the shawl has been muddied with the passing of time:

Simpson, being on 'special duties' at the time of the double murder, had gone to Mitre Square with several other officers from both the City and Metropolitan forces, and with another policeman accompanied the body of Catherine Eddowes as it was wheeled to the City mortuary in Golden Lane. Seeing the shawl, he asked one of the senior officers if it was fine to take it, as he thought his wife Jane might find the silk useful for dressmaking. David believes that it was his rank, Acting Sergeant, that allowed him to have the shawl. When Simpson showed the bloodstained shawl to Jane, she understandably wanted nothing to do with it. Regardless of Jane's opinions, it was not disposed of: and that's one of the first and most important pieces of luck in this sequence of events. Some time prior to his death in 1917, Simpson passed the shawl to his sister, Mary Simpson, David Melville-Hayes' great-grand-mother, and on her death in 1927 it was given to her daughter Eliza Mary Smith. When she in turn died in 1966, the year I was born, the shawl once again moved down a generation to her daughter, Eliza Elise Hayes, David Melville-Hayes' mother. At the age of eighty-four, in 1986, Eliza Elise moved to Australia and before leaving offered the shawl to David's two brothers. Again, the shawl had a lucky escape, as the brothers, with little interest in its story, intended to burn it, which prompted David to take it off their hands and rescue what he felt was an important piece of history.

That is the basic version set out by David according to the original family story, but over the years he has added new observations; for example, he believed that it was possibly his grandmother, Eliza Mary, who had cut the large chunk from the shawl to be rid of the heavy bloodstains and that she may also have attempted to bleach out other smaller stains. He also remembers seeing the shawl for the first time when he was about eight or nine years old and that it was kept in a large wooden sea chest with 'waxed handles' which was also used to store the family's 'Sunday-best' clothes, and which David still owns. One element of the story is more problematical: David states that Amos Simpson gained access to the shawl because he was the first officer at the scene in Mitre Square and it has even been said that he discovered the body himself. This version of events has also surfaced in the media from time to time. That he was the very first on the scene seems unlikely.

To remind us, the police reports state that, as we've seen, it was PC Edward Watkins who found Catherine Eddowes' body that morning, and went for help to George Morris, the nightwatchman at Kearley and Tonge. After Morris, an ex-Metropolitan police officer, raised the alarm a number of officers swiftly arrived at the scene, including PC James Harvey who had been near the entrance to Mitre Square only five minutes earlier and PC Frederick Holland. Also alerted were City detectives Edward Marriott, Robert Outram and Daniel Halse who were standing at the bottom of Houndsditch nearby.

As the word of another savage murder of a prostitute was spread along the police lines of communication, senior officers would have arrived at the scene and further police reinforcements would have been sent from Bishopsgate and other City police stations to perform various duties. Owing to the loss of City police files on the Ripper case, it is impossible to know exactly how many policemen would have been present at any one time, and it is likely that apart from those directly involved following the immediate discovery of the body, not all would have been recorded. In effect, the fact that Amos Simpson's name does not appear in any of the few surviving reports does not necessarily mean he was not there at some point, even early on. Catherine Eddowes' body was removed from Mitre Square at 2.20 a.m. and according to the story passed down by his descendants, Amos Simpson accompanied it. But Simpson was a Metropolitan police officer, so what was he doing on City police territory?

Amos Simpson was born in 1847 in Acton, Suffolk, the fourth child of eleven born to agricultural labourer John Simpson and his wife Mary. I found out from talking to his descendant, David Melville-Hayes, that the malting house where Sally and I lived was only three villages away from Amos's birth place. Amos was working with his father on a farm at Barrow Hill by the time he was fourteen years old, but the desire to branch out and go to the big city must have been great, and he joined the Metropolitan police in 1868 aged twenty-one, where he was first posted to Y Division (Holloway). In 1874 he married Jane Wilkins (who was born in 1848 in Bourton-on-the-Water, Gloucestershire) at the ancient Old St Pancras Church in London and together they had two children, Ellen and Henry. Simpson was promoted to acting sergeant in 1881 and five years later transferred to N Division (Islington) where he was still based at the time of the Ripper murders. Later in his police career, he moved to Cheshunt in Hertfordshire and served with the Hertfordshire Constabulary until his retirement, when it appears that he and Jane, with daughter Ellen and her children, returned to the farm in Barrow Hill to continue the work of his father who had died in 1892. In the 1911 census, Amos is recorded as a Metropolitan police pensioner and retired farm labourer, ably assisted in the running of the farm by the large Stearns family (his daughter's family).

Amos Simpson was remembered as an upright and moral man by his family and was greatly respected in the community. The report of his death in the *Suffolk and Essex Free Press* of 18 April 1917 said:

> His wife died 5 years ago and since then he has been attended to by his devoted daughter who lost her husband (killed in action) on September 13th 1916 leaving 5 young children. His son and daughter in law came to spend the Easter with him and they had a pleasant time. Mr. Simpson was very cheerful on the Monday morning and sang "The Last Rose of Summer" to the monophone. He was taken suddenly ill in the evening and died on Tuesday morning at 8 o'clock leaving 1 son, a widowed daughter, a daughter in law, 5 grandchildren and many relatives and old friends to mourn their loss.
>
> He will be greatly missed by all, being a devoted husband, loving father and a warm friend.

According to the family story attached to the shawl, on the night of Catherine Eddowes' murder, Simpson was on 'special duties', when regular officers were transferred temporarily to undertake specific responsibilities, such as protecting public offices and buildings, dockyards, military stations, as well as the premises of private individuals and public companies. So although Simpson was based in N, or Islington Division, the execution of 'special duties' often meant moving from one police division to another and he could easily have been in H Division's territory, which comes very close to Mitre Square, within earshot of a police whistle. Another officer we know was in a similar situation was PC Alfred Long who found the fragment of Catherine Eddowes' apron and the 'Juwes' graffiti on the wall of Wentworth Dwellings in Goulston Street on the morning of the double event. PC Long was actually from A Division (Westminster) and was one of many officers who had been drafted into the Stepney H Division during the murders to increase manpower on the streets.

We know from surviving reports and accounts that officers did cross the City/East End boundary, a good example being City Detective Constable Daniel Halse, who was walking around Goulston Street, Whitechapel (Met territory), not long before PC Long found the piece of Eddowes' apron and the wall-writing there. It appears that during these difficult times, the borders between the City and Metropolitan police areas were, by necessity, becoming fluid.

There is an alternative possibility for such surveillance work outside of the Ripper investigation; I had previously thought that Simpson's presence near Mitre Square was because his special duties were related to the hunt for the Ripper. However, when I spoke to David Melville-Hayes about this subject, he categorically stated that Amos Simpson had been there on the lookout for Fenian terrorists. This was the family story, and he was sure it was true. The 1880s were a time of great political and social upheaval, particularly in the East End, where conditions had provoked the masses of unemployed and chronically poor to, on occasion, rise up and cause great unrest and damage in the West End. Allied to this was the growth of Socialism as a valid political force, as well as Anarchism, both of which had followings among the waves of eastern Europeans who had rapidly and recently made their homes in East London.

As well as this unrest, the rise of the Home Rule movement during the mid-1800s had led to an outbreak of terrorist acts by the Fenians (a collective term for the Fenian Brotherhood and Irish Republican Brotherhood) throughout the decade in protest at the United Kingdom's governance of Ireland. The most extreme acts were committed by 'Dynamitards' who used explosives to create havoc, and significant damage was done to Clerkenwell Prison in 1867 when members of the Irish Republicans attempted to free one of their members who was being held there on remand.

After a lull in attacks during the 1870s, the Fenians stepped up their campaign in the 1880s, targeting many important buildings such as major railway termini, Buckingham Palace and Trafalgar Square. In 1885, two men, James Gilbert Cunningham and Harry Burton, were involved in attempts to bomb several railway stations in the capital: Victoria, Ludgate, Paddington and Charing Cross. Only the bomb at Victoria went off but various errors in setting the device made it ineffective. On 24 January, a bomb went off at the Tower of London, even then a busy tourist attraction. Cunningham was the man responsible, as Burton was attempting to do the same at the House of Commons at the time.

The Tower was within the jurisdiction of H Division and Frederick Abberline was on the case, and through some impressive detective work came to the conclusion that Cunningham was the culprit and arrested him. Burton was soon also apprehended, and it interested me to note that, during the plot, Burton had been lodging at several East End addresses, including Prescott Street in Whitechapel and 5 Mitre Square. As a result of these arrests, Abberline, who would be so important to the Ripper case a few years later, was awarded £20 and gained one of his many career commendations for his efforts.

There may not be written evidence from the time that categorically proves the family story of how Simpson came into the possession of the shawl, but equally it cannot be disproven and there appears to be no deliberate attempt at deception. Indeed, the story has pretty much stayed the same over the years and if we ignore the misreporting that Simpson *found* Eddowes' body and stick to the story as it was passed down to Amos Simpson's descendants, then his presence in and around Mitre Square on that fateful morning of 30 September 1888 is not unreasonable and, in fact, not at all unlikely.

But before I track the later movements of the shawl, I want to mention two interesting references which suggest that knowledge of its existence goes back a lot further than Paul Harrison's tip-off from Chief Inspector Mick Wyatt in 1988. The first, and least important, one is a rather curious article about a 'Whitechapel Club' in Chicago, and the story dates from 1891.

The Whitechapel Club is interesting because it underlines how far the story of Jack the Ripper spread, and what a hold it had on people. The club was formed in 1889 by a small group of journalists and lasted a mere five years. The core membership was made up of newspapermen, but also included artists, musicians, physicians and lawyers. Inside, the club resembled some kind of Black Museum with decor including Indian blankets soaked with blood, nooses and knives that had been used in murders. Skulls, often for drinking out of, were everywhere. Their president was supposedly Jack the Ripper himself, although of course he never attended and so all meetings were chaired by the vice-president. These meetings were usually ribald, drink-fuelled affairs, during which members would tell stories, jokes, poems or monologues amid a great deal of good-natured insults and heckling. References to the club often appeared in the Chicago press, and one article, written by Bill Nye and published in the *Idaho Statesman* on 3 May 1891, made mention of an artefact from one of the Ripper murders in a supposed communiqué from their never-present leader back in London:

> Perhaps I am as well off here amongst friends, suppressing vice and evading the keen eyed police, as I would be in America, where the social evil does not as yet own the town.
>
> Do all that you can to make the club cheerful and bright. I send by this steamer a grey plaid shawl, stiff with the gore of No. 3. It will make a nice piano cover, I think. Could you not arrange with the city to combine your dining room with the city morgue, so that rent could be saved and your dining hall have about it a home-like air which money alone cannot procure?

It was obviously just another of the hoaxes club members played on each other, but the reference to a shawl, albeit from 'No. 3' – one would assume it meant Elizabeth Stride, the other half of the double event – was interesting nonetheless, even if the 'plaid' description was far from my silk shawl.

The second near-contemporary reference, and certainly a more intriguing one, was from an article in an American magazine called *The Collector: A Current Record of Art, Bibliography, and Antiquarianism*, a specialist magazine that contained regular reports from London, Paris, Berlin and other places on collections and collectors. The article, published on

2 November 1892, was from their London correspondent and concerned a meeting he had had with a London collector who was not named.

> But the grisliest freak of a local collectorship which has recently come to light is that of a native who is making a museum of mementoes of Jack the Ripper . . . My acquaintance with him is due by accident. Having some business in Fleet Street the other day, I turned in to the The Cheese [the Old Cheshire Cheese pub in Fleet Street, one assumes] for a chop, and there met a couple of men who exercise editorial functions on certain of our daily papers. In the course of conversation one of them mentioned a rather odd thing which had occurred to him that morning. His landlady had requested permission to speak to him when she sent up his breakfast, and this being accorded, she had stated in substance: There was some person in London who bought things connected with the Ripper murders, and the charwoman whom she employed owned a shawl which had been worn by one of the victims. She wished to dispose of it, and on principle that journalists know everything, or ought to, the landlady inquired of her lodger where this collector could be found. The lodger promised to look the matter up, when he had time to spare for the search after such a needle in a haystack.
>
> He had hardly finished telling us about it when a fat – paunched and rosy – looking man of the middle age, who had been gobbling a steak with marrow bone sauce at the next table, came over to us and introduced himself. He gave us his card, which showed him to be engaged in coals as a business, and stated that he was the Jack the Ripper

collector, and stood ready to negotiate for the charwoman's relic. At his invitation I accompanied him to his abode, which was an old house where he also had his office, at the head of the wharf where his barges landed with freight. He occupied the upper portion of the house alone, being long a childless widower, as he explained, and he had his Ripper museum arranged and ticketed in an old bookcase behind glazed doors. It was a sickening collection of rags and dirty trifles generally, and included even some stones and packages of dirt picked up at the scenes of the hideous crimes they commemorated. When he informed me, in a voice husky with pride and marrow-bone sauce that one special envelope of dirt had blood on it, 'Yes, sir; blood genuine blood,' I was glad enough to remember an engagement and leave him to the study of his unique and unenviable collection.

The name of the 'charwoman' who supposedly owned the shawl is missing from the story. If the tale is genuine (and it is almost too bizarre to have been invented) and the shawl mentioned was actually the one supposedly taken from Catherine Eddowes, then the identity of the 'charwoman' could have been Amos Simpson's wife, Jane, who we know did not like or want the shawl.

Records of Jane's employment status are very thin on the ground; in the census records for most of her adult life, the relevant section was left blank, as it was on her marriage certificate. However, in the 1871 census, Jane (Wilkins) of Bourton-on-the-Water, aged twenty-three, is listed as housemaid to John Bundy and his daughter Elizabeth at their home at 46 Crowndale Road, St Pancras. Jane Wilkins would marry Amos Simpson at Old St Pancras Church three years later in the presence of Elizabeth Bundy, and perhaps by the early 1890s, working as a domestic elsewhere, she was giving serious consideration to getting the shawl out of her home, a plan that never reached fruition. Although she was married to a policeman and had two children to care for, like many women Jane may have worked as a cleaner to add to their income, although this is purely supposition on my part. The *Collector* article is a possible near-contemporary reference to the shawl. It may simply be a coincidence, but David Melville-Hayes told me when I met him that he believed a relative, possibly Amos's son, worked at the Cheshire Cheese pub at around the time that the shawl was offered for sale in 1891, staying there until 1900.

By the time Bill Waddell at the Scotland Yard Black Museum was made aware of the shawl's existence a hundred years later, David Melville-Hayes had removed two pieces and framed them for John and Janice Dowler. David first approached the museum in late 1991: he felt the museum was the right home for such a bizarre item as the shawl. Waddell was interested in finding out more, and so Hayes was invited to Scotland Yard to show the shawl. Impressed, Waddell asked Hayes if he was prepared to let them have the shawl as part of their collection and Hayes agreed, on the proviso that it was strictly 'on loan'. With the museum not open to the public, the shawl spent the next six years hidden away, safe but inaccessible to all but those privileged visitors to 'The Black'. It was in 1997 that Andy and Sue Parlour became involved.

The Parlours' interest in Jack the Ripper was sparked around 1992 when, during research into Andy's family tree, they discovered that he was descended from George Nichols, the cousin of Mary Ann Nichols. Andy himself hailed from the East End and had moved with his family to Essex in the 1960s, as many East Enders had done before (and still do). From there on, the Parlours began researching the murders in earnest, visiting the crime scenes and archives across the country, as well as creating their own research business, ASP Historical Research, and Ten Bells Publishing, named after the famous Spitalfields pub.

Living in Clacton-on-Sea, the Parlours had heard the story that a local resident owned a shawl associated with one of the Ripper's victims. By now, the framed cuttings had passed from the Dowlers to an antiques dealer in Thetford and the Parlours were able to buy them from there. The hunt was soon on to find the mysterious owner of the rest of the shawl. They found him, but not in a way they would have anticipated.

One Sunday morning, early in 1997, the Parlours were at a local antiques fair, looking for old London prints and other related ephemera, when they fell into conversation with a stall owner, a distinguished-looking gentleman who asked them why they were specifically looking for items relating to the East End. Hearing that they were researching the Ripper murders, the stallholder said that he had a connection to the story, adding that he was in possession of an artefact directly relating to Catherine Eddowes. By some amazing stroke of serendipity, the Parlours had found David Melville-Hayes. Letting him know that they were the current owners of the framed sections, they asked where the rest of the shawl was and he told them that it was in the Black Museum at Scotland Yard.

At that time, the Parlours were working on a book about the Ripper murders, which was being written with author Kevin

O'Donnell, the book I first saw at the auction. In late 1997, the Parlours and O'Donnell made arrangements to visit the Black Museum to see the shawl for themselves, accompanied by respected Ripper and true-crime researcher Keith Skinner, who had very close links with the museum. By this time, the curator was John Ross, an ex-Metropolitan police officer. Ross retrieved the shawl from his office – it was obviously not on display – and showed it to the visitors. He admitted that he was not convinced that the shawl had once belonged to Catherine Eddowes, going on to say that the Black Museum only kept artefacts that were unequivocally proven to have been connected with famous crimes. After a few minutes of looking at it, the shawl was taken back to whatever obscure storage area it was being kept in.

The visit to Scotland Yard that day left the Parlours bemused: they felt the shawl was not being given its due by the museum. Back in Clacton, they told David Melville-Hayes that the shawl was not on display. He was disappointed and decided that, as the museum wasn't doing anything with it, he might as well have it back. He entrusted the Parlours to make the arrangements to have the shawl returned, and they contacted John Ross on his behalf – who in the end seemed reluctant to let it go. Nonetheless, the shawl was 'on loan' and David Melville-Hayes could have it back whenever he chose and so a date was arranged for it to be picked up. The Parlours were advised to bring a letter of confirmation from David, which they did. Before leaving with the shawl, Ross asked the Parlours when they would be bringing it back, and they replied with a diplomatic, 'We'll have to speak to the owner.' Before they returned the shawl, Scotland Yard had also taken a small sample of their own, which measured 2 by 4 inches.

Once David had the shawl back in Clacton, he decided to let the Parlours look after it, which they were more than pleased to do. The shawl was kept by the Parlours for many years and generated great interest. It was displayed in a glass case at the Royal Festival Hall on the South Bank, and in 2001 it went to Bournemouth where it was shown (with other Ripper ephemera, including the famous 'Dear Boss' letter) at the annual Jack the Ripper conference. These conferences, first held in Ipswich in 1996, provide Ripper experts and enthusiasts with the chance to get together, hear speakers on the subject and share information and ideas. For many years the venues alternated between Britain and America, where interest in the Ripper has never abated.

Despite all the interest in the shawl and its potential importance in the case, it had never been authenticated or scientifically tested. In 2006, Atlantic Productions, a television company specializing in factual programmes, asked if they could feature it in a documentary they were working on. Executives from the company met the Parlours, explaining that they would like to have the shawl tested for DNA by an expert, on camera for the programme. David Melville-Hayes gave permission but insisted on being present at the examination.

Testing took place at the Parlours' home in Clacton on 30 August 2006. That morning, the film crew from Atlantic arrived, followed by John Gow, a leading DNA forensics expert and his assistant Jennifer Clugston, who were flown in from Glasgow to conduct the testing. The shawl was laid out in a spare room and John and Jennifer spent much time examining it, surprised by its size and concluding that the large, torpedo-shaped stains appeared to be dried blood that had spattered across the surface. Several swabs were taken from the areas that John and Jennifer believed were stained with blood, human or otherwise. Interviews with Gow and David Melville-Hayes were filmed and eventually the film crew packed up their equipment and the experts were driven to the airport for their return flight to Scotland.

The finished documentary was aired in November 2006 and strangely, despite being featured quite a lot, there was hardly any specific discussion about the shawl. One of the interviewees, John Grieve, the Metropolitan police's first Director of Intelligence, was asked if he felt that the shawl was genuine.

'The DNA testing was inconclusive,' he answered.

This was a big disappointment and the Parlours and David Melville-Hayes have never been given the DNA test results by Atlantic. Apparently they had been taken away by a police officer based in Glasgow. Frustratingly, nothing had been proved: they were no nearer knowing whether the shawl belonged to Catherine Eddowes, whether it had been found at Mitre Square or indeed whether it had any link whatsoever to the Ripper story.

By the beginning of 2007, David Melville-Hayes had made the decision to sell the shawl. Now in his seventies, suffering from poor health and with his own two sons not interested in taking on custody of the shawl, he felt it was time to pass this peculiar family heirloom on to a permanent owner who, appreciating its potential significance, would look after it as well as he had done. He told me that whenever he took the shawl out of its wrapping he felt a coldness descend on the room, and a strange feeling would come over him, which strengthened his resolve to sell it. An auction seemed to be the logical step forward and Melville-Hayes decided that proceeds from any sale would go to the Royal National Lifeboat Institute. This is where I came into the picture.

My belief in the importance of the shawl increased the more I knew about it: the provenance sounded authentic, although I am always cautious of stories that have been handed down through families. But here there was enough powerful detail to convince me. The next, obvious, step was to take up where the TV documentary failed: I determined to find scientific proof to back up the history of the shawl. Despite their inconclusive testing, I was convinced that the key lay in the scientific developments of recent years.

CHAPTER EIGHT

FINDING HUMAN BLOOD

I was driving along the M6 on my way to North Wales, where my business was based. I had to make an important phone call at 6.30 p.m., so I pulled into the service station on the toll road that loops around Birmingham, and called the number.

'We can't nail this until we can test a living descendant of Catherine Eddowes,' said Ian Barnes, Professor of Molecular Palaeobiology at the University of London. I had called Ian soon after I started my search for a scientist who could investigate the shawl for possible DNA. It was the summer of 2007, and I had approached Mark Thomas, Professor of Evolutionary Genetics at University College London. Professor Thomas was an expert in ancient DNA and in 1994 was one of the first people to read the DNA sequence of the extinct woolly mammoth. He put me on to Ian Barnes, one of his colleagues and another specialist in ancient DNA.

Ian was very enthusiastic about the project, and we chatted more over the phone over the next few days. I was keen to find out if the stains on the shawl were human blood.

But it was the phone call I made from the service station car park that shifted my research up a gear. Ian told me then that the only value of extracting DNA from the shawl would be if there was something to compare it with, and we would need the DNA of a direct descendant of the victim. Just getting DNA from the shawl was a pointless exercise: it proved nothing unless it could be tied to Catherine Eddowes.

So this had to be my next effort. I am not a trained researcher, although I have become much better over the years since I started this quest, but I soon heard about a book which gave family trees for the descendants of the Ripper victims. It was out of print, and I found that there were only a couple of places in the country where I could see it. One was the Cambridge University Library, which was where I chose to go, as we were living in Newmarket at the time. I went into the hallowed library on a day pass, having been photographed, issued with a badge, and told that I had to make notes in pencil (to prevent books being defaced) and that I could not photocopy more than 10 per cent of the book. I ordered the book, waited about twenty minutes until it arrived, and then began excitedly tracing Catherine's family.

To my great disappointment the family tree ended with Catherine Sarah Hall, who was descended from Catherine Eddowes' daughter, and who died in Blackheath in the 1950s. It was interesting to see that the name Catherine had come down through the family, but ultimately very frustrating because I was no closer to finding a living descendant. Then I wondered if the author of the book had deliberately kept the family tree short of the present generation, perhaps to protect the family from unwanted attention.

I managed to make email contact with him, tracing him through a Jack the Ripper website. His response to my request for help was a sharp rebuff. The message was clear: leave well alone. I was disappointed and annoyed at his attitude at the time, but today I can understand that he was protecting the family members. Interest in anybody descended from a victim (or suspect) in the Ripper case is very strong and the author of the book had spent many years gaining their trust and treating their stories with sensitivity. He probably felt that the last thing he needed was some newcomer to the field barging in and potentially spoiling the relationship. At the time, however, it was quite a blow. All my attempts to find a living descendant had stalled. I felt, as I have done at several points on this journey, as if I was trying to run uphill in flip-flops and the hill was getting steeper all the time.

For a time it went on to the back burner, because I was completely absorbed in family matters and business problems. I put the shawl out of my mind but I never forgot about it, and would from time to time take it out and look at it, but it was certainly not centre stage in my life.

I was trying to sell my care homes business, and the sale was long and protracted, and took more than six months, and was a time-consuming and complicated affair. The shawl and the Ripper were not at the forefront of my mind. Eventually the sale went through in the spring of 2008, and I made a good enough profit to be able to take some time off from business and decide what I was going to do next.

A couple of years after Alexander was born we decided to try for another baby, because we didn't want him to be an only child. There were major gynaecological problems, and again we had to use IVF. We were excited when we heard Sally had conceived twins, boys, at the beginning of 2008, but we were warned immediately that one of them had a heart defect and would not survive. The other one was healthy, but at risk because of the position of the other baby and the medical team told us that there was only a slight chance of the baby surviving.

We lived with it day by day: is this going to be the day when we lose our babies? It was a harrowing, unbearably painful time. It was the only thing we could focus on. The day came when Sally felt less movement and she knew, deep down, that one of the babies had died. It was the healthy baby who had died. His twin could not survive without open-heart surgery immediately after being born. We had to make the heart-rending decision to put our poorly baby to sleep, and then Sally had to go through the hell of an induced labour after carrying our dead twins inside her for almost a week.

We had, at the time, moved into our apartment in Brighton Marina, and we were living there when we lost the twins. It was while we were there that something happened to rekindle my enthusiasm for the search for the Ripper. In Brighton I joined a gym, mainly to distract me from the moment-to-moment agony of worrying about the twins. Going to a gym is a very normal thing to do, but one that set me off again on my pursuit, for the oddest of reasons. When I went for the induction, the session where a fitness trainer assesses what you are capable of, the young man running the session said to me: 'Do you have any hobbies? What do you do in your spare time?'

He was only making polite conversation, in the same way that hairdressers always ask if you've got any holidays lined up. I replied with similar platitudes about going to the cinema, and out for restaurant meals. Then I added, 'And I've got this strange, rather geeky interest.'

I don't know why I said it, because I knew from experience that other people tended to find my interest in the Ripper rather ghoulish. But naturally he asked what it was, and I told him.

'Oh, that's very interesting. I'm descended from one of the suspects, Aaron Kosminski,' he said.

I was floored. Not only was he claiming to be descended from a suspect, it was *the* suspect, the one Alan McCormack had told me with great certainty was the Ripper. Had fate just handed to me another amazing connection?

It turned out to be a complete red herring. Another blind alley for me to stumble down. There was a story in the young man's family about Kosminski being their ancestor, but research proved it to be completely wrong, confirming my innate suspicion about family yarns, even though I was following my hunch about the shawl on the basis of just such a yarn. But the young man had told me in good faith, and although I wasted a lot of time, I am grateful that he rebooted my interest in the case, and also reminded me that as well as the shawl's connection with Catherine Eddowes, I also had the Kosminski angle to pursue.

Thanks to the fitness trainer, I started on a substantial amount of research into Aaron Kosminski's life and background. For a time, this was the main thrust of my research, and Catherine Eddowes was pushed into the background.

Soon after we moved back from Brighton to our Hertford-shire home, I was working on maps of the East End, trying to sort out in my head where Kosminski had lived, and how close it was to the places the victims were murdered. It was hard to find maps of the area as it was in the 1880s, but I discovered Booth's maps 'descriptive of London poverty', a series of maps made between 1886 and 1903 by the philanthropist and social reformer Charles Booth as part of his crusade to influence government policy towards the poor. The maps are available online, and proved to be a lot more use to me than Google street maps.

It was on Halloween, 31 October 2008, that I was finally able to look at the layout of the area, and I was blown away by what I saw, realizing how close Greenfield Street (now renamed Greenfield Road) where Kosminski lived is to the scene of the third murder. It is less than a minute's walk from the scene to his door. I couldn't sleep, and jumped into my car in the early hours of the morning and drove to the East End. I stood at the corner of Greenfield Road looking over at Berner Street, and was filled with an immense sense of being right, of having found the Ripper, even though I had no more proof than anyone had for any of the other suspects. But I also had a deep conviction that one day, whatever it took, I *would* have the proof.

This was when I first walked his routes through the streets, timing them to see just how easy it was for him to slip around the area and then take refuge back at home.

But before I could go further with my Kosminski research – or any other Ripper research – I was again overtaken by family life. The great news is that Sally became pregnant, and this time it was a normal, healthy pregnancy which resulted in our daughter Annabel, who was born in June 2009. I also embarked on a series of new business ventures, building up a property portfolio, and once again the shawl and everything to do with Jack the Ripper was very much on the back burner.

Then, in April 2011, I received an email from Andy and Sue Parlour who had always fronted the ownership of the shawl for me. They had been approached by a TV company to take part in a documentary. The programme was to feature former Metropolitan police detective and forensics expert Robin Napper conducting a 'hunt' for Jack the Ripper. The TV company said that Napper would be concentrating on the suspect Frederick Deeming and he was going to use cutting-edge forensic techniques to link Deeming with the Whitechapel murders.

Deeming had, as I've said, at one time been my top choice as the likely suspect, and I was not the only person who favoured him: for many years, the Black Museum in Australia exhibited his death mask as that of Jack the Ripper. Despite claims of Deeming being in South Africa at the time of the murders, research for the documentary showed he was possibly in Hull in the north of England at the time. When Deeming's skull was located in Australia, the potential to extract DNA material from it for a new investigation would, clearly, make compelling television. But, as I had learnt, they needed something to compare that DNA with, and that meant some piece of contemporary evidence from 1888. As far as the programme makers were concerned, this meant either the alleged Ripper letters or the shawl. In the end, they tried both.

I agreed with the Parlours that, although I had turned down several approaches from television companies, this one was worth doing. I knew they were wrong about Deeming, after the information I had been given by Alan McCormack and my subsequent research into Kosminski (of which more later) but I was interested in them having DNA from Deeming: it was the solid scientific approach I felt needed to be taken, and if they got DNA from the shawl at least I would know if the stain was blood, and if it was human. So I agreed to cooperate with the programme makers.

In the documentary, Napper met the Parlours who showed

him their framed portions of the shawl and Napper, in a contrived dialogue, asked where the rest of it was, and was told that I had it. For the filming, I took Napper to a 'secret location', a property I was developing at the time, so he could inspect the shawl. From here it became a bit of a farce. Napper looked at the shawl, enthused about it resembling the 'published descriptions' and then dropped the big question: 'Would you be happy to have it forensically tested?' he asked me.

I had been expecting it, but I was genuinely concerned about damage to the shawl by any invasive testing. The film crew assured me that no damage would result, and that I could be there to watch and voice my concerns, should I have any. So with my agreement in May 2011 the analysis went ahead at Liverpool John Moores University (LJMU) and was filmed for the show.

On the day of filming we discussed what testing was to be conducted and I realized that the work was going to be mainly superficial. There were going to be surface samples of one of the stains taken, and some samples from one of the edges of the shawl, which was explained to me as being the most likely point where the killer would have held it.

It was clear that the tests were not invasive, and although I was relieved that the shawl was not being damaged, even a layman could see they were also likely to be ineffectual. I remember thinking 'This doesn't look like it's going to cut it . . .' The scientists were shown pointing out ideal areas for analysis, basically the stains that everybody had been saying for years were bloodstains, and then proceeding to rub cotton buds over the patches in an attempt to gather material from which DNA could be extracted.

I found out later that all they were likely to get from this method was dead skin cells, dust or somebody else's dandruff – superficial and recent detritus and hardly a definitive examination of a deep, ingrained century-old bloodstain. This method is the standard way to obtain samples from textiles for DNA analysis in recent cases, but it is wholly inadequate for an item as old as this, with many years of possible contamination from everyone who had handled the shawl. The scientists had not seen the shawl before, and were given a very short time frame, and short notice. Not surprisingly, the documentary declared that the results were inconclusive.

Interestingly, after taking samples from the back of a stamp that was attached to an envelope that had once contained a Ripper letter, the analysis showed that the person who licked the stamp was definitely not Frederick Deeming, because it was the DNA of a woman. Apparently it would have been common in the nineteenth century for somebody posting a letter to take it to a post office where a counter clerk would put the stamp on, making any attempts to get the Ripper's DNA from the saliva on the back of a stamp a complete waste of time.

The 'tests' conducted on the shawl in May 2011 were no better than those done in the earlier 2006 documentary, and no results of the tests were included in the programme. So once again we had a Ripper documentary with high production values, lots of talk about 'hard evidence', 'reinvestigating the case', 'new suspect' but no evidence that actually solved anything. I was disappointed, because I was even more convinced that the answer to this whole case lay in science, the science that the shawl could, I believed, provide.

But making the documentary was a seminal point in this story, because it was on this film set that I met a man who has become a vitally important part of my search for the Ripper, the man whose scientific expertise, allied with my determination to get all possible evidence out of the shawl, has meant that we can now lay the Ripper case to rest.

When I first saw Dr Jari Louhelainen my initial thought was 'scientist'. He looks what he is: he's a giant bear of a man, with spectacles and tousled hair, and a Scandinavian pragmatism that makes him seem like an absent-minded professor. I have come to know him well, and there is much more to him than this: he has a hinterland. He is an ex-ice hockey player, an avid skier, he is married to another scientist, Riitta, and he has two young daughters. He left his native Finland in 1994 when he moved to Sweden to finish his PhD at the internationally renowned Karolinska Institute, one of the world's leading medical universities (which is also one of the Nobel Prize-awarding bodies). This is where Jari met his wife and where their first daughter, Rebecca, was born in 1997. After staying in Sweden for six years, he moved to England in 2000.

On Jari's part, when he first saw me he thought I was 'eager and intense'. Those are good words to describe how I felt: I wanted to get on with decoding the information I was sure the shawl contained. Since that first meeting we have become allies in the quest, with me being the driving force while Jari was, and still is, the neutral, balanced expert who did not always understand my need for everything to be done as quickly as possible.

He says: 'When I met Russ, he was so different to the scientists and policemen I normally deal with, who have no personal interest in what they are doing, and are sometimes dispassionate. He was so enthusiastic, I did not know what to make of it all. At first, I didn't take it too seriously.'

Jari had heard of Jack the Ripper: he really is a global brand. In Finland he is known as 'Viiltaja Jack', which translates as Ripper Jack.

'I did not know too much about the case, it had not been of great interest to me,' he says. 'When I was asked to take part in the programme I regarded it just as another job.'

Jari is a Senior Lecturer in Molecular Biology at LJMU, as well as Associate Professor of Biochemistry at the University of Helsinki and he has two major lines of research: forensic genetics and medical/mammalian genetics. The latter includes gene studies of top athletes, in collaboration with the university's Department of Sport Science.

If you ask him why he is working in two such different fields he explains that the methods used in medical genetics are very similar to those used in forensic science, so it is not difficult for him to juggle the two disciplines. There are obvious advantages as well, as he has brought quite a few methods which are used in medical genetics into his forensic work: medical genetics is a well-funded field and at the edge of scientific discovery, whereas forensics lag behind. In his résumé on the LJMU website, his expertise in the forensic area includes 'determination of age of forensic samples', ' applications of Next Generation sequencing for forensics', 'forensic imaging applications' and 'human identification using novel genetic methods'.

He came to England for a post-doctoral position in cancer genetics, based at Cancer Research UK in Leeds, and his wife started working at Leeds University. In 2002 their second daughter, Sophie, was born, and they moved to Bradford, which was a good base for their outdoor activities and close enough to Leeds to commute. Soon after, Jari took up a post at Oxford University, and moved from there to Liverpool John

Moores University because the journey to and from Oxford was difficult and time-consuming.

Jari spends four nights a week in Liverpool and the weekends with his family in Bradford. He works on unsolved forensic cold cases for Interpol, Western Australia Police and Merseyside Police, and he is one of the supervisors for a Roman dig in Chester, the site where the Cistercian Poulton Abbey once stood. There are hundreds of skeletons on the site from the medieval period, so this is a long-term project for him. The aim is to establish who these people were, and where they came from. He is also involved in a research project analysing remains from the *Mary Rose*, the warship from the reign of Henry VIII. He was recruited to the TV programme when Robert Napper asked a contact of his who would be the best person, and was told, 'If there's anyone in the world who can do it, it's Jari.'

Even on that first day when we met for the TV programme, I picked up on his dry sense of humour: there was a funny moment when on camera I was asked to hand him a bag that was supposed to contain the shawl: in fact, because the shawl was still carefully preserved between the sheets of cardboard, the bag was full of my socks and undies.

Jari maintained a very professional approach during the testing and filming, but I could sense that, like me, he felt the work he was being asked to do, in one day, was superficial and scientifically speaking a waste of time. But although he was not particularly interested in the Jack the Ripper story, Jari was fascinated by the possibility of a piece of fabric as old as the shawl which clearly contained some information in its stains. He told me, that same day, that we should take things further, away from the cameras.

So a few days after the filming I telephoned Jari to ask about the cost of a really serious set of tests. They were substantial. On the spur of the moment I said no, in that case I did not want to do them. I had the feeling I have had so often on this quest: I had hit a brick wall, and I did not want to throw a lot more money at it. As so often before I told myself, 'Maybe you are not meant to do this. You've had a crack, it's not working, let it be.' I was disappointed, but as usual told myself to get on with the rest of my life and put Jack the Ripper behind me.

But the following week Jari called me back, saying that he could do these tests in his own time for me, free, as long as he could write a paper on his findings when it was all over. I was delighted to accept: the very fact that he wanted to do this made me feel that, if a scientist of Jari's standing was willing to do this work, there must be a real chance that we would find something. Suddenly, from that one phone call, my enthusiasm was back to full strength.

I realized this was probably just another research project to Jari, but we agreed that this was going to be our project, with no outside interference. Our partnership was established, informally, and from then on Jari joined me in the pursuit of the Ripper, even though he probably did not at this stage appreciate the full implications of what we were embarking on.

I met Jari at his laboratory at LJMU on the morning of 14 June 2011 and he gave me a full explanation as to what he was going to do during the primary analysis. This included taking a strand from one end of the shawl to try and establish a date when the shawl was made, as well as special photographic analysis under different lighting conditions to establish what the stains on the shawl were.

I left the shawl with him, and because I was on Merseyside I went off to spend the day with my mum. Jari spent the day examining the shawl using different forensic light sources, outside the usual visible light range, and also using special photography equipment, including a camera which was able to see in the infrared region.

Jari took the shawl into a special room which has a sterile, dust-free vacuum environment, with an extractor to take out all contaminants, and which can also be blacked-out to make it free of any unwanted light contamination. Bloodstains on floral (as in the shawl) or other complex patterns are often undetectable in normal conditions. In the vacuum room, the hunt for previously undetected bloodstains started with a set of different infrared filters ranging from 720–950 nanometres (nm).

Normal human vision is in the region of 400–700 nm. This is called 'visible light'. The same applies to light sources we use: the main output from standard bulbs or other light sources are in the visible light region. Taking a photograph with a normal camera (film or digital) results in a photograph which corresponds closely with what we see with our own eyes. Normal digital cameras have an in-built filter on top of the image sensor which blocks the infrared region (over 700 nm) and camera lenses usually block most of the invisible light regions, including ultraviolet (UV – less than 350–400 nm), which helps the photographs look as natural as possible.

In forensics, using non-visible light for recording something unseen by the naked eye is a very useful tool. The infrared light can reveal hidden writing, or inks and dyes which have been obscured by other substances. For example analysis of old paintings can find the previously erased brushwork of sketches beneath the visible surface. This type of photography uses a camera which is sensitive to infrared but does not capture the visible or UV light. In other words, the camera records light well above the 700 nm wavelength and all visible light is blocked.

Another type of special photography is 'reflective UV photography' which uses a UV light source together with a UV-blocked camera. So, the camera cannot actually see UV light at all, but if that light makes something emit fluorescence in the visible region (above 400 nm), it will record it. We are all probably familiar with the visual effects of UV lights, usually for theatrical or display purposes, where they are sometimes used in concerts or nightclubs. Our white shirts glow brightly under this light because the shirt contains materials or compounds known as 'phosphors' which fluoresce under such conditions. UV light is used in forensics because many natural substances, including those from the human body, also contain phosphors and will fluoresce in a variety of ways. For example, semen stains will emit a bright fluorescence and can be recorded using this method. This is called a presumptive test, a first step in identifying substances, as there can be other molecules present (both natural and artificial) which will fluoresce as well.

Using this special equipment, the shawl itself looked pattern-less and quite light-coloured overall. The infrared light also revealed a previously undetected, very dark, slim, almost rectangular mark in the middle of the larger stain, the one in the middle of the shawl. This pattern was very clearly visible, with high contrast, on both sides of the shawl, even though the actual stain itself was barely visible to the naked eye. It did not correspond to the visible patterns on the shawl. Jari speculated that this mark could be blood, but as it was rectangular, it was quite unusual. Jari still does not know what this is, but he speculates that the shawl could have been pressed with a blunt object but is mystified as to why it left a mark. If it was oil or tar it would be easily identified.

With the reflective UV he could not see anything fluorescent on the reverse side of the shawl; however, when it was turned over he could see a set of fluorescent stains which were very possibly semen. It is known that urine and saliva fluoresce under ultraviolet light but they tend to give off an orange hue, whereas seminal fluorescence is usually greenish. The stains Jari spotted had a clear green cast. When moving further towards the other end, a set of darker stains could be seen. Again, in a typical forensic analysis these would be candidates for blood-stains.

When I got back to the lab at 4.30 p.m. Jari told me that in his opinion the shawl held bloodstains that were 'consistent with arterial blood spatter caused by slashing'. He said the distribution of the stains was key to this finding of 'slashing': his experience working with crime enforcement agencies and training crime scene investigators meant he recognized the pattern. The white spots that I, in my ignorance, had put down to the ageing process were in fact blood spatter. He explained to me that the pattern is consistent with medium-velocity blood spatter, coming from an angle that shows the blood was not just dropped on the shawl. Spatter like this is often involved with beating or stabbing. High-velocity spatter could be caused by shooting, and low-velocity by blood dripping onto the object. There was no evidence of dripping on the shawl, and Jari concluded that the blood spatter was 'compatible with the details of the killing'. I was thrilled to hear this.

He also said that one of the other stains was fluorescing under his lights in a way that made him think it could be semen, although he was, as a true scientist, very non-committal and cautious.

As I heard his words, delivered in his unemotional way, I felt a surge of excitement, my heart racing. Of course, the presence of blood could not be definitely proved using just photography. Of course, it could be animal blood, it may not be as old as 1888, there were all sorts of possibilities. And, of course, Jari had to do more testing before we would know anything definitive. But it looked to me, the layman, very promising.

He took me into the scientific vacuum room to see for myself. I was kitted out head to toe in a plastic boiler suit and goggles, so that I felt as if I belonged on the set of *Ghostbusters*. We looked at the shawl with the naked eye under normal lighting conditions and then I put on the goggles, which made the room pitch black. Then Jari showed me how the stains showed up under different lighting: it felt spooky and weird. There was one larger (approximately 2–3 inches in diameter) stain in the middle and smaller stains near one end of the shawl. Some other stains were also detected near the edges of the shawl, and Jari pointed out to me odd patterns not visible to the naked eye.

As I drove home down the motorway that evening the words 'blood spatter consistent with slashing' played through my brain. I knew what the Ripper had done to the body of Catherine Eddowes: it all seemed to fit in. It felt like we were on track, things were going in the right direction at last. But I had to contain my exhilaration. There was nobody who would understand my excitement. The only person on the journey with me was Jari, and he was a dispassionate scientist who at this stage did not understand my sense of urgency.

Now that we had started, I was very keen to get more tests done as soon as possible, but because Jari was doing the work on the shawl alongside his regular workload, I had to be patient – and, of course, I understood his problems, especially when one of his daughters was unwell, and when his car was smashed into by another driver. But every time the work had to be set back, the frustration for me was intense. The delay was torture.

It was in the New Year, 20 January 2012, that I went back to Liverpool with the shawl again, this time travelling by train, leaving my home in Hertfordshire at 4.30 a.m. It didn't bother me getting up so early: I was so excited it was hard to sleep. I delivered the shawl to the lab at 9 a.m., and again left Jari to get on with it. It was a grim, rainy, cold day, and I had nothing to do but to wander around Liverpool. I went to the Tate Liverpool, I went to John Lewis and every other large store, just to get into the warm and out of the rain. I texted Jari after a few hours:

'Are you ready yet?'

'No, another hour.'

That's how it went all afternoon.

It was 5 p.m. when I was finally summoned back to the lab, and the first thing I saw, and which sent my spirits soaring, was a big grin on Jari's face.

'How did you get on?' I asked.

'Look at this,' he said.

He showed me one of the large stains on the shawl and told me it contained 'evidence of split body parts', and then he said some very encouraging words. 'This would be very difficult to forge.'

He had used different equipment, and the day was not an unqualified success. The initial presumptive blood tests proved to be inconclusive, the main reason being that the dyes used in the shawl inhibited any firm result. He took swabs and tested for an enzyme method reaction (known as the KM method), which works well with fresh samples. It is the first stage of analysis and Jari had explained to me that finding a positive trace for blood was a long shot due to the age of the stains, but it was worth performing the process. If Jari could establish the presence of blood it would give him something to work from, and hopefully DNA material could be extracted and we could move on to the next stage. If not, we would have to use other, more complicated, methods. Unfortunately this technique did not work for us, but all was not lost: there was more work he could do. (In fact, science moves so fast that there is already another process available today which would probably have worked for us.)

I'd been reading up about the significance of DNA 'fingerprints', and although I didn't understand everything Jari said, I knew some of the science. A genome is all of a living thing's genetic material, and contains the entire set of hereditary instructions for building, running and maintaining an organism, and passing life on to the next generation. The genome of an individual will contain forty-six chromosomes, inherited half from the father and half from the mother. The genome also contains genes, which are packaged in those chromosomes and have the specific characteristics of the organism: a little like a Russian doll, with smaller dolls inside bigger dolls, the genome is divided into chromosomes, those chromosomes in turn contain genes, and the genes are made of DNA. Every chromosome has its own specific genes. For example, our chromosome 13 has several hundred genes and one of them is the breast cancer gene BRCA2. On the other hand, chromosome 15 has a gene which affects our eye colour.

Each one of earth's species has its own distinctive genome: the dog genome, the wheat genome, the genomes of the frog and so on. Genomes belong to species, but they also belong to individuals. Though unique to each individual, a human genome is still recognizably human. The genome differences between two people are much smaller than the genome differences between people and close animal relatives such as chimpanzees, but unless you are an identical twin, your genome is still different from that of every other person on earth – in fact, it is different from that of every other person who has ever lived, although, because you inherit so many genes from each of your parents, and thus from your ancestors, there are many points in common, and it is the exact combination that is unique to you. In modern paternity and maternity tests, elements of a child's DNA can be compared with that of a putative parent (usually the father) to detect if traces of their DNA are present in the child's sample.

For standard forensic cases, the genomic DNA is used, as in most cases the DNA is fresh and has not had time to become fragmented, or broken. When looking at DNA which is old and therefore fragmented, the amount of the genomic DNA available is often so low that it cannot be reliably analysed. However, all human cells still have something called mitochondrial DNA. Mitochondrial DNA (mtDNA) is present in the mitochondria, small structures in cells that generate energy for the cell to use as food. Unlike genomic DNA which is created from *both* parents, mtDNA is passed down the generations exclusively through the female line, via the mother's ovum, because the mitochondria in sperm is destroyed during fertilization. Thus the mtDNA of a female will be passed completely intact down the line of direct female descendants for many, many generations.

Forensic laboratories occasionally use mtDNA comparison to identify human remains, and especially to identify older unidentified skeletal remains, and it is so consistent that it has been employed on ancient, often extinct, animal remains to establish evolutionary links into the present day. Statistically, mtDNA is not as powerful as genomic DNA because it is only a small strand, but it still gives a high probability for human identification. The advantage of mtDNA is that it is much more abundant than the genomic DNA. In each human cell we have one copy of genomic DNA but in the same cell we can have *a thousand* copies of mtDNA, which means that even if the genomic DNA has degraded, there should still be enough mtDNA which can be analysed.

Jari explained that further tests on the suspected bloodstains required a different and more effective method of extraction than swabbing, to ensure that the original DNA material could be pulled from the very depths of the stains. He used his own in-house technique which we called 'vacuuming' – this is not the scientific word, but a description that helped me understand the process. Jari's method used a modified sterile pipette filled with a liquid 'buffer' which is injected into the material for testing. The 'buffer' dissolves material trapped in the weave of the fabric without damaging any cells and the pipette sucks it out rapidly. The process of injection and suction takes place in a flash. On an item like the shawl, this would be much more suitable than swabbing, which picks up all sorts of surface contamination such as dust or, worse, dead skin cells from any number of sources – just think how many hands the shawl had passed through in its life.

This vacuuming method ensured that specimens collected would not contain just superficial contamination, but would suck out material like dried cells and biological debris from cells that had been trapped in the shawl for a considerable time. Eventually, Jari was able to confirm that the stains on the shawl contained human genetic material as they gave positive signals for both human genomic and mitochondrial DNA.

Jari had also discovered during the different-light analysis that the large stain in the middle of the shawl, the one with the secondary oblong shape in the middle, showed evidence of different bodily fluids owing to the way the stain fluoresced. The results clearly suggested to him that residue – such as faeces or intestinal fluid – from split body parts was present, and this was why he had been grinning so widely when I got back to the lab. At this stage it was impossible to deduce which specific body parts they were from because it was not possible to differentiate DNA from the liver, from, say, lung tissue. Tissue-type can be determined using so-called 'gene expression profiling' but given the age of the samples involved with the shawl, Jari thought that this would not be possible to do as RNA (ribonucleic acid) would be needed, and RNA is known to degrade even more readily than DNA.

The traces of split body parts were a clear reminder of what Jack the Ripper did to mutilate Catherine's body. What was also interesting was that the stain that indicated different fluids appeared to be replicated at the other end of the shawl, suggesting that the shawl had been folded over the object that left those marks. This was incredible stuff, and I was particularly thrilled by the words, 'This would be very difficult to forge.' Even Jari's sangfroid was momentarily overcome.

Great progress had been made. To summarize, we had now confirmed that there was human blood on the shawl, possibly semen and, most excitingly, evidence of split body parts. Remember, Catherine Eddowes had had her uterus and left kidney removed. I felt we were close to establishing a proper, scientific link between the events in Mitre Square and what appeared on the shawl, which at the time of its retrieval must have been in quite a mess. There was, of course, so much more to be done, but things seemed to be moving in the right direction.

CHAPTER NINE

FINDING DNA

While I was waiting for Jari to do more testing, I set off on another leg of the research: I decided to find out about the shawl itself. After all, it was no good finding it had human blood and semen on it, if it then turned out not to be old enough to date back to the time of Jack the Ripper. I was sure it was at least that old, but I needed to prove it.

Not long into my research I made another, massive discovery, a leap forward that I had not expected.

Considering where it was found, it seemed logical to assume that the shawl had been made in Spitalfields, which was known as a centre for the silk-weaving trade around the eighteenth century, when the Huguenot silk weavers colonized the area, and built the beautiful town houses that have now been preserved. From the late 1600s onwards the area to the east of the City of London, where open fields provided perfect conditions for growing mulberry trees (for silkworms) and the laying out of tenter grounds (for drying and stretching cloth), silk weaving was the major occupation in what is now the East End. The Huguenot houses can be identified by the long windows in their attic spaces, designed to capture as much light as possible for the delicate weaving process. Throughout the seventeenth and eighteenth centuries, Spitalfields silk was highly prized thanks to the skill of the craftsmen, and the area itself built up into a very prosperous neighbourhood.

A mixture of the industrial revolution, when new mechanized weaving technology replaced the traditional looms, and changes in the laws regarding the importation of silks from abroad signalled the end of Spitalfields silk's halcyon days. The Huguenots gradually left the area for the suburbs and Home Counties and the district gradually fell into a deep decline and, as we've seen, by the 1880s was known for its poverty, crime and vice. Those weavers who remained lived in considerably less salubrious surroundings than their predecessors and ultimately the East End translated their traditions into the general 'rag trade'. This line of work was eventually picked up by the eastern European Jewish immigrants and, later still, by settlers from Bangladesh.

Even to my unpractised eye, the shawl seemed to be of high-quality fabric, so I felt it was a remnant of the glory days of the silk weaving trade. By this time in my Ripper quest I had become a tenacious and more experienced researcher, and so I set out on my own silk road, and in the course of one afternoon I sent a blizzard of emails which, with results coming in over the next few weeks, changed my direction entirely.

My first contact was with the Huguenot Library in London who directed me to a number of publications relating to such silks and pattern-books where I might be able to find something similar to the design on the shawl. Searching online I discovered that Spitalfields silk designs were very distinctive, featuring a much more 'open' floral pattern, in contrast to the tightly packed Michaelmas daisies on the shawl. I could not see anything that even vaguely looked like my shawl.

I contacted the textiles department of the Victoria and Albert Museum, but even though I was passed from one expert to another, I ended up, after some weeks, with no definitive information from them.

I received some information from Christie's and Sotheby's, the big auction houses, when I sent them photographs of the shawl. The Director of the Textiles Department at Christie's dated it at around 1800 to 1820, and said it could have come from Spitalfields or Macclesfield, another centre for silk weaving, although it was not a typical pattern. She added, 'It could equally be continental.' The Sotheby's expert thought the shawl could be later in the nineteenth century, and possibly French. They were working without handling and looking at the shawl, so I was not expecting them to be able to give me more than this.

But in the meantime I had struck gold. I discovered a website devoted to English and French antique textiles run by a lady called Diane Thalmann, a noted expert on shawls, who lives in Switzerland. Having sent her photographs of the shawl, she said: 'I am fairly sure this shawl is early 1800s. However, it is not really familiar to me, and not English. I'm sure you realize that, as it is in pieces, it has no value. What a terrible shame! It would only be suitable for use for documentation or crafts. The quality of silk, as far as I can see, is typical of silk circa 1810 to 1830, but more I can't say.'

It was that phrase 'not English' that inspired me to make a great mental leap, especially as it was backed up by the Christie's expert saying it could be continental. It had been staring me in the face since I had hit on the relationship between the last three murders and the dates of Michaelmas.

What if this shawl did not belong to Catherine Eddowes at all? What if it had been left at the scene of the crime by the Ripper himself?

It suddenly made so much sense. Catherine was very poor, and the day before her death she and her partner John had pawned a pair of his boots, no doubt very worn, for enough money to buy themselves some food. Surely, if she'd had an expensive silk shawl, they would have pawned that for considerably more money? And where would she, with her history of poverty and privation, have acquired an expensive shawl?

I also realized that, for the Michaelmas daisies to have real significance, they had to be connected to the Ripper. Perhaps he had left the shawl at the scene of the crime as an obscure clue to the police as to when he would strike again. Perhaps he had intended to take it away with him, but was using it in his disturbed mental state because of its Michaelmas symbolism. Whatever he meant by leaving it there, it suddenly seemed blindingly obvious that it was nothing to do with Catherine and was entirely to do with him. He had taken the shawl with him on the night of 29 September, with the intention of killing, and he signalled that he would kill again, on the Michaelmas date that was (if he was Aaron Kosminski, as I strongly believed) part of his own background and the culture of his homeland, not this new Michaelmas he had had to learn in England.

Kosminski's family were certainly not wealthy, but they were not semi-destitute, as Catherine was. And in the escape from Poland the shawl could easily have been brought along among his possessions.

I was bowled over by the realization, but there was a lot

more work to be done. I emailed Diane back immediately.

'One last thing, could the shawl have originated in Poland or Russia?'

I knew, from the research I had done into Aaron Kosminski, (which we will get to in due course) that he had lived in Poland when it was under Russian rule (hence the need for the Jews to flee) and also possibly in Germany – we know some of his family moved to these countries, and we're unclear at that stage of his life who, among his siblings, he had lived with.

Her prompt reply said: 'I honestly can't say, but it is possible. I don't usually have a problem identifying shawls from Western Europe, but this is a bit of a mystery to me – yes, it could be either. Russia of course had a culture of high fashion at the beginning of the 1800s especially.'

I hit the internet. One of the greatest manufacturers of textiles in Eastern Europe throughout the nineteenth century was based at Pavlovsky Posad, sixty-eight kilometres from Moscow, a fact that I very quickly uncovered. The town of Pavlovsky Posad was founded in 1845 on the site of a number of villages, namely Pavlovo, Dubrovo, Zaharovo and Melenki. From the very beginning the textile industry was its main business, particularly because the original village of Pavlovo had the Pavlovo Posad factory which produced shawls and handkerchiefs. It had been founded in 1795 by Ivan Labsin, a farmer who set up a small workshop to produce silk shawls. Although demand for silk shawls has dwindled over the decades, this factory still operates, mainly making woollen shawls, scarves and kerchiefs, and Russian Orthodox women use the colourful, floral shawls to cover their heads in church.

Patterns of daisies were one of the popular flower motifs in the production of shawls and scarves at Pavlovsky Posad. The choice of daisies was not surprising, since the religious make-up of the region was Eastern Orthodox Christian, which celebrates Michaelmas as a major feast. Although it was by no means the only possible manufacturer of the shawl, Pavlovsky Posad was a good example of the eastern European silk manufacturing tradition, and my gut instinct took over again, telling me I had found the place where the shawl was made. I was now totally convinced that I was heading full speed in the right direction.

I was very excited, and again the only person I could share my breakthrough with was Jari. I sent him a message there and then, with a link to the website:

> I've just had a breakthrough. Shaking actually. This is strictly between us. I went back to the specialist who told me the shawl isn't English, and I asked if it could be Russian or Polish. She confirmed it could well be. It has nothing to do with the Huguenots at all. Pavlovsky Posad made shawls from the early 19th century and deeply religious Eastern orthodoxy is where we get the Michaelmas daisies from. He brought it over from Poland with him, and now we have a trail to him.
>
> Need a pint!!!!

Jari, as usual, responded encouragingly: 'Definitely the same style, and the material looks similar.' He stressed, in typical Jari style, that this new information was not going to influence him or his work. Quite right, but I was desperate for even more progress. I'd been immersed in the Ripper case for twelve years at this point, and it felt as if I was on a pebble beach, turning over every pebble to find something. Every so often, I turned the right pebble and the case moved forward.

Now the big question facing us was: we knew that the stains on the shawl appeared to contain human DNA, most likely to originate from human blood and other bodily fluids, including semen. We also knew that the shawl almost certainly predated 1888, the year of the Ripper. But could we link the garment conclusively with the murder in Mitre Square? To discover if the DNA recovered from the shawl was truly that of Catherine Eddowes, I would have to find a living descendant who was willing to give us a reference DNA sample for comparison. But my previous research into the Eddowes family tree had hit a dead end.

And then, fortune stepped in yet again. Although I have gone down many blind alleys, and most of the achievements in this quest have been the result of dogged, time-consuming research, I also know that from time to time I have some good luck. This was one of those occasions.

Throughout late 2011, the digital TV channel Yesterday had been broadcasting a programme called *Find My Past*. Each episode set out to reveal how three people were related to characters from a significant historical event by searching the records on www.findmypast.co.uk. Usually, the programme would take on one specific theme per episode, such as the Dam Busters raids, the Gunpowder Plot, the *Titanic* and the mutiny on the *Bounty*. Often the characters from these events had some interaction with each other; in a programme about Dunkirk, for example, the story of how one soldier saved the life of another was covered and their descendants introduced to each other.

The outer side of the shawl showing the Michaelmas daisies.

The reverse side of the shawl with
Michaelmas daisy section folded inwards.

Martha Tabram, possibly
the first Ripper victim.

A typical Whitechapel dosshouse.

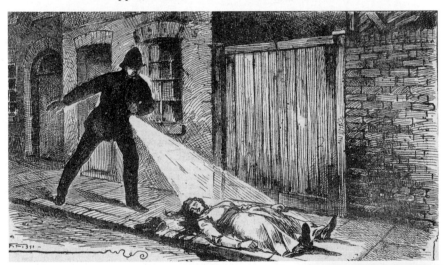

Above The discovery of
Mary Ann Nichols.

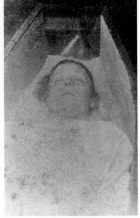

Right Mortuary photograph
of Mary Ann Nichols.

Right Mortuary photograph
of Annie Chapman.

Below The front of 29 Hanbury Street.
The door directly under '29' was the
passageway to the backyard where
Annie Chapman was murdered.

Bottom The backyard of 29 Hanbury
Street. Annie Chapman's body was
found between the step and the fence.

THE STREETS ARE COLOURED ACCORDING TO

Lowest class.
Vicious, semi-criminal.

Very poor, casual.
Chronic want.

Poor. 18s. to 21s. a week
for a moderate family.

A combination of colours—as dark blue and black, or pink and red—indicates tha

The Booth Poverty Map.

Mortuary photograph
of Elizabeth Stride.

An artist's impression
of Elizabeth Stride, as shown
in *The Illustrated Police News*.

Artist's impression of Louis Diemschutz
discovering the body of Elizabeth Stride.

Berner Street. The gateway is where Israel Schwartz saw
a man attacking Elizabeth Stride shortly before her murder.

Artist's impression of
Catherine Eddowes.

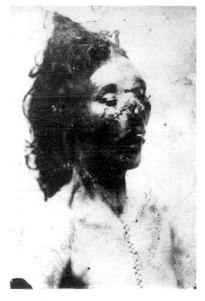

Mortuary photograph
of Catherine Eddowes
showing the gruesome
nature of her injuries.

SCENE OF THE MITRE SQUARE MURDER
THE † INDICATES THE SPOT WHERE THE
BODY WAS

Above Mitre Square
murder scene.

Left Goulston Street
doorway. The graffito
was written on the inner
wall and the piece of
bloodied apron found
on the floor below.

Left Inspector Frederick Abberline.

Right Amos Simpson, Acting Sergeant of the Metropolitan police at the time of the murders.

Chief Inspector Donald Swanson.

An artist's impression of
Mary Jane Kelly.

Dorset Street, where
Mary Kelly was living
at the time of her
murder.

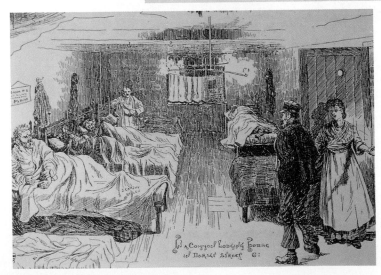

A sketch of a
dosshouse on
Dorset Street.

Mary Jane Kelly crime scene. This is the only photograph of a Ripper victim as she was found.

13 Miller's Court.

The Swanson marginalia, naming
Aaron Kosminski as a suspect.

Colney Hatch Asylum.

Colney Hatch Asylum's
observations of Kosminski.

Leavesden Asylum.

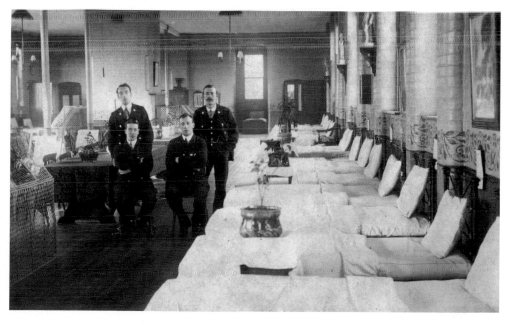

Attendants at Leavesden Asylum pose for a photograph.

Jari in the lab.

Jari taking samples from the bloodstained shawl.

The shawl laid out in the lab for testing.

Russell and Jari look at the shawl's stains under a UV light.

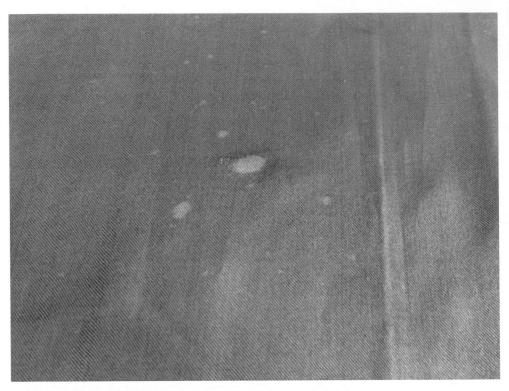

Close-up of various stains being tested.

A vial containing a
captured cell ready for testing.

Russell and Karen.

In the sixth episode of the first series, first broadcast in November 2011, the theme was Jack the Ripper. Three descendants of people directly linked to the Ripper case were featured: Oliver Boot, the great-grandson of journalist Henry Massingham, deputy editor of the radical *Star* newspaper which created so many sensational stories during 1888; Dan Neilson, whose ancestor George Hutt was the duty officer at Bishopsgate Police Station the night Catherine Eddowes was taken there for being drunk and incapable the evening before her death; and finally, Karen Miller, the three times great-granddaughter of Catherine Eddowes herself.

I missed the programme when it was first broadcast but saw it online in April 2012, after hearing about it from a Ripper website.

Catherine Eddowes' only daughter, Catherine 'Annie' Conway, had married Louis Phillips in Southwark in 1885 and together they had seven children. Their eldest daughter Ellen (born 1889) married Joseph Wells in 1912 and they had six children, one of whom was Catherine Annie Wells who married Albert J. Foskett in 1943. In turn their daughter, Margaret Rose, married Eric Miller in 1965 and to them Karen Elizabeth was born in 1971. I now had my *direct* living descendant of Catherine Eddowes.

I couldn't believe what I was seeing. A descendant of Catherine's was, at that moment, my Holy Grail. And there she was, on the screen, talking openly about the tragic incident in her family's past. Following clues in the programme and doing some detective work of my own, I discovered where Karen worked and quickly found her contact details.

The thought of cold-calling a direct descendant of Catherine Eddowes to tell them about the blood on the shawl *and* ask for

DNA samples was rather a daunting one. At first, I felt that somebody else should do it, somebody I could find who would have perhaps more gravitas or standing in historical research than I did and therefore could add the required authority to the request. My lack of confidence was mainly because of the abrupt response I had received from the researcher with links to the victims' families. I did not want to frighten her off, and see another door close in my face. In the end, I opted to do it myself, schooling myself to be as sensitive as possible.

I knew this phone call to Karen Miller could go either way – acceptance and cooperation, or the conversation cut short by the sound of the receiver being slammed down. On the positive side, I had seen a couple of Ripper documentaries that were made with the cooperation of the other victims' families and they appeared to accept their lineage. One showed a Ripper expert taking a direct descendant of Mary Ann Nichols around the East End, even showing her the site where her ancestor had met her death and kick-started history. After the initial shock of discovering they were descended from a Ripper victim it seemed these descendants were keen that the memory of their ancestors should be kept alive because, regardless of the terrible ends these women met, it was history on a wider stage, as well as their own personal family history.

Still, despite this encouragement, I was aware that this had to be approached correctly and unsensationally. In May 2012, I bit the bullet and made the call. I made it clear to Karen early in the conversation that I am a married man with children: I didn't want her to think I was a stalker or loner living in a garret with the walls covered in Ripper photos and memorabilia.

I need not have worried: Karen is a lovely person, and she was very receptive to what I had to say. She, too, could see the importance of directly linking the shawl to her great-great-great grandmother. She said she was very happy to supply me with a sample of her DNA, on swabs taken from inside her mouth.

In criminal cases, the use of DNA evidence has become increasingly common and we read about it all the time in court cases. Where evidence of DNA is found at a crime scene, reference samples are required from a relevant party for comparison purposes. The preferred form of reference sample is a buccal or oral swab. Buccal cells are found inside the mouth, lining the cheeks (*buccal* is Latin for cheek) and are easy to collect; collection devices are simple to use, inexpensive, and most importantly buccal cells are a reliable source of DNA, hence their frequent use.

I wrote a letter of confirmation to Karen to effectively seal the deal and then sent her the clean and sterile swabs in their required storage containers with a stamped-addressed envelope to return them to me. And then nothing happened. I was anxiously checking the post every day, and nothing came. I was very worried, convincing myself that she had had second thoughts, that she had talked to someone who had persuaded her against helping. I was on tenterhooks. Thank goodness for my wife Sally, who took a much more sensible perspective, and told me not to bombard Karen with phone calls, texts or emails until at least two weeks had elapsed. I found it hard being patient: here was vital evidence, and it was dangling just out of reach.

But Sally was right. After the prescribed two weeks, in which I kept myself busy and tried not to think about it, I texted Karen, asking, 'Is everything all right?' Back came the reply: it seemed my swab containers had arrived just before she went away for a fortnight's holiday. It was a salutary reminder to me that normal life went on outside my project, and I could not expect others to share my urgency.

Before long, two sealed samples of Karen's DNA, taken from her mouth, were sitting in my freezer to protect them from any contamination or degradation, ready to be worked on. I delivered them to Jari, and was only happy when I knew they were safe in his freezer. I knew that if Karen's DNA matched that of Catherine Eddowes, we could prove, once and for all, that this old piece of stained clothing was the only genuine, verifiable artefact in the Ripper case that could really lead somewhere. But progress on this strand of the investigation would have to wait until Jari had time.

In the meantime Jari turned his attention to acquiring evidence from the stains that had fluoresced green and which suggested the presence of semen, although as ever Jari was cautious and pointed out that there were other possibilities. The worst case scenario was that the stain was washing powder, but we were both convinced by this stage that the shawl had never been washed.

Talking about luck: that has got to be one of the greatest strokes I, and anyone else interested in solving the Ripper case, could possibly have had. After all the hands it has passed through, and after the story that the original owner, Jane Simpson, hated it because of the bloodstains, it is nothing short of remarkable that nobody, in the shawl's long history, has ever tried to clean it up by washing it. If they had, all the vital evidence would have been lost.

I knew that the presence of male bodily fluids on an item that could be linked to a murder meant a strong likelihood that the killer's DNA was on it. There are murder cases, particularly serial killer cases, where the murderer obtains sexual gratification from the act of killing or mutilation and promptly ejaculates, either on the body of the victim or on clothing belonging to them. One that I had known about for some time was the case of Peter Kürten, the 'Düsseldorf Vampire', who killed men, women and children in a series of sexually motivated murders in 1929. Kürten obtained sexual gratification from his crimes and the amount of times he stabbed his victims often depended on how long it took him to achieve orgasm. The sight of blood was an integral part of his pleasure and a famous story about Kürten is that he wished to hear his own blood gushing into a bag immediately following his beheading. Dennis Rader (the 'BTK Killer' – Bind, Torture, Kill), Andrei Chikatilo (the 'Rostov Ripper') and Peter Sutcliffe (the 'Yorkshire Ripper') are other notorious serial killers whose horrific acts culminated in ejaculation. Semen and the DNA contained within it has been used to secure criminal convictions and also, in other cases, to exonerate the accused. A good example of this is one of the earliest uses of forensic DNA comparison in Britain in the 1980s, in a case that became known as the Enderby murders.

In November 1983, a fifteen-year-old schoolgirl, Lynda Mann, was found dead on a river towpath in Narborough, Leicestershire, having been strangled and raped. The only clue was a semen sample taken from Mann's body from which forensics deduced that the owner's (and most likely the killer's) blood group was Type A, but in the absence of any other evidence, the case went unresolved. Almost three years later, another young girl, Dawn Ashworth, was found raped and murdered on another footpath in Enderby, only a mile from where Lynda Mann had died. Again there were traces of semen which was analysed and which showed the same blood group as that found on the previous victim. This made it highly likely that it was the same man who raped and murdered the two girls.

Following extensive investigations, a man named Richard Buckland was arrested and confessed to the second murder, but strongly denied any involvement in the first. Investigators decided to try a new and untested technique: 'genetic finger-printing' through DNA analysis. Such testing had already been used in paternity suits to determine the real identity of a child's father, but it had never before been used in a criminal case. It was felt that this 'genetic fingerprinting', would solve the case, as well as confirm the technique's viability, so a sample of Buckland's blood was taken for analysis. To everyone's surprise, there was no match between his DNA and those taken from the semen found on the bodies of the two girls, and Buckland became the first person in criminal history to be *proven innocent* based on a DNA test.

With the search to find the killer now back on, all the men from the area around where the bodies were found who had Type A blood were asked to voluntarily submit to a DNA test. Over 5,000 men agreed to do it, but the object was actually to find any man who would not willingly take the test because they had something to hide. Colin Pitchfork, who had previous convictions for indecent exposure and who was already of interest to the police, wanted to avoid detection and so persuaded a friend to take the test in his place, providing him with false identification and a cash payment of £200 for his troubles. Unfortunately, when the friend foolishly bragged in a public place about what he had done, he was overheard by a woman who immediately contacted the police. With attention now on Colin Pitchfork, he confessed and his genetic fingerprint turned out to be identical to that found in the semen at the crime scenes. In September 1987 he became the first person to be *convicted* of murder based on 'genetic fingerprinting'.

Since then the use of DNA in forensics has become a standard detection tool, and the science has improved exponentially. Naturally, it was the way forward for us to connect the shawl with both victim and murderer.

In autumn 2012 I took the shawl back to Jari. It was my children's half-term holiday from school and we were staying with Sally's family in North Wales. I drove to Liverpool with the shawl and left it with Jari, going back to join my children at the swimming pool in Prestatyn. Later in the day I went back to Jari's lab, taking my father-in-law with me, to collect it again. There was nothing Jari could tell me there and then, other than that he had taken the samples he needed.

He had used the same extraction method he'd used to take the blood samples from the shawl. Material from the possible semen stains was extracted from the relevant locations and placed into three separate vials. As routine procedure, they were put into a special freezer at minus 80°C for maximum preservation. The likelihood of sperm surviving this long was extremely slim and the standardized forensic methods for sperm detection tend not to work with samples as old as the ones we had. When ejaculated sperm ages, the tails are lost first, so the hypothesis Jari explained to me was that if the sperm had dried quickly, and the cells were trapped within the textile, we might be lucky and find at least a few sperm heads which had avoided natural degradation.

Once again, we had a stroke of luck. Jari had been to dinner with a colleague and old friend from Leeds University, David Miller. David is the Reader in Molecular Andrology at the Reproduction and Early Development Group at the University of Leeds Institute of Genetics, Health and Therapeutics. Quite a mouthful, but the importance to us is that David is, in Jari's words, 'a world class expert in sperm head analysis', one of very few in Britain. He is a specialist in fertility and the causes of infertility. They met when Jari and his wife rented David's huge Victorian mansion in Leeds in 2001. David contacted Riitta when he heard they were looking for somewhere to live, as David was going to Detroit to work, and he wanted tenants he could trust: he chose Jari and Riitta in preference to some burly Australian sportsmen. The house was newly renovated and although Jari was initially put off by its age, the minute he saw it he said 'Where do I sign?'

By coincidence, at that time Jari was doing DNA microarrays (don't ask me!) for Cancer Research in Leeds, and David was invited to do similar work in Detroit. The two families are now close friends.

'Over dinner we talked science, of course. That's what scientists do,' Jari said.

'I asked him if he thought sperm heads could survive for so long, and he told me it was possible, as sperm heads are very stable.'

What's more, David was willing to work on our samples. When they had coordinated dates, Jari took the three vials home with him to Bradford, and temporarily stored them in his home freezer before Riitta delivered them personally to David as she was working on the same campus.

It was on the 12th day of the 12th month of 2012, as I was driving into London, that my car phone lit up with the information there was an incoming call from Jari. I pulled over, because I know from experience that I need to concentrate when talking to Jari. I can't take in scientific details while I'm negotiating London traffic.

'We've got some cells,' he said.

It was a massive moment, and I was speechless.

Jari went on: 'They are not sperm heads, they are squamous cells, from the epithelium.'

Somewhere in the dark recesses of my memory I knew I had heard the word 'epithelium' when I was doing A level Biology, but if I ever knew what it was, I had certainly forgotten by now.

'What does it mean?'

Jari explained as simply as he could to me.

The epithelium is one of four basic types of tissue which is present in the human body, either outside or inside. The epithelium is widespread in living organisms – in humans it coats or lines numerous organs and can be found on the insides of the lungs, the gastrointestinal tract and the reproductive and urinary tracts, among other places. Jari told me there was a strong possibility that these cells had come from the urethra during ejaculation, because they originated in a stain that fluoresced like semen under his lights.

The most important piece of information he gave me was, 'We can probably get DNA from these samples.'

I sat in my car at the side of the road, stunned. It seemed now we could have access to the DNA not just of the victim, but of the Ripper himself. It was hard to take it in.

Jari told me that David Miller was concerned about the absence of sperm in the sample; however, the evidence of squamous cells meant that it could not be ruled out that some sperm could have been there (which could be revealed in some future analysis). For the moment he felt that finding the epithelial cells meant that no further investigation was necessary.

When I got home I rang David to confirm what Jari had told me, and to thank him for doing the work for us. He talked me through the testing he had done, then followed up by sending me an email, complete with images of three views taken down a light microscope with 400x magnification. He gave me a detailed explanation of the procedure he had followed, and then he wrote:

> The fact that I didn't find any sperm does not automatically exclude their presence, but considering that squamous cells are a minor component of a typical semen sample (they get into the semen by mechanical sloughing from the urethral epithelium during ejaculation), I would have expected to see them if they had been there. On the other hand, squamous cells like these are also found in other bodily fluids including saliva, sweat etc (basically any fluid that washes over or bathes an epithelial surface).

'Mechanical sloughing' in this case means that when ejaculation occurs, epithelial cells from around the urethral tract are dragged out with the semen and will be part of the resulting ejaculate. As far as I was concerned at that moment, the most important bit was that the cells could provide us with the crucial DNA. And because the stain fluoresced like semen under Jari's forensic lights, it was the likeliest candidate as a source.

I immediately emailed David to make absolutely certain I understood the main fact: 'From what I gather from our conversation, you can get DNA from the cells you have found. Is that correct?'

Two minutes later his reply pinged into my inbox.

'Yes, that's correct.'

I was thrilled. I knew getting the DNA would be difficult. There were twelve cells isolated altogether, and David had placed them on microscope slides ready for any further testing and potential extraction of DNA. There would be an extremely limited amount of DNA and the microscope slide might have contaminants from the shawl which could ruin the whole process, but in principle it could be done. We were on our way with another vital strand of the whole investigation. That portentous date, 12/12/12, had lived up to its promise.

I think the news that we had been successful in Leeds with the sperm head analysis, which had found the epithelial cells, helped Jari understand the importance of the whole project. He says himself, 'I got hooked at this point.' He, too, could see that we were on the brink of something very big, and he stepped up a gear. He had always been willing to do my research when he could, alongside his day job: now he was prepared to go above and beyond the call of duty to get on with it.

One thing he wanted to do before embarking on the DNA comparison was to definitively age the shawl. The DNA work would be time-consuming and costly, but in the meantime he could get on with this. From my research I was sure it was a silk shawl from the Russian factory of Pavlovsky Posad, and Diane Thalman had confirmed it was in all probability early nineteenth century. But that didn't amount to proof, and both Jari and I understand that to make this case watertight, we need scientific proof at all levels, not just expert opinion.

So on 2 January 2013 I drove to Liverpool again with the shawl. The university was still on its Christmas break, but Jari went into his lab specially to do an absorption test. Previously while taking the DNA samples, Jari had noticed that the blue dye of the floral pattern appeared to be highly water soluble, and came off easily, whereas the brown dye did not come off at all. Where the stains were mixed in with the dye, Jari had to separate the dye out in order to get samples from the stain. The first attempt at the absorption test failed, as the colour just disappeared before Jari could start testing it.

The fact that the blue dye came off so easily told us one piece of information: the shawl could never have been used as an outer garment, because rain would have made the blue dye leak. This underlined that it could not have belonged to Catherine Eddowes: with her itinerant lifestyle it would certainly have been exposed to rain. Just before her death she and her partner John had walked back to London from the hop fields in Kent, and because she had nowhere to live she had all her clothes on when she was murdered: there is no possibility that the shawl would never have been wet if it was hers.

The difference between the two dyes also suggested that the shawl was not machine printed, but that the dye was hand-applied. Now Jari was going to test it to find out the type of dye used, which would help date it.

While Jari was working on it I wandered into the museum next door to his department at the university. It was somewhere to keep warm, as it was a bitterly cold day. The place was full of parents and children: it was still the school holidays. I strolled around, trying to occupy myself looking at the exhibits, while all the time thinking about what was going on in the lab.

Jari carried out an absorption test using a spectrophotometer on the blue area of the shawl. The test shows where the fabric is absorbing light, which differs between dyes. For example, 6,6'-dibromoindigotin is considered to be one of the oldest (if not *the* oldest) pigments. It is a major component of Royal Purple or Tyrian Purple, which is known to have been very expensive. This was one possibility for the blue dye. Another candidate was indigo. With just one microlitre of the dye extract (one twentieth of a small droplet of rain, barely visible to the human eye), Jari could see that the dye spectra closely resembled the known spectrum of indigo, with a peak of 620 nanometres but not the dibromoindigo (Royal Purple). Looking at the absorbance spectrum did not give a full confirmation of the chemical composition of the dye but it showed that only one compound was applied to the blue section, and therefore we knew that the shawl was definitely not screen printed, which was very encouraging news. Screen printing was introduced in 1910, and if it had been dyed in this way the game would have been over.

When I returned to Jari's lab he showed me a graph with the blue peak. He told me that the best way to proceed was to look at the fabric with a nuclear magnetic resonance instrument, and for this we would need to enlist the help of a colleague of Jari's, Fyaz Ismail, who is the Senior Lecturer in Medicinal Chemistry, Drug Design and Discovery Module Leader at LJMU. Fyaz is a lovely, jolly character who we nicknamed The Chemist. So later I took the shawl back up the motorway to Liverpool. I knew that The Chemist would need an actual sample of the shawl, but the size of the sample took both Jari and me by surprise: the test needs two samples, one of each colour, each about a centimetre square. I was horrified: by now I was so protective of the shawl that it felt like a piece of my own body was being cut off, and Jari said that the expression on my face looked as if I was about to have a heart attack. Nonetheless, it had to be done. Jari shared my surprise if not my horror: he is used to working in a micro/nano scale with everything.

The NMR instrument is huge and would fill an average size living room. It costs around half a million pounds and has very strict safety protocols because it can be deadly. The strong magnetic fields near the instrument can stop not just watches but pacemakers, defibrillators, and can pull out metal surgical implants or prosthetics, and can make hairpins fly at high speed. Anyone wearing a metal necklace can be choked to death.

NMR can help determine the structure of the material being analysed as well as additives used in textile products. It is a research technique that exploits the magnetic properties of certain atomic nuclei and determines the physical and chemical properties of the atoms or molecules in which they are contained, thus providing information about the structure, dynamics, reaction state and chemical environment of molecules. This is achieved by bombarding the samples with radio waves of a fixed frequency. The nuclei contained within the molecules absorb that radio frequency when an external magnetic field is introduced and reaches an appropriate level. When the radio waves and magnetic field are at the right level, the nuclei can absorb those radio waves. Different nuclei absorb radio waves at different rates, dependent on the environment the nuclei are contained in and it is the rates of such absorption which gives us clues as to what the molecules are. The results appear as a form of graph with peaks and troughs, and from this graph we can determine the nature of the molecules under study. In other words, NMR can tell us what something is made of.

The results of the NMR analysis of the shawl showed the composition of the dye used on it. The molecules were very complex and this suggested that it was a natural dye not a synthetic one (which would have a much simpler profile). Also, as the dye was soluble in water, it again suggested natural pigment. Natural dyes are the oldest types in use and were invariably derived from sources such as roots, berries, plants and fungi. The blue dye samples taken from the shawl had similar properties to woad, a very common blue dye derived from the plant *Isatis tinctoria* which has been used for thousands of years. This was a massive boost, another huge step along the road, and I was beginning to feel that luck was definitely on my side.

While Jari was working in his lab I went on to one of his computers to research the origins of synthetic dye. It was first created, by accident, by William Perkin in 1856 and caught on swiftly, replacing natural dyes by the 1870s: synthetic colourants cost less, offered a huge range of new colours and they gave better visual qualities to the materials they were used on (I discovered that William Perkin actually lived in the East End, in Cable Street, and I have since been to look at the blue plaque on his house, grateful that his discovery helped us determine the age of the shawl).

Natural dyes also required a mordant which would fix the colour and a variety of natural substances were used to do this. The most common were alum, tin, chrome and iron, but sometimes human urine was used. The mordant improves the fastness of the dyes; however, they were not as water-resistant as synthetic dyes. Because of this, items like shawls were not necessarily washed, and often just given a good airing or an application of some fragrant plant such as lavender. As Jari told me, if my shawl had ever been put into a modern washing machine the entire blue section would have dissipated, and even gentle hand washing would have seen most of it leak out. The fact that it was a natural pigment, not synthetic, also explained why the small stains which were believed to have been made by semen affected the dye in the way they did, effectively giving the spots a 'bleached' look where the semen had made the natural pigment deteriorate. Natural dyes absorb more: a synthetic dye would have repelled the stains, and they would probably not have survived.

So the natural dye used on the shawl strongly suggested a date in keeping with the probability that it existed before 1870, which tied in with what the experts at Christie's and Sotheby's had told me when I asked for their advice. But now we had more than expert opinion, we had proof. Even more excitingly, Fyaz Ismail felt that the dye also had characteristics similar to those he had seen before which came from Russia, notably the St Petersburg area.

Dyes apparently have different properties owing to the different ingredients available for their synthesis in any given locale. Also, silk dyeing was a competitive and secretive business, and very little was written down – the recipes were handed down from generation to generation. Consequently they all differed, and it was possible to pinpoint a specific area. This was another significant and exciting discovery which made me feel that fate was on my side, and that my gut feelings were being transformed into real evidence. I remember thinking: I keep unpeeling this onion, and as every layer comes off it's a massive, breathtaking moment. Is this all too good to be true?

*

We were now ready for what was going to be the most important test so far – the comparison of the DNA extracted from the bloodstains on the shawl with that of Karen Miller.

To do this it was vital that we had what are called 'control samples' from various individuals who had handled the shawl over the previous twelve months, in order to eradicate any potential recent traces of anybody else's DNA. These samples were taken from myself and all the members of the team who had worked on the shawl, including Jari. Along with the sample from Karen Miller, all were purified, meaning that the DNA itself from each sample was isolated using a combination of physical and chemical methods. Since the shawl was over a hundred years old, unsurprisingly, the genomic DNA from it was found to be fragmented and not appropriate for use. Fortunately, we also had samples of the mitochondrial DNA (mtDNA), which is of course passed down intact over many generations via the female line. We therefore had a direct, uninterrupted genetic link along the female line between Karen Miller and Catherine Eddowes and thus Karen's mtDNA should, we hoped, be identical to that of Catherine.

Due to the age of the material on the shawl, the human mtDNA was amplified in seven small segments to facilitate the analysis. If Jari had tried to amplify a larger DNA fragment in one go, there was a high chance of a double strand break (i.e. the DNA is cut into two pieces) somewhere in the segment and the polymerase chain reaction (PCR) would fail. By doing smaller segments, there was a higher chance of finding an intact fragment. This approach is normally required with ancient or damaged DNA samples, because of the risk of fragmentation with age, even when properly stored. PCR is currently the standard method used in DNA base forensics and also medical diagnosis. It basically replicates a single section of DNA strand millions of times, thus giving a sound base to work from. The amplification process was performed with a method which responded specifically to human DNA samples, so that any stains consisting of animal blood would not produce a result.

To find out the possible matches and mismatches, DNA needs to be sequenced. The DNA is made of four components called nucleotides which are adenine (A), guanidine (G), cytosine (C) and thymine (T). In DNA these are arranged in a chain which can have any of these in any order (or there can be a stretch of nucleotides which are the same, for example like AAAA or GGGGGG). Between two individuals the DNA sequence is identical for a vast majority of the sequence which is why it is necessary to select an area which is known to have some variation between individuals of the same species. In mtDNA there are two areas called hypervariable region I and hypervariable region II, which are known to contain variations in a normal population, so when two normal individuals are compared there are likely to be differences. The mtDNA segments which were amplified were all in these two regions. When this was performed on our control samples and to the samples extracted from the shawl, we could then compare them by looking at the order of those nucleotides.

Six out of seven of the mtDNA segments subjected to DNA sequencing analysis were successful, in other words, we had six complete DNA profiles that could be used for profiling. Only results fulfilling the highest quality control were accepted and this was done using the Phred quality score, a widely used method of measuring the quality of a DNA sequence. The most commonly used method is to work with a Phred score of 20 or above, which dictates that the level of accuracy will be 99 per cent or higher.

The result of the first complete DNA profile was an incredible 'Eureka!' moment, and confirmed that the shawl contains human mtDNA identical to Karen Miller's, based on that particular mtDNA segment.

Jari was still being a scientist, and stressing caution. He had to stay neutral, but even he was admitting it was a very good match. For me, it was cause for a celebration and I must admit to visiting the pub and sinking a few pints. Just occasionally, I had to let my hair down and revel in how far we had got.

When work started analysing the other mtDNA sections, it was found that two others showed contamination from fresh DNA (matching with one of the reference samples). However, this is a well-known and well-documented problem with ancient DNA samples as fresh, non-fragmented DNA amplifies much more readily than older DNA and so contamination like this is known to occasionally take place. However, such contamination could not be responsible for the match between the mtDNA sequences from the shawl and that of Karen Miller.

One of the amplified mtDNA segments from the blood found on the shawl matched Karen's, and had a sequence variation which gave a match with the mtDNA of Karen Miller *only* and did not match any of the other control samples. The variation is known as a Global Private Mutation, a rare gene variation that is usually found only in a single family or a small population. According to the database of the Institute of Legal Medicine and based on the latest information available, the variation that both Karen's DNA and the DNA from the bloodstains on the shawl shared has a frequency estimate of only 0.000003506, in other words, it is present in only 1 in 290,000 of the world's population.

To put the genetic variation discovery into context, it means that as the United Kingdom currently has a population of around 63,750,000, Karen Miller is one of only around 223 people in the *country* who possesses this genetic variation. If that ratio was the same back in 1888, when the UK population would have stood at about 36,000,000, Catherine Eddowes, whose blood (also containing that variation) appears to be on the shawl, would have been only one of about 136 people in the country with that variation. To work proportionally with that statistic, Catherine would have been one of only about a dozen people with that variation in London in 1888 when the population stood at about 4,000,000. Karen Miller is one of about twenty-five people in London with the variation today. Considering that Catherine Eddowes' daughter Annie's descendants stayed in the same area of London (Bermondsey and Southwark) for generations, and Karen herself was born in South London too, this really does narrow down the field.

Jari sent me a summary of his findings, which more or less repeats what I have explained, but may be of more interest to any scientists reading this:

> The shawl was first visually inspected, both in visible light and also using special forensic light sources, i.e. different wavelengths of ultraviolet and infrared using a customised forensic camera with specific band pass filters. Using these methods several differentially fluorescing stains were identified, suggesting presence of various biological sources (for example, blood/saliva/semen). A total of six of these stains

were sampled for DNA using a novel in-house method developed for this purpose. The DNA from these samples were purified, as well as control reference samples from Karen Miller (descendant of Catherine Eddowes), Russell Edwards (the owner of the shawl) and the laboratory personnel who have been known to handle the shawl. Due to the age of the shawl, the human mitochondrial DNA (mtDNA) was amplified in seven small segments to facilitate the analysis. This approach is normally required with ancient or damaged DNA samples, since the DNA is known to fragment with age, even when properly stored. The amplification was performed with a system, which is specific to human DNA, so stains created with animal blood etc. would not produce a result.

Six out of seven mtDNA segments subjected to DNA sequencing analysis were successful. Only results fulfilling the highest quality control (so called Phred20 score) were accepted. One of these amplified mtDNA segments had a sequence variation which gave a match between one of the shawl samples and Karen Miller's DNA only; i.e. the DNA sequence retrieved from the shawl did not match with control reference sequences. This DNA alteration is known as global private mutation (314.1C) and it is not very common in worldwide population, as it has frequency estimate of 0.000003506, i.e. approximately 1/290,000. This figure has been calculated using the database at Institute of Legal Medicine, GMI, based on the latest available information. Thus, this result indicates that the shawl contains human DNA identical to Karen Miller's for this mitochondrial DNA segment. According to the history of this shawl, a maximum of six persons have handled it in the past twelve months. Because the garment is made of silk, skin cells from those handling it prior to the last twelve months will no longer be there (in the case of wool, the cells would remain for far longer). Based on the DNA work above, we know that at least two of these persons do not have this specific mutation (314.1C). Hence the analysis above strongly suggests that the shawl could contain the DNA of the Jack the Ripper victim Catherine Eddowes. When analysing the other mtDNA sections, we found two other mtDNA segments to have apparent contamination from fresh DNA (matching with one of the reference samples). However, this is a well-known and documented problem with ancient DNA samples as fresh, non-fragmented DNA amplifies much more readily than old DNA. So contamination like this is known to take place occasionally. However, contamination cannot explain the match described above.

So there it is, in Jari's dispassionate prose: 'Hence the analysis strongly suggests that the shawl could contain the DNA of the Jack the Ripper victim Catherine Eddowes.'

Science appears to have proven that the shawl was what it was said to be. It *must* have been at the scene of the crime back on 30 September 1888 and shows traces of Catherine Eddowes' blood, proven to match that of her direct female descendant. On its own, this makes the shawl probably the single most important find in Ripper history; no knife, diary or letter has ever been linked with these murders so conclusively. For me this was an incredible 'wow' moment. Despite all the peaks and troughs of this journey, things were suddenly going in a way that vindicated the shawl and my reasons for buying it.

But there was still a long way to go. Research had shown that the shawl was the right age, was most likely eastern European in origin and was present at the Eddowes murder. My feeling that it had come from the killer himself was growing stronger by the day and the figure of Aaron Kosminski was looming larger in my thoughts. We knew the shawl also contained other human material, and this time we would be using this evidence not to prove simply that the shawl was genuine and had been at the scene of the crime, but to solve the greatest murder mystery of all time: the true identity of Jack the Ripper.

CHAPTER TEN

NARROWING DOWN
THE SUSPECTS

It was in 2007, soon after Alan McCormack gave me the name, that I started my research into Aaron Kosminski. But then the other aspects of the investigation took centre stage, and it wasn't until many years later that I started looking at him in earnest again. There was still a niggling doubt in my mind: yes, we had almost certainly got the Ripper's DNA. But what if the Ripper was not Kosminski? I was going on what Alan had told me, but there were other plausible cases made for suspects who seemed, at first sight, to be just as possible as him.

So before I go into the story of Kosminski, let's look at the other possible Rippers.

The official files were not released to the public until the 1970s, and the detectives and senior policemen who were on the case in 1888 left nothing more than oblique references in their memoirs, so the case was wide open to all sorts of mad theories being put forward. With so little actual evidence, it was possible to make a case for almost anyone, many suggestions bizarre and almost laughable.

In the years since the last victim's death, the Whitechapel murderer has been a Jewish slaughterman, an escaped lunatic, a mad medical student, an avenging doctor, a homicidal midwife and even a member of the royal family. One early theory was that the killer was several men who came from Portugal on the cattle boats. It wasn't ruled out by the police, and it joined a slew of other tip-offs about foreign sailors who worked on ships that were berthed on the Thames. Extensive searches of the docks and the ships that were moored there on the nights of the murders were made and every man was expected to account for himself.

A popular belief was that the Ripper was an escaped lunatic, and this story was even more sensational if the lunatic also happened to be foreign. In the official files now held at the National Archives, there are numerous reports of suspects in this category. Jacob Isenschmid, known as the 'mad butcher' and who had spent some time in an asylum, became a suspect after the murder of Annie Chapman when the police were tipped off about his unusual and often aggressive behaviour. Inspector Abberline heard about Isenschmid, and he was promptly found and incarcerated while the police made their enquiries. In fact Abberline went so far as to believe that he sounded just like the man that Mrs Fiddymont and friend had seen in the Prince Albert pub on the morning of the Chapman murder. From what we can see from the reports, Isenschmid was an individual of great interest to the police, but he was believed to be so insane that the doctors would not allow him to be used in an identity parade. Eventually the fact that he was safely out of circulation in custody when the later murders occurred proved his innocence, if not his sanity.

Charles Ludwig was another strange character mentioned in

the files. A highly volatile and violent German hairdresser, he had pulled a knife on a woman in a dark alley in the Minories, just south of Aldgate, on 18 September 1888. Avoiding arrest, he then went to a coffee stall and promptly threatened an innocent bystander with the knife, and this time was caught and held. He was still in custody on the night of the double murder, which ruled him out as a suspect. His landlord told the newspapers that he was:

> A most extraordinary man, is always in a bad temper, and grinds his teeth in rage at any little thing which puts him out. I believe he has some knowledge of anatomy, as he was for some time an assistant to some doctors in the German army, and helped to dissect bodies. He always carries some razors and a pair of scissors with him . . .

The man was obviously mentally ill. The same could be said about Oswald Puckeridge who, apart from having a history of mental illness which saw him put away in asylums many times, was declared as being 'a danger to others'. He was described in the official files as 'educated as a surgeon' and at one point had threatened to 'rip people up with a long knife'.

There were loads of other suspects. Nikaner Benelius was a Swedish-born traveller who had recently come to England from America and who, despite having very little in the way of similarities to the descriptions of men wanted for questioning, was nonetheless interrogated after the death of Elizabeth Stride. He was arrested again after behaving suspiciously in Buxton Street, Mile End, but again was exonerated of all suspicion that he was Jack the Ripper.

Police time was wasted on a large manhunt following a suggestion that three medical students from the London Hospital, all believed to be mentally unwell, had gone missing. Two were soon accounted for, but much time and legwork was taken up tracing the final missing student whose mother claimed that he had gone abroad.

The police were also plagued by timewasters, whose stories had to be checked out just in case. Another medical student at the London Hospital, William Bull, confessed to the murder of Catherine Eddowes. He was drunk when he made the confession and it was soon established he was in bed at his family home when the murder happened. A whole slew of letters was sent to the police with suggestions of how to improve the investigation, theories about how the killer got away and the names of suspicious individuals. Some were interesting, but some were plainly ridiculous, including accusations that either Sgt William Thick or PC Edward Watkins was the Ripper. Some were malicious: people getting even with anyone they had a grudge against. Some writers claimed to have visions of the killer or that the entire mystery could be solved if they were allowed to use their psychic abilities to assist the police. One woman wrote of her conviction that the murders were committed by an escaped ape which, after committing his foul deed, would hide the murder weapon up a tree and then slink back to whichever private menagerie he had managed to sneak out from.

Some of the information was undoubtedly given in good faith, as in the case of suspect G. Wentworth Bell Smith who lodged with a couple in the Finsbury area of London and would apparently recite religious tracts, espouse the evils of prostitution, claiming that these women should be drowned and, rather alarmingly, would stay out all night and return home in a great frenzy, foaming at the mouth. Again, sound alibis proved he was not the Ripper.

Robert D'Onston Stephenson, an eccentric journalist and occultist who was staying at the London Hospital at the time of the crimes, wrote to the police regarding his own theories, namely that the Ripper was French and that the uterus of a prostitute was considered of some use to this Frenchman. Stephenson's interest in the case turned him into a suspect himself years later, accused of using the organs of the mutilated victims for arcane rituals and occult practices. Those who espouse the case of Stephenson as the Ripper note that, with the exception of Mary Kelly, the murder locations make the sign of a (sacrificial) cross.

By the time the Whitechapel murders came to a sudden halt, many individuals had been either arrested and released, or accused without serious evidence. A list of all the suspects who were considered by the police would have been very long. Hardly a day seemed to pass without some newspaper following up a suspect lead, but in the end, that is all they seemed to be: suspect.

There was no shortage of ideas: as Inspector Frederick Abberline told one newspaper in 1892, four years after the killing ended: 'Theories! We were almost lost in theories; there were so many of them.'

As time went on, and no culprit was found, the public fascination with the case deepened. In the years since the Ripper roamed the streets, many, many more names have been put forward. It seems that after the passage of a certain amount of time, a good case can be made for almost anyone.

Author Leonard Matters claimed in 1929 that a 'Dr Stanley' was the Ripper, killing prostitutes out of revenge for the death of his beloved son who died after contracting a sexually transmitted disease from a prostitute. The story hinged on an account of Dr Stanley's own confession which Matters claimed he had seen in a journal published in South America. There is no evidence that Dr Stanley actually existed, and this is also the case with a later 'doctor' suspect. In 1959 another author, Donald McCormick, named the murderer as Dr Alexander Pedachenko, an insane doctor sent by the Ochrana (Tsarist secret police) in an effort to discredit the Metropolitan police.

One theory that gained quite a lot of support was that the murderer was a woman, Jill the Ripper, probably a midwife who, through performing illegal abortions, had access to the women of the East End.

With the evolution of television and other mass media, a welter of other Ripper suspects have appeared, the more sensational the name the more coverage that can be guaranteed. At the top of the suspect popularity pile must be Prince Albert Victor (or Prince Eddy), grandson of Queen Victoria. His candidacy as the Ripper has naturally captured the imagination of the public and media alike for many years, and the popularity of this theory has never completely diminished.

Prince Eddy was first put forward in 1970 when Dr Thomas Stowell, a distinguished London physician, alluded to the Prince suffering from syphilis and claimed that the madness his illness induced caused him to venture into the East End and murder prostitutes. Involved was Sir William Gull, the Queen's physician, who was charged with following Eddy around and after the night of the double event, Gull incarcerated Eddy, by now a deranged killer. Apparently the Prince escaped to commit one last crime (Mary Kelly) before being taken out of circulation.

Despite the historical record stating that Eddy died of influenza in 1892, theorists have concluded that it was actually syphilis that brought about his end: plausible, because the death certificate of someone so close to the throne would have been written with care to avoid embarrassing the queen. But even though Buckingham Palace was able to supply his whereabouts on the nights of the Ripper murders from court records – on the night of Mary Kelly's murder, the Prince was celebrating his father's birthday at Sandringham – it was such a far-out idea that the media exposure was considerable. The combination of the biggest murder case ever and a member of the Royal Family was irresistible, and it struck a chord with the public, who love conspiracy theories.

Within a few years, a new version of the royal hypothesis emerged, this time with the women being killed by Sir William Gull himself, in an attempt to prevent them from going public about a potentially monarchy-damaging scandal that involved the Prince. According to this theory, Mary Kelly was witness to a marriage between Eddy and a Catholic commoner, Annie Crook, and became the nanny to the couple's secret daughter, Alice. Once the couple were separated on the orders of the Queen, Kelly supposedly exiled herself to the East End where she shared the story with several other prostitutes. Mary Kelly, as the focus of the assassination plot, was the last and most horribly butchered.

Interwoven into the tale, as first told in a BBC TV series in 1973 and then in a bestselling book by Stephen Knight (*Jack the Ripper: The Final Solution*, 1976), was Sir Robert Anderson, Assistant Commissioner CID and willing collaborator,

Walter Sickert, the British impressionist artist, plus a generous helping of Masonic ritual and references. So popular has this version of the case remained over the years, despite being roundly disproven, that it has spawned three feature films, including the Twentieth Century Fox blockbuster *From Hell* with Johnny Depp (the one that awakened my interest in the whole case) and a two-part television drama starring Michael Caine.

Walter Sickert himself became a suspect in his own right in a number of theories, the most well-known being that put forward by crime novelist Patricia Cornwell, who invested her time and a lot of money in state-of-the-art forensic analysis in pursuing him as the Ripper.

The next big case to enthral the public was that of James Maybrick, a Liverpool cotton merchant who was allegedly the victim of murder in 1889 when he was apparently poisoned by his young American wife Florence. Suddenly, Maybrick became a prime Ripper suspect when the so-called *Diary of Jack the Ripper* was released to the world in 1993. The diary, given to a man named Mike Barrett by a friend in 1991 was, to all intents and purposes – if the content is anything to go by – written by Maybrick himself, detailing the murders and his reason for committing them: a vengeful, arsenic-fuelled campaign against prostitutes in response to his wife's perceived infidelities. Soon after the diary was discovered a watch appeared, inside which was scratched the initials of the canonical five victims, Maybrick's signature and the words 'I am Jack'.

The 'diary' has been scrutinized and subjected to innumerable tests, as has the watch, with no firm conclusion and it is still hotly debated today. It could be a genuine diary written by

Maybrick for his own reasons, or a modern hoax perpetrated around the Ripper centenary in 1988, or even a hoax made nearer the time of the murders themselves. Maybrick is still a popular suspect who continues to capture the public imagination.

Mary Kelly's former boyfriend Joseph Barnett has been put forward as the Ripper, killing prostitutes to deter Kelly from working on the streets. The plan failed and Barnett eventually butchered her in her own squalid room as the only way he could stop her. Unbelievably, having destroyed the woman he had tried so hard to protect, he went on to live an unremarkable life in the East End: not the usual pattern of a serial killer.

One of the last people to see Kelly alive, her friend George Hutchinson, has also been accused of her murder and the detailed description he gave after the Kelly inquest of the man he saw accompanying her during the last hours of her life has been seen as a smokescreen to divert the investigation away from his own guilt. What was interesting about these two theories, Barnett and Hutchinson, is that they reintroduced characters directly related to the original events. A criminal profile of the Ripper that was created by the FBI in the centenary year, 1988, showed that Barnett seemed to fit many of the criteria and it signalled a new way of approaching the Ripper case, namely using modern forensic methods to treat the Whitechapel murders as a 'cold case', which is what Patricia Cornwell subsequently did. This is the route that I have now pursued with, I believe, considerably more success than anyone else, thanks entirely to the shawl.

There have been many bizarre suggestions for Ripper candidacy. Lewis Carroll, William Booth (founder of the Salvation Army), Arthur Conan Doyle, King Leopold of the Belgians and former prime minister William Gladstone have had their names dragged in. Joseph Merrick, the famous 'Elephant Man', was suggested by a contributor to an internet site who attempted to make a good case, regardless of the pitfalls of naming such a distinctive character as the Ripper. Merrick resided at the London Hospital and thus would have access to surgical knives, he resented women because his appearance prevented meaningful relations with them and he went about unrecognized because he wore a hood in public . . .

There are many more names, and many books detailing their credentials. But there are a few much more credible suspects, the ones the police who were working on the case at the time took seriously. These are the main rivals to Aaron Kosminski as serious contenders, and they remain the most likely to rival him. They were the ones the police considered very carefully at the time, and they have continued to be the preferred choices of most serious researchers. I had read about all of them before I spoke to Alan McCormack, and although at that time I favoured Deeming, I could have been persuaded by the arguments in favour of any of them. I never gave any serious consideration to the wilder theories, but these are the names which topped the police list then and, to this day, top the list of possible Rippers.

All of these suspects were mentioned by senior police officials with direct links to the Ripper case. They are: Montague Druitt; Francis Tumblety; George Chapman; Michael Ostrog and 'Kosminski' (my man).

George Chapman was mentioned by Inspector Abberline in a newspaper interview in 1903. This was the year that Chapman (real name Severin Klosowski) had been hanged as the 'Borough Poisoner' after cruelly killing three 'wives' in succession, usually to get hold of their money. Chapman was a barber-surgeon from Poland who had been living and working in Cable Street, Whitechapel in 1888. He later ran a barber-shop from the cellar of the White Hart pub at the corner of Whitechapel High Street and George Yard, where Martha Tabram was murdered on 7 August 1888 (the pub proudly promotes its connection to the case, and is a feature of the Ripper tours). In the interview that Abberline gave around the time of Chapman's arrest and trial, he said:

> . . . there are a score of things which make one believe that Chapman is the man; and you must understand that we have never believed all those stories about Jack the Ripper being dead, or that he was a lunatic, or anything of that kind. For instance, the date of the arrival in England coincides with the beginning of the series of murders in Whitechapel; there is a coincidence also in the fact that the murders ceased in London when 'Chapman' went to America, while similar murders began to be perpetrated in America after he landed there. The fact that he studied medicine and surgery in Russia before he came here is well established, and it is curious to note that the first series of murders was the work of an expert surgeon, while the recent poisoning cases were proved to be done by a man with more than an elementary knowledge of medicine. The story told by 'Chapman's' wife of the attempt to murder her with a long knife while in America is not to be ignored . . .

It is hard to know whether Abberline *really* believed that Chapman was the Ripper or was just getting caught up in the heat of the moment, as he said in a later interview that the police were no nearer to knowing the killer's identity in 1903 than they were in 1888. George Chapman, despite changing his method of killing (often thought unlikely for a serial killer according to today's research into the psychology of serial killing) still has his supporters, and an alleged comment by Abberline to arresting officer Sergeant Godley after Chapman was apprehended – 'You've got Jack the Ripper at last' – continues to fuel his candidacy, although this remark by Abberline was first reported only years later, in a book that came out in 1930.

Fuelling the speculation, and as alluded to in Abberline's newspaper interview, is the fact that Chapman moved to Jersey City in the USA in 1891, following which it has been claimed that several murders of a comparable nature to the Ripper crimes took place – in fact, there was only one murder of a prostitute that could have fitted the Ripper's modus operandi. Chapman returned to Britain the following year to begin his poison murders. These are so different from the brutal, seemingly random violence of the Ripper that I find it hard to believe they were all the work of the same man.

The next suspect to be named by a senior policeman at the time is 'Dr' Francis Tumblety, an American 'quack'. Tumblety's name had been linked with the Whitechapel murders as far back as 1888, mainly in the American press, but many subsequent researchers had missed the frequent references to his possible guilt that were made contemporaneously after he fled from London that year. Tumblety was an unusual character and always seemed to attract trouble. He had been linked to the assassination of Abraham Lincoln and apparently had connections with Irish Fenian activities. He was a homosexual, or at least bisexual, and was arrested on 7 November 1888 for 'acts of gross indecency' with several other men, and was given bail for what was legally classed as a misdemeanour. Soon after, he skipped bail, left Britain and, via France, returned to his homeland under the alias of 'Frank Townsend'. Once there, the press was full of stories about him being Jack the Ripper, something Tumblety – who enjoyed the notoriety – was more than happy to address, admitting that he had been a suspect and that he had been questioned by the British police but insisting he wasn't guilty.

His prominence as a worthy contemporary suspect was not truly appreciated until the discovery of a letter, written by former Special Branch Chief Inspector John Littlechild to journalist George R. Sims in 1913, which came to light in the early 1990s during a sale from the collection of crime historian Eric Barton. The letter's provenance was sound and led many researchers scurrying back to the archives to find out more about this peculiar man.

Tumblety is a credible suspect and high on the list of possible Rippers. There were many press articles in which associates and those who had crossed Tumblety made it clear that he had a great dislike of women. Littlechild himself mentions this in his letter, saying that Tumblety's feelings against women were 'remarkable and bitter in the extreme, a fact on record'. But, as with all the suspects, the evidence that exists today is well short of conclusive. For example, it is possible Tumblety was still in police custody on 9 November 1888, in which case it would have been impossible for him to have murdered Mary Kelly: some researchers dedicated to the Tumblety candidature have got round this by suggesting that Kelly was murdered by a copycat, and that Tumblety was responsible only for the other victims. As with George Chapman, the so-called Ripper-like murders in the USA in 1891–2 which led many to believe that Jack had crossed the Atlantic, have been blamed on Tumblety who spent the rest of his life there before his death in 1903. In his defence, it is unlikely that Tumblety, as a homosexual, would have murdered women as homosexual serial killers usually only target men. But this is all supposition.

In 1894, six years after the murders, the *Sun* newspaper claimed it knew the name of the Ripper and that he had been convicted of malicious wounding in 1891, deemed insane and incarcerated at Broadmoor, the hospital for the criminally insane in Berkshire. The newspaper did not actually give the man's name, but said the identity was known to Sir Melville Macnaghten, the Assistant Chief Constable of the Metropolitan police CID, who had been appointed in 1889 after a career running his father's tea plantations in India. Macnaghten took up his post at the height of Ripper mania, because the police and public did not know then that the killings were over, and there was still a state of alarm in the East End. He would certainly have been privy to all the information the police had gathered. After the *Sun* articles he wrote a memorandum, which was eventually put into the Scotland Yard files. The memorandum was not written for public consumption. In it Macnaghten exonerated the man alluded to in the newspaper, Thomas Cutbush, of the crimes and then, importantly, named the three men he felt more likely to have been the Ripper than Cutbush. He described them as, in his words:

(1) A Mr M. J. Druitt, said to be a doctor & of good family, who disappeared at the time of the Miller's

Court murder, whose body (which was said to have been upwards of a month in the water) was found in the Thames on 31st Dec. – or about 7 weeks after that murder. He was sexually insane [probably a reference to homosexuality] and from private info I have little doubt but that his own family believed him to have been the murderer.

(2)   Kosminski, a Polish Jew, & resident in Whitechapel. This man became insane owing to many years indulgence in solitary vices. He had a great hatred of women, specially of the prostitute class, & had strong homicidal tendencies; he was removed to a lunatic asylum about March 1889. There were many circs connected with this man which made him a strong 'suspect'.

(3)   Michael Ostrog, a Russian doctor, and a convict, who was subsequently detained in a lunatic asylum as a homicidal maniac. This man's antecedents were of the worst possible type, and his whereabouts at the time of the murders could never be ascertained.

I had first heard of the Macnaghten memorandum from Alan McCormack, and had read it straight away. It is a vital plank of genuine evidence, written as it was by a senior ranking police officer who would certainly have known all there was to know, at the time, about the investigation. For me it was the mention of Kosminski that was of prime importance, but for other researchers Druitt, because he was named first, was given the top slot.

Macnaghten's original notes, upon which he based the final memorandum, were in the possession of his daughter, Lady Christobel Aberconway, and she showed them to broadcaster

Daniel Farson when he was researching a TV programme, *Farson's Guide to the British*, in 1959. When the programme was aired, emphasis was placed on Druitt as Macnaghten's favourite, but he was only referred to as 'MJD'.

Montague John Druitt was a teacher and barrister who, as Macnaghten mentioned, was found dead in the Thames on New Year's Eve 1888. He was not a doctor as Macnaghten wrote, which illustrates the cautious way we have to treat evidence, even when it comes with such good provenance. His mother had been plagued by mental illness and, according to a note found on his body, Druitt feared he was going the same way. His suicide gave a perfect reason for the Ripper murders stopping when they did. Other authors in the late nineteenth century, usually from the police or press, also alluded to the Druitt suicide without mentioning him by name: we can deduce from this that he was a favoured suspect among those who were close to the case.

Sometime before Macnaghten wrote his memorandum, a story about the Ripper's supposed suicide appeared in the press saying that a 'West of England' member of parliament had solved the Ripper case and that the murderer committed suicide on the date of the final murder suffering from 'homicidal mania'. Another reference to a Ripper suicide came from the journalist George R. Sims who spoke for several years from 1899 about a suspect who had drowned himself in the Thames at the end of 1888. Two books, written by Tom Cullen (*Autumn of Terror*, 1965) and Daniel Farson (*Jack the Ripper*, 1972), made the case for Druitt. For some years he was suspect number one, until he was eclipsed by the sensational royal conspiracy theories.

*

The third suspect, Michael Ostrog, is the least likely of the triumvirate. He was a petty thief, conman and fraudster, with a long history of arrests and prison sentences behind him by 1888. But he had never been violent – the closest he came was pulling a revolver on a police superintendent after one of his arrests – and there is nothing to support Macnaghten's allegation that he was a homicidal maniac. When he was on a couple of occasions detained in an asylum rather than in prison, he was found to be suicidal, but not a threat to others. Even his stays in the mental asylums were probably part of his well-practised ability to con: he possibly feigned madness to get a softer place to stay than prison. Some reports have him in prison in France at the time of the Ripper killings, although other researchers disagree. But nothing about him seems to fit what we know about the Ripper: he was in his mid-fifties at the time of the murders, and he was too tall at 5 foot 11 inches to fit any of the descriptions.

Which brings us to Macnaghten's views on Kosminski.

In his memorandum, Macnaghten describes Kosminski as a Polish Jew whose insanity was brought on by years of indulgence in 'solitary vices', which we can assume is a typically coy Victorian euphemism for masturbation, and as a result he was sent to an asylum. In 1892 Robert Anderson, who at that time was still Assistant Commissioner CID, said in an interview in *Cassell's Saturday Journal* that the Whitechapel murderer was undoubtedly a homicidal maniac. Three years later, the writer Alfred Aylmer said in the *Windsor Magazine* that Anderson had a very specific idea of the identity of the Ripper: 'He has himself a perfectly plausible theory that Jack the Ripper was a homicidal maniac, temporarily at large, whose hideous career was cut short by committal to an asylum.'

Anderson put his ideas into print in 1901 in an article on penology and in a book published later about his life as a senior police officer. He stated that 'the inhabitants of the metropolis generally were just as secure during the weeks the fiend was on the prowl as they were before the mania seized him, or after he had been safely caged in an asylum', presumably because he believed the victims 'belonged to a very small class of degraded women who frequent the East End streets after midnight', leaving respectable citizens safe. So, early on, Anderson was making a stand for the identity of the Ripper having been known and that he had been safely taken out of circulation, which seems to confirm what Macnaghten said in his memorandum. But it did not end there: in 1910, when Anderson published his memoirs, he put his cards on the table. In *The Lighter Side of My Official Life* he made an assertion, without any sense of doubt whatsoever, that he and his force were aware of the identity of the Ripper:

One did not need to be a Sherlock Holmes to discover that the criminal was a sexual maniac of a virulent type; that he was living in the immediate vicinity of the scenes of the murders; and that, if he was not living absolutely alone, his people knew of his guilt, and refused to give him up to justice. During my absence abroad the Police had made a house-to-house search for him, investigating the case of every man in the district whose circumstances were such that he could go and come and get rid of his bloodstains in secret. And the conclusion we came to was that he and his people were certain low-class Polish Jews; for it is a remarkable fact that people of that class in the East End will not give up one of their number to Gentile justice.

And the result proved that our diagnosis was right on every point. For I may say at once that 'undiscovered murders' are rare in London, and the 'Jack-the-Ripper' crimes are not within that category. And if the Police here had powers such as the French Police possess, the murderer would have been brought to justice. Scotland Yard can boast that not even the subordinate officers of the department will tell tales out of school, and it would ill become me to violate the unwritten rule of the service. So I will only add here that the 'Jack-the-Ripper' letter which is preserved in the Police Museum at New Scotland Yard is the creation of an enterprising London journalist.

Having regard to the interest attaching to this case, I am almost tempted to disclose the identity of the murderer and of the pressman who wrote the letter above referred to. But no public benefit would result from such a course, and the traditions of my old department would suffer. I will merely add that the only person who had ever had a good view of the murderer unhesitatingly identified the suspect the instant he was confronted with him; but he refused to give evidence against him.

In saying that he was a Polish Jew I am merely stating a definitely ascertained fact. And my words are meant to specify race, not religion. For it would outrage all religious sentiment to talk of the religion of a loathsome creature whose utterly unmentionable vices reduced him to a lower level than that of the brute.

It was strong stuff and upset several people when the memoirs were serialized in *Blackwood's Magazine* prior to publication, particularly the editor of the *Jewish Chronicle* who said that

Anderson had no proof that the killer was a Jew. Anderson replied to the objection and was unrepentant, arguing that 'When I stated that the murderer was a Jew, I was stating a simple matter of fact. It is not a matter of theory. In stating what I do about the Whitechapel Murderer, I am not speaking as an expert in crime, but as a man who investigated the facts.'

So Robert Anderson, Assistant Commissioner CID of the Metropolitan police in 1888 and a man who knew the full facts of the Ripper investigation, publicly insisted that the Ripper was a 'low-class' (i.e. a poor, lower working-class) Jew, driven insane by 'unmentionable' and 'solitary' vices and who had been identified by a witness who had clearly seen him but who had refused to testify or give any further assistance to the authorities.

Anderson's confident claims were not echoed by all the other officials involved with the case. It was later suggested that Anderson's opinions were the cloudy recollections of an elderly man and others have even said they believed that he was lying outright. Anderson was self-serving and boastful at times, but it is unlikely he would come out with blatant lies, considering his position. He had strong religious principles which would also militate against him lying: since 1860 he had been a devout fundamental Christian and believed in the imminent coming of Christ. He was the author of innumerable books on religion and interpretation of scripture. His convictions regarding the Ripper did not seem to waver, even in light of strong criticism.

Robert Anderson's definitive judgement on the outcome of the Ripper case seemed to stand alone until the discovery of a copy of his 1910 memoirs which had once been in the possession of Chief Inspector Donald Swanson. Swanson was the detective who was pretty much in charge of the

Ripper investigation while Anderson was on sick leave, and consequently it would be hard to find a better informed source: every shred of evidence, notes of every police interview, every statement given, arrest made and any and all theories were presented to him at the time. He was a career policeman, like Abberline, who rose through the ranks from being a beat constable, unlike Macnaghten, Anderson and Warren who were recruited at a high level from the world of the military or the colonies. Well versed in procedure, Swanson would have been closely familiar with every twist and turn in the case, and his opinion on any Ripper-related matter, had he chosen to write his memoirs (which he did not, unfortunately), would have been of enormous interest. So when this copy of Anderson's memoirs turned up in the 1980s, riddled with Swanson's own annotations written between 1910 and his death in 1924, including a part where he *actually named* Anderson's Ripper suspect, the revelations were of maximum importance to historians and researchers.

The book had passed to Swanson's spinster daughter, Alice, following his death, and when Alice herself died in 1981, it came into the possession of her nephew, Jim Swanson. Despite the book being in the family for generations, the notations (or 'marginalia' as they have since become known) had escaped attention until Jim Swanson acquired the book and his brother, Donald, noticed the pencilled notes. A story about the marginalia was sold to the *News of the World* in 1981 for £750, but the newspaper never published it: there was no reason given. This meant that the marginalia languished in relative obscurity, of interest only to experts in the case, until the book was presented to Scotland Yard's Black Museum in July 2006. When the press heard about it, it was treated as a brand-new discovery: the *Daily Telegraph*, for example, used a large photograph of Donald Swanson in old age, with the headline: 'Has this man revealed the real Jack the Ripper?'

The significant annotations related to the passage where Anderson claims that the suspect was a male Polish Jew, living in Whitechapel, who had people (probably meaning family or fellow members of his community) protecting him. The passage ended: 'I will merely add that the only person who ever had a good view of the murderer unhesitatingly identified the suspect the instant he was confronted with him; but he refused to give evidence against him.' From here, Swanson had written in pencil underneath and in the margin:

because the suspect was also a Jew and also because his evidence would convict the suspect, and witness would be the means of murderer being hanged, which he did not wish to be left on his mind. And after this identification which suspect knew, no other murder of this kind took place in London . . .

The rest of the relevant notes continued in the endpaper of the book and read:

. . . after the suspect had been identified at the Seaside Home where he had been sent by us with difficulty in order to subject him to identification, and he knew he was identified. On suspect's return to his brother's house in Whitechapel, he was watched by police (City CID), by day and night. In a very short time the suspect with his hands tied behind his back, he was sent to Stepney Workhouse and then to Colney Hatch and died shortly afterwards – Kosminski was the suspect. DSS.

The content of the marginalia was probably the most important discovery since Dan Farson was introduced to Macnaghten's memorandum in 1959, which led to Montague Druitt becoming the prime suspect for many years. Here at last was what seemed to be a direct reference to the identity of the Whitechapel murderer, the so-called 'Jack the Ripper', put forward by men who were actually in a position to know the real background story. It is easy to see why Alan McCormack of the Black Museum would claim in our conversations that Scotland Yard knew who the killer was and always had done. The book with its notes was, in effect, the 'documentation' that McCormack had told me about.

As with any important document, there is always the issue of provenance. For the 'Swanson Marginalia' it appeared excellent, as the book had remained with Swanson's immediate family and descendants. Also, the presence of the notes was not unusual, as Donald Swanson appeared to be a compulsive annotator of books, as could be seen by looking at other volumes in the family's possession. What really needed to be confirmed, just to be on the safe side, was whether the notes in Anderson's book were actually written by Swanson.

Tests were arranged and in 1988, Dr Richard Totty, Assistant Director of the Home Office Forensic Science Laboratory, was given a photocopy of the relevant pages along with copies of other known examples of Swanson's writing. Dr Totty's results were a surprise, as he felt that the marginalia had not been written in the same hand as the sample writing. It turned out that this was because the sample handwriting was not Swanson's, but was written by a secretary on his behalf and merely bore Swanson's signature. Replacement samples were provided which were in Swanson's actual hand, and Totty confirmed that they matched.

When the copy of Anderson's book was donated to the Black Museum in July 2006, another set of tests was initiated, again to satisfy curator Alan McCormack that what they had was bona fide. Using one of Donald Swanson's notebooks from the family collection for comparison, the analysis was performed by Dr Christopher Davies who at that time was one of the senior document examiners in the London Laboratory of the Forensic Science Service. In his report, he said:

> What was interesting about analysing the book was that it had been annotated twice in two different pencils at different times, which does raise the question of how reliable the second set of notes were as they were made some years later. There are enough similarities between the writing in the book and that found in the ledger to suggest that it probably was Swanson's writing, although in the second, later set, there are small differences. These could be attributed to the ageing process and either a mental or physical deterioration, but we cannot be completely certain that is the explanation. The added complication is that people in the Victorian era tended to have very similar writing anyway as they were all taught the same copybook, so the kind of small differences I observed may just have been the small differences between different authors. It is most likely to be Swanson, but I'm sure the report will be cause for lively debate amongst those interested in the case.

He concluded that 'there is strong evidence to support the proposition that Swanson wrote the questioned annotations in the book *The Lighter Side of My Official Life*.' But for some, 'strong evidence' is not conclusive evidence and the slight trace of hesitancy by Dr Davies means that, for some Ripper investigators, the authenticity of these annotations is still in question. They fight their corner in internet forums, with exasperatingly long arguments which are sometimes shut down by administrators once they become libellous. Several people have been accused of interfering with the document in order to put Kosminski in the frame. The whole debate shows how passions are inflamed by the Ripper mystery, and the lengths some enthusiasts will go to prove a point.

Eventually, thanks to all this acrimony, a new set of tests was conducted by Dr Davies in 2012, this time with newly found material from the Swanson family collection which had samples of Donald Swanson's handwriting at different stages of his life. By this time, the copy of Anderson's book had been removed from the Black Museum at the suggestion of the family because they felt there was no point it being displayed in a place where nobody could see it (just as happened with the shawl, which was removed in 1997). Dr Davies' new report claimed that 'there is very strong support for the view that the notes towards the bottom of page 138 in Donald Swanson's copy of *The Lighter Side of My Official Life* and the notes on the last leaf in this book were written by Donald Swanson.' And as for the key phrase 'Kosminski was the suspect', Dr Davies answered critics who felt that it had been added on purpose by Jim Swanson at a later date:

I have concluded that there is no evidence to support the view that the final line on the last leaf of the book was added much later to a pre-existing text. I have also found no evidence to support the view that this line was written by Jim Swanson.

The Swanson marginalia is one of the few artefacts from the Ripper story that has been subjected to physical scientific scrutiny, along with several Ripper letters, the Maybrick Diary and now, of course, the shawl. It is, I firmly believe, the genuine article, and I think my view is now vindicated. All attempts to rubbish the marginalia have been refuted by qualified analysis, and therefore I believe we can say that what is contained within it must be considered the important words of an important man involved in the Ripper case.

Around the time that the Anderson book and the Swanson marginalia were in limbo and before much information about them had been published, in 1986–7, freelance writer and broadcaster Martin Fido was preparing his own study of the Ripper case and, drawing from Anderson's claims, undertook an extensive trawl through asylum records looking for the suspect. Aware that a 'Kosminski' had been put forward by Melville Macnaghten, he found an Aaron Kosminski in the records of Colney Hatch Asylum, where he had been incarcerated in February 1891, a date that was at odds with Macnaghten's assertion that he had been 'removed to a lunatic asylum about March 1889'. Fido also felt that Aaron Kosminski was little more than a harmless imbecile and certainly not the homicidal maniac that the Ripper was meant to be. He also did not die shortly after being sent to Colney Hatch as was claimed in Swanson's marginalia.

Fido duly picked out another Jewish inmate, David Cohen, who died in October 1889; this man was from Whitechapel and was extremely violent and thus, in Fido's opinion, fitted the bill better than Kosminski. But Cohen's candidacy was not without its problems either: most obviously, the name was wrong. Fido got round this by suggesting that 'David Cohen' was perhaps a 'John Doe' name, in other words a blanket title given to those eastern Europeans with names that were difficult to pronounce. Also, according to Swanson, the identification took place at the 'Seaside Home', which is popularly believed to refer to the Police Convalescent Seaside Home in Hove on the Sussex coast, near Brighton. As this establishment opened in 1890, Cohen could not have been identified there as he had died the year before.

Another boost to the case for Kosminski, apart from his presence at Colney Hatch as stated by Swanson, was the reason for his internment – 'self abuse' – a very specific diagnosis which obviously made a direct link with the 'solitary' and 'unmentionable vices' put down by Anderson and Macnaghten.

It was all enough to confirm to me that Kosminski was the most likely suspect, and so I began to renew my research into his life which I had started in 2007. The most pressing need was to get a sample of his DNA, to compare it with the shawl.

This was now my biggest task.

CHAPTER ELEVEN

WHO WAS AARON KOSMINSKI?

From the moment Alan McCormack uttered those words: 'We know who the Ripper is. We've always known,' I have felt strongly that Aaron Kosminski is the right suspect. I've looked at all the others, and although there are some discrepancies among the assertions of the police involved in the case, I think the compelling evidence leads to him. So who is he? What do we know about him?

The answer is that we don't have a very full picture of this man who is the most famous murderer in the world. Records from the 1880s are shadowy at best, and with a foreign immigrant, even more so. But we do have an outline of his life.

Soon after I bought the shawl I started the search for him, which led me in 2008 to the London Metropolitan Archives (LMA), which are housed in the Farringdon area of London, and are the main archive for the Greater London area. The archives contain 105 kilometres of documents, maps, books, film, pictures and photographs of London, some of it dating back to 1067.

I went to the archive because I discovered that the records of Colney Hatch Asylum, one of the two asylums he was held in at the end of his life, were stored there, and I spent a day trawling through them, photographing all the references to Aaron Kosminski. But I hit a wall when it came to getting the archives from the other asylum to which he was later transferred, Leavesden. I was not able to get into these archives because they were too fragile to be handled by a member of the public; however, I paid one of the professional archivists to do the research for me (see Appendix for a selection of documents). I was not the first researcher in the archives there: I saw Martin Fido's name above mine in the log of who had been looking at Aaron Kosminski's records, the man who had rejected him in favour of David Cohen as the Ripper. But I still find it remarkable that in all the years since he was put on the list of three top suspects, so little research had been done into him before.

So what do we know? Who was Aaron Kosminski, and what triggered his gruesome attacks on the prostitutes of the East End in a few terrible months in 1888?

Aaron Mordke Kosminski was born in Klodawa, in the Province of Kalish in central Poland, on 11 September 1865, the son of tailor Abram Josef Kozminski and his wife, Golda Lubnowski. They were described in an undated entry in the Klodawa Book of Residents as 'petty bourgeois', which suggests that they had a reasonable standard of living. Aaron was the youngest of seven children, although his oldest sister, Pessa, only lived until she was three, and died long before he was born. His next sister, Hinde, was born seventeen years before he was, in 1848, followed by a brother, Icek (who later adopted the Anglicized name of Isaac), born in 1852. Next was a sister, Malke (who also changed her name to Matilda), and then another sister, Blima, born in 1854. Closest in age to him was his brother Woolf who was five years his senior. By the time Aaron was born, his mother Golda was forty-five, and she had spent twenty years giving birth and rearing children.

Klodawa is a small town about ninety miles from Warsaw, with a salt mine which formed the backbone of its economy, and which is still the largest salt mine in Poland. The town has a chequered and mostly unhappy history of being invaded and handed around between different states: in the seventeenth century it was destroyed by the Swedes, then it was ruled by Prussia, followed by a spell as part of the Duchy of Warsaw. It was part of the Congress Kingdom of Poland, an autonomous state ruled by the tsars of Russia, from 1815 until a rebellion against Russia in 1863, which was suppressed and the area became a province of the Russian Empire. It formally became part of Russia in the year that Aaron was born.

If his home town had a fractured history, the Jewish community within it had an even more troubled past, having at times been expelled from the town. By the time of Aaron's birth, almost a quarter of the population was Jewish. His father Abram was a tailor, and from everything we know about the work his sons did when they came to London, it's clear he apprenticed them to his trade.

In about 1871, when he was twenty, Isaac was the first of the family to move to London, with his young wife Bertha, probably moving to escape the poverty of Klodawa, and to work in a larger population: there may not have been enough tailoring work in a town of less than 3,000 inhabitants.

Aaron was only eight or nine years old when his father died, at the age of about fifty-four, after Isaac had already left Poland. We don't know the cause of his death, but the impact on the family must have been huge. Hinde and Matilda were married by then, and no longer living with the family. Their father's death certificate lists him as leaving a widow and three children living at home, presumably the youngest three, Blima, who was sixteen at the time, Woolf, fourteen, and the much younger Aaron.

They must all have felt the death of the father acutely, for financial reasons as well as emotional ones. But perhaps Aaron, so much the youngest, was more affected than the others. I am not going to attempt to explore the psychology of separation and loss at such an early age in any depth, but we know today how profoundly children's lives are influenced by losing a parent at a crucial stage of their development.

In a patriarchal society, the head of the family was now Woolf, a young teenager who had to support his mother, sister and little brother. Aaron was no doubt recruited to work: it was normal for children as young as ten to be employed. Blima may also have worked in the family business until her marriage.

We know almost nothing about the life of his sister Blima, although she changed her name to Bertha Held, from which we can deduce that she married and also, because of the anglicized first name, left Eastern Europe. Matilda married her cousin Mosiek (later changed to Morris) Lubnowski. They moved to Germany where their first two children (they had four) were born and after at least two years there they moved to London.

His oldest surviving sister, Hinde, married Aaron Singer, another tailor, in Poland and had two children there, born when their uncle Aaron was only ten and then twelve years old.

Other than this, very little is known about Aaron's childhood in Poland. What we do know is that brother Woolf and his wife Brucha (another cousin, who also anglicized her name to Betsy) emigrated to London in 1881, when Woolf was twenty. Fifteen-year-old Aaron probably went with them and joined the thousands of Jewish refugees who were now descending upon the East End to escape the pogroms, the Russian violence towards Jewish communities.

Whether Golda travelled with them is not known: she may have come later with her daughter Matilda, who lived in Germany when she first left Poland (and it's a possibility that Aaron, too, went with her) because we have records of Golda living with Matilda in London, and she is buried there. Hinde, who now went by the name Helena (and later was known as Annie) also travelled to London with her family at about the same time. It is possible that her husband came earlier: there's a reference to him fleeing Poland after a scandal, and he appears to have been a bit of a ladies' man who, much later, deserted his wife and family. The Singers stayed in London for two or three years, where two more children were born, before leaving for America in 1885, where they settled in Boston.

The journey from Klodawa to London was undoubtedly horrendous, with border guards demanding bribes and robbers taking advantage of the defenceless travellers. Crossing the North Sea typically took two or three days, crammed with other emigrants in dirty, smelly conditions. The Kosminskis were fortunate compared to most of their fellow travellers: they had somewhere to go in London, and someone to greet them. Isaac was living there with a successful tailoring business, and he was relatively comfortably off in his new homeland. By 1885, three of the Kosminski siblings, Isaac, Matilda and Woolf, were renting houses in the East End in Greenfield Street (now Greenfield Road), off Commercial Road, and which was described as a relatively respectable street for the neighbourhood, inhabited by 'a rather superior class of people', according to Charles Booth's survey carried out in 1888. Before they left for America, Helena and her family, the Singers, also lived in Greenfield Street.

With their new anglicized first names, the Kosminskis changed their surname to Abrahams, simply because it was easier to pronounce and spell than Kosminski, although Aaron, at least, seems to have preferred the old name. Perhaps he felt he had lost so much already – his father, his homeland, his language – that he was not prepared to surrender his name, too.

Woolf and his family, and Matilda and hers, may have found it harder to settle in London than Isaac did. Both families are recorded as moving to different addresses, all either in Green-field Street or very close by, in the next few years (Woolf lived at four different houses in the street, as well as in the nearby Providence Street, Yalford Street and Berner Street, where he had lived next door to the scene where Elizabeth Stride would later be murdered). We don't know which of his siblings gave Aaron a home: perhaps they all took care of their youngest brother at different times, but as they all had children themselves, and Golda to house, conditions must have been cramped. It would be unlikely he lived separately: young single people in those days would normally live with family.

Isaac was prospering in a small way, and by 1888 he had fourteen employees and a workshop in the yard behind his house, one of fifteen similar workshops along one side of Greenfield Street, which shows that the Jewish tailoring busi-ness was well established. One reason for this is that they were making clothes for women: previously all tailoring in Britain had been done for men, and women were dressed by home dressmakers.

However, with so many people in the business, and keen competition, it is understandable that relative newcomers like Woolf struggled to make a mark. Matilda's husband Morris was a shoemaker, and he too appears to have found it hard to make ends meet in the early days in London, probably because shoemaking again was not a new trade in the area and there would be established competition.

Although the East End was a popular place for the Jewish settlers to congregate, they were, by 1888, experiencing a backlash of anti-Semitism, being accused of stealing jobs from unemployed British-born nationals; of undercutting each other on price so much that the wages they paid were not enough to sustain their employees; and there were firebrand Jewish Socialists condemning the low-waged rag trade workshops. It was an unsettling time for the immigrants, and it must have seemed to the Kosminski/Abrahams family that they had lived their entire lives under anti-Semitism.

Whichever branch of his family he was living with, in 1888, when the Ripper murders happened, Aaron was close enough to the scenes of all the crimes to have easily got there and to have escaped. I've traced the routes, I know these short distances well. On the night of the double murder, when he was interrupted at Dutfield's Yard, he was compelled to strike again, and I believe he was only successful because of the proximity of his home to the scene. There was a hue and cry in the streets, with police and public hunting him, yet he *needed* to strike again on that significant date. Living just on the edge of Whitechapel meant he could commit the murder with time to carry out his ritual mutilations, and still get back to the safety of his home, which would be either in Greenfield Street (with Isaac or Matilda), or Providence Street or Yalford Street, where we know Woolf was living at about this time (we know he lived in both streets from the dates his children attended local schools, but we don't know exactly when he moved to each new address). All these streets give easy access to the crime scenes.

Immediately after the murders, the records on Aaron Kosminski are scanty, with just one tantalizing glimpse of him. In December 1889, he appeared in court after being arrested for walking an unmuzzled dog in Cheapside. Fear of a rabies outbreak had led to a law requiring all dogs to be muzzled. Aaron's appearance in court was reported in the press. *Lloyds Weekly News* said:

> Police-constable Borer said he saw the defendant with an unmuzzled dog, and when asked his name gave that of Aaron Kosminski, which his brother said was wrong as his name was Abrahams – Defendant said that the dog was not his, and his brother said it was found more convenient to go by the name of Abrahams, but his name was Kosminski – Sir Polydore de Keyser imposed a fine of 10s and costs, which the defendant would not pay as it was the Jewish Sunday and it was not right to pay money on Sunday. He was given 'til Monday to pay.

Another report in the *City Press* said:

> Aaron Kosmunski appeared to a summons for having a dog unmuzzled in Cheapside. When spoken to by the police he gave a wrong name and address. Defendant: I goes by the

name of Abrahams sometimes, because Kosmunski is hard to spell (Laughter). The defendant called his brother who corroborated that part of the evidence relating to his name. The Alderman said he would have to pay a fine of 10s and costs. Defendant: I cannot pay, the dog belongs to Jacobs, it is not mine. The Alderman: It was in your charge and you must pay the fine, and if you have no goods on which to distrain you will have to go to prison for seven days.

The brother present at the court was probably Woolf, who was certainly using the name Abrahams. It is interesting that Aaron, who was twenty-four, was accompanied by his older brother; it is not clear why he had to come along and there doesn't seem to be any reason to assume that Aaron was having any sort of difficulty, either with language or ability, to understand what was happening, although he probably needed help paying the fine.

From there, Aaron Kosminski disappears briefly from the historical record. When he reappears in 1890, it is in the records of the Mile End Old Town workhouse. On 12 July, Aaron was taken there by one of his brothers, again probably Woolf. The exact reason why he was taken there is not clear, although it was probably because Aaron had begun to show unmistakable signs of being mentally disturbed and Woolf may well have hoped there was treatment available, or at least to get a diagnosis: the record shows that the 'cause of seeking relief' was 'Qy Insane' which meant 'query insane', a common enough entry for pauper admissions at the time. Workhouses were institutions providing basic care for those who had reached the very bottom of the social ladder, with no means of support and no accommodation. They were also used to house the mentally ill and the elderly, and they were dirty, overcrowded, unsanitary places: a refuge of last resort.

On admission Aaron was described as 'destitute'. We can only guess that he was behaving sufficiently unusually for the family to be worried enough to seek help. His occupation was given as 'hairdresser' and his address was 3 Sion Square, Woolf's home. His religion was recorded as 'Hebrew', and he was classified as an 'able bodied man' in terms of which meagre diet he would be allocated.

There is nothing in any records I have found to show that he ever worked as a hairdresser, and with the family history of tailoring it is a surprising occupation, but there is equally no reason to doubt the information given on his admission papers to the workhouse: perhaps he did, at some point, work as a hairdresser. He was discharged back into the care of his brother three days later and it is unlikely that he saw a doctor or was given any help. Perhaps the family felt guilty about leaving him there, perhaps they worried that without more secure accommodation he would be able to resume his murders. We will never know.

Six months later, Aaron was readmitted to the workhouse, and this time his address was given as 16 Greenfield Street, the home of his sister Matilda and her husband Morris Lubnowski, which shows the family probably shuttled him around between their homes. The date was 4 February 1891, and it appears that his mental health had now deteriorated to a state that the family, who had been sheltering and supporting him, could no longer cope. On his admission the register of patients stated that he was suffering from 'mania' and he was examined by a doctor, Edmund Houchin, who wrote a report on his findings and declared Kosminski insane:

> I personally examined the said Aaron Kosminski and came to the conclusion he is a person of unsound mind and a proper person to be taken charge and detained under care and treatment.

a) *Facts indicating insanity observed by Medical Man, viz:*
He declares that he is guided and his movements altogether controlled by an instinct that informs his mind, he says that he knows the movements of all mankind, he refuses food from others because he is told to do so, and he eats out of the gutter for the same reason.

b) *Other Facts Indicating Insanity Communicated by Others*
Jacob Cohen, 51 Carter Lane, St Paul's EC says that he goes about the streets and picks up bits of bread out of the gutter and eats them, he drinks water from the tap & he refuses food at the hands of others. He took up a knife and threatened the life of his sister. He says that he is ill and his cure consists in refusing food. He is melancholic, practises self-abuse. He is very dirty and will not be washed. He has not attempted any kind of work for years.

Houchin ended his report with the words: 'The said Aaron Kosminski appeared to me to be in a fit condition of bodily health to be removed to an asylum, hospital or licensed house.'

The decision to commit him is recorded as 'unchallenged', which means that nobody in his family opposed him being locked up: if they had (as I am sure they must have had) suspicions about him, they probably felt great relief at the responsibility for him being taken from them.

Jacob Cohen, who gave the information about the attack on a sister (who must have been Matilda, unless the report inaccurately uses 'sister' for 'sister-in-law') and the way that Aaron was behaving, was Woolf's business partner, and could also, perhaps, have been Woolf's brother-in-law. Woolf's wife Betsy had a brother Jacob who took the name Cohen after he left Poland, and although he lived and worked (successfully, as a butcher then a draper) in Manchester, it is possible that he was an investor and partner in Woolf's business venture, and visited London because of the business. The address he used when he gave the information about Aaron Kosminski is the address of Woolf's business. But this is speculation: I think it sounds plausible, but nobody has established the true identity of Jacob Cohen, and Ripper researchers have worked hard at it.

The siblings may have asked Jacob Cohen to give the details of Aaron's progressive degeneration because he would be seen as more independent of the family. Possibly the family also gave evidence and this simply wasn't recorded. Houchin would have been dealing with many cases, and we are lucky that such a detailed report has survived.

When Aaron was arrested for walking the unmuzzled dog he said in court that the dog was 'Jacob's', and this is probably another reference to Woolf's partner.

From the workhouse, he was taken to Colney Hatch Asylum on 6 February 1891. This institution was opened at Friern Barnet in July 1851 as the second pauper lunatic asylum for the county of Middlesex. Designed in the Italianate style by S. W. Dawkes, it had 1,250 beds, making it the largest and most modern institution of its kind in Europe. Within ten years it was enlarged to take 2,000 patients. It had its own cemetery (closed in 1873 after which the patients were buried in the Great Northern Cemetery in New Southgate), its own farm on which many patients were employed, its own water supply, and its own sewage works built after the local residents complained of untreated sewage from the asylum flowing into a nearby brook.

The Colney Hatch admission register describes Kosminski as twenty-six years of age, Hebrew, single and, again, a hairdresser. The cause of his condition, originally entered as 'unknown', was amended in red ink to 'self abuse' and the period of his current 'attack' was initially listed as '6 months' but again amended to say '6 years', suggesting that Aaron had been showing mental health problems since 1885, when he was twenty. It was recorded that he was not deemed to be a danger to others. Brother Woolf was again listed as nearest relative.

Through my own research at the LMA I have copies of his notes, and they show him ranging between quiet, morose periods and episodes of great excitement:

FORM OF DISORDER: *MANIA*
Observations
Ward 9.B3.10

On admission patient is extremely deluded & morose. As mentioned in the certificate he believes that all his actions are dominated by an 'Instinct'. This is probably mental hallucination. Answers questions fairly but is inclined to be reticent and morose. Health fair. *F. Bryant*

1891 Feb 10: Is rather difficult to deal with on account of the dominant character of his delusions. Refused to be bathed the other day as his 'Instinct' forbade him. *F. Bryant*

April 21: Incoherent, apathetic, unoccupied; still has the same 'instinctive' objection to the weekly bath; health fair. *Wm Seward*

1892 Jan 9: Incoherent; at times excited & violent – a few days ago he took up a chair, and attempted to strike the charge attendant: apathetic as a rule, and refuses to occupy himself in any way; habits cleanly: health fair. *Wm Seward*

Nov 17: Quiet and well behaved. Only speaks German [?Yiddish]. Does no work. *Cecil J. Beadles*

1893 Jan 18: Chronic Mania: intelligence impaired; at times noisy, excited & incoherent; unoccupied; habits cleanly; health fair. *Wm Seward*

April 8: Incoherent; quiet lately, fair health. *Cecil J. Beadles*

Sept 18: Indolent, but quiet and clean in habits, never employed. Answers questions concerning himself.
Cecil J. Beadles

1894 April 13: demented and incoherent, health fair.
C. Beadles

April 19th: Discharged. Relieved. Leavesden. *Wm Seward*

This last note shows that Aaron Kosminski was transferred to the overcrowded Leavesden Asylum near Watford in Hertfordshire in 1894, where conditions were far worse than at Colney Hatch. No reason was given for the transfer, but it is possible that his intractable condition meant that he was never going to be rehabilitated. When he was admitted to Leavesden his bodily condition was noted down as 'impaired'. For the first time, his mother Golda is listed as his next of kin, her address given as the house where his sister Matilda and her family lived.

The sparse notes taken at Leavesden relating to the last years of his life, which were procured for me by the archivist at the LMA, show that his behaviour continued to fluctuate, and later on his physical health also began to deteriorate. The notes below from Leavesden have been compiled from various loose sources in the records and have been arranged in chronological order to give a better sense of Kosminski's decline:

10/9/10: Faulty in his habits, he does nothing useful & cannot answer questions of a simple nature. BH [bodily health] poor. AKM

29/9/11: Patient is dull & vacant. Faulty & unhealthy in habits. Does nothing useful. Nothing can be got by questions. BH weak. H.C.S.

15/4/12: Didn't test negative. FH

6/9/12: No replies can be got; dull & stupid in manner & faulty in his habits. Requires constant attention. BH weak. AKM

16/1/13: Patient is morose in manner. No sensible reply can be got by questions. He mutters incoherently. Faulty and untidy in his habits. BH weak. AKM

1/4/14: Patient has hallucinations of sight and hearing, is very excitable and troublesome at times, very untidy, bodily condition fair.

16/7/14: Incoherent and excitable: troublesome at times: Hallucinations of hearing. Untidy – BH fair. G.P

14/2/15: Pat merely mutters when asked questions. He has hallucinations of sight and hearing and is very excitable at times. Does not work. Clean but untidy in dress. BH fair. DNG.

1/3/15: No improvement.
Weight taken on 17 May 1915, 7st 8lb 10oz

1/11/15: Patient has cut over left eye caused by knock on tap in washhouse.

2/2/16: Patient does not know his age or how long he has been here. He has hallucinations of sight and hearing & is at times very obstinate. Untidy but clean, does no work, B.H. good. JM

8/7/16: No improvement.

5/4/17: No improvement.

26/5/18: Patient put to bed passing loose motions with blood and mucous.

27/5/18: Transferred to 8a.

3/6/18: Diarrhoea ceased. Ordered up by Dr. Reese.

28/1/19: Put to bed with swollen feet.
Weight in February 1919, 6st 12lb.

20/2/19: Put to bed with swollen feet and feeling unwell. Temp 99°.

13/3/19: Hip broken down.

22/3/19: Taken little nourishment during day, but very noisy.

23/3/19: Appears very low. Partaken of very little nourishment during day.

24/3/19: Died in my presence at 5.05 a.m. Marks on body, sore right hip and left leg. Signed: S. Bennett, night attendant.

According to Aaron Kosminski's death certificate, the cause of death was gangrene. He was fifty-three when he died, and weighed less than seven stone, probably the result of refusing to eat and years of inactivity. The marks on his hip and leg could well have been bedsores. From the sparse notes we can deduce he was in a near catatonic state much of the time, but we do not know whether he was drugged. Although anti-psychotic drugs were not developed until the 1950s, workers in the noisy, understaffed asylums routinely sedated patients to make caring for them easier.

Aaron's body was passed into the possession of 'I & W Abrahams', his two brothers, Isaac and Woolf. He was buried by the Burial Society of the United Synagogue on 27 March 1919 at East Ham Cemetery at a total cost of twelve pounds and five shillings, and his address was given as 5 Ashcroft Road, Bow, which was at that time the home of his brother-in-law Morris Lubnowski and sister Matilda. The inscription on the gravestone read: 'Aaron Kosminski who died the 24th of March 1919. Deeply missed by his brother, sisters, relatives and friends. May his dear soul rest in peace'.

Although the gravestone refers to only one brother, Isaac was alive for another year – so it is likely the gravestone was added later, after Isaac's death. The siblings and their mother Golda are all buried together, in a different cemetery, and their surnames are all recorded as Abrahams. So despite the loving inscription, it seems the rest of the family were happy to keep their mentally ill brother separate from them, even in death.

Looking at these records, it is understandable that Martin Fido and others find it difficult to reconcile this steadily deteriorating and sad figure with the dreaded Jack the Ripper. Yet Aaron Kosminski is the only 'Kosminski' in the asylum records fitting the time period, and a 'Kosminski' was named by Melville Macnaghten as 'a strong suspect'; Robert Anderson was convinced that the Ripper was a poor, insane Polish Jew who had been identified as the Ripper and sent to an asylum and Donald Swanson appeared to agree with him, albeit misnaming Mile End Workhouse as 'Stepney Workhouse', and then named him. I believe there are enough circumstances to make the police's 'Kosminski' and Aaron Mordke Kosminski one and the same, and that is why, in my pursuit of the scientific evidence to prove who the Ripper really was, I made him my prime target.

There is other material that backs up the claims by Macnaghten, Anderson and Swanson. Robert Sagar joined the City of London police in 1880 and swiftly rose through the ranks. By 1888 he was a Sergeant, becoming a Detective Sergeant the following year. Major Henry Smith, Acting Commissioner of the City police at the time of the double murder, said, 'a better or more intelligent officer than Robert Sagar I never had under my command'. In 1905, on Sagar's retirement, a number of newspapers featured his involvement in the Ripper case, and their reports threw up interesting snippets of information that have some bearing on the Kosminski claims. One, from the *City Press*, suggests that not only was the killer believed to be a 'madman' but also that evidence to convict him had not been forthcoming and he was taken out of circulation by being put in an asylum:

His [Sagar's] professional association with the terrible atrocities which were perpetuated some years ago in the East End by the so-styled 'Jack the Ripper' was a very close one. Indeed, M. Sagar knows as much about those crimes, which terrified the Metropolis, as any detective in London. He was deputed to represent the City police force in conference with the detective heads of the Metropolitan force nightly at Leman Street Police Station during the period covered by those ghastly murders. Much has been said and written – and even more conjectured – upon the subject of the 'Jack-the-Ripper' murders. It has been asserted that the murderer fled to the Continent, where he perpetrated similar hideous crimes, but that is not the case. The police realised, as also did the public, that the crimes were those of a madman and suspicion fell upon a man who, without a doubt, was the murderer. Identification being impossible, he could not be charged. He was, however, placed in a lunatic asylum and the series of atrocities came to an end.

Reynolds News took a similar line when talking about Sagar in 1946:

Inspector Robert Sagar, who died in 1924, played a leading part in the Ripper Investigations. In his memoirs he said: 'We had good reason to suspect a man who worked in Butchers' Row, Aldgate. We watched him carefully. There was no doubt that this man was insane – and after a time his friends thought it advisable to have him removed to a private asylum. After he was removed, there were no more Ripper atrocities.'

Frustratingly, Sagar's memoirs have never been traced and as far as we know Kosminski did not work in Butcher's Row, a section of Aldgate High Street named for its prevalence of butchers and slaughterhouses. However, what Sagar is alleged to have said about friends removing the suspect to a private asylum has parallels with Kosminski's fate, even though, again as far as we know, he was not in a *private* asylum at any point before he was admitted to Colney Hatch.

Another City detective, Harry Cox, wrote in *Thompson's Weekly News* following his retirement in 1906 that he too was involved in the surveillance of a suspect. He revealed that the suspect was Jewish and that after a time the Jews in the area where the man lived became wise to who he was:

The man we suspected was about five feet six inches in height, with short, black, curly hair, and he had a habit of taking late walks abroad. He occupied several shops in the East End, but from time to time he became insane, and was forced to spend a portion of his time in an asylum in Surrey.

While the Whitechapel murders were being perpetrated his place of business was in a certain street, and after the last murder I was on duty in this street for nearly three months. There were several other officers with me, and I think there can be no harm in stating that the opinion of most of them was that the man they were watching had something to do with the crimes. You can imagine that never once did we allow him to quit our sight. The least slip and another brutal crime might have been perpetrated under our very noses. It was not easy to forget that already one of them had taken place at the very moment when one of our smartest colleagues was passing the top of the dimly lit street.

The Jews in the street soon became aware of our presence. It was impossible to hide ourselves. They became suddenly alarmed, panic stricken, and I can tell you that at nights we ran a considerable risk. We carried our lives in our hands so to speak, and at last we had to partly take the alarmed inhabitants into our confidence, and so throw them off the scent. We told them we were factory inspectors looking for tailors and capmakers who employed boys and girls under age, and pointing out the evils accruing from the sweaters' system asked them to co-operate with us in destroying it.

They readily promised to do so, although we knew well that they had no intention of helping us. Every man was as bad as another. Day after day we used to sit and chat with them, drinking their coffee, smoking their excellent cigarettes, and partaking of Kosher rum. Before many weeks had passed we were quite friendly with them, and knew that we could carry out our observations unmolested. I am sure they never once suspected that we were police detectives on the trail of the mysterious murderer; otherwise they would not have discussed the crimes with us as openly as they did.

These accounts appear to support the claims of Anderson and Swanson – both Sagar's and Cox's recollections hint that the identity of the murder was known to friends or family and that they appeared reluctant to give him up to 'gentile justice' as Anderson said. When Cox refers to 'the last murder' we do not know which one he means, but possibly it was that of Alice Mackenzie, who is not today thought to be a Ripper victim, but was bracketed with the other deaths at the time. Swanson's marginalia talks of surveillance by City police prior to the suspect's incarceration.

I have used these sources to produce a logical timeline of events surrounding Aaron Kosminski's apprehension and incarceration.

On 12 July 1890, clearly showing signs of mental illness, his family took him to Mile End Workhouse where his sanity was queried. On his release he went back to his brother Woolf's house where the family took care of him and, if they had suspicions about his involvement in the crimes, they presumably did their best to keep him out of harm's way and from the authorities.

Soon after, in response to intelligence or possibly even a tip-off regarding the alleged attack on his sister with a knife mentioned by Dr Houchin (who, interestingly, was a police surgeon for the Whitechapel Police Division, and may have been involved with the police work on the Ripper case, and therefore on the lookout for anything suspicious), Aaron Kosminski was taken in by the police to be identified by a witness who had seen him with one of the victims on the night of one of the murders. A positive identification was made, but owing to religious reasons, the Jewish witness refused to give incriminating evidence and thus the police had little option but to release Kosminski into the care of his family, at which the City police begin their surveillance.

On 4 February 1891, by now exhibiting serious mental problems, he was taken back to the workhouse, deemed insane and went to Colney Hatch and, later, Leavesden.

Some researchers focus on the discrepancies in the various stories, but they were all recalled from memory at later dates, so this is understandable. There are many common themes and I think there is enough evidence to support my interpretation of events, which I am offering only as a justification for going down the route of pursuing Kosminski as the most likely suspect. If this was all I had to base it on I, like so many others, would simply be putting forward a theory, arguing a case. And however convincingly I argued it, there would always be doubt, a counter theory. But I was using *my theory* about Kosminski only as a shortcut to take me to the right man, in terms of scientific proof. All the way through my quest for the Ripper, it is science, not theory, that has been my ally.

Like so many other researchers, I was intrigued by the assertion that there was a witness who identified the Ripper and there was a mysterious venue where this happened. I had a second conversation with Alan McCormack in 2009 when he suggested I should do some digging into who the witness was, so this was the next avenue I went down.

Swanson said the identification took place at the 'Seaside Home' which on the face of it seems an unusual place to hold such an important event. However, during the Whitechapel murders, whenever news got out that a suspect had been taken to a police station, large crowds and interfering journalists would descend in numbers, so with a situation as sensitive as this, discretion would have been paramount. It makes sense that the police might look for a location outside London which was not a police station and yet was under their control, with staff who would understand the importance of not talking about it.

Most researchers today accept that the 'Seaside Home' refers to the Convalescent Police Seaside Home in Hove, East Sussex. 51 Clarendon Villas (its correct address) runs parallel with Church Road, yards away from the corner of Sackville Road, and only a short stroll from the seafront. The building is still there today and is now private flats. Convalescent homes were often built by the coast, where patients could benefit from the clean air while they recovered from illness: philanthropic employers set them up for the benefit of their staff, especially those who worked in heavy industries or in cities with little access to country air (in later years, unions would provide them for their members). I have been to stand outside it twice, the first time when I initially established that it was the right place, having found it in the Brighton archive library. I went again, much later, when I was well and truly on Kosminski's trail, and this visit caused a much stronger reaction in me. I felt myself shudder involuntarily, as I stood outside, knowing that he had been in one of those rooms.

The logistics required to get the suspect from his home to the Seaside Home may explain Swanson's use of the phrase 'sent by us with difficulty'. East London was still buzzing with Ripper rumours and Ripper paranoia in 1890, and any obvious arrest of a suspect would have been seized upon by the voracious press – who wanted to keep the sensational story running – and the nervous public, so spiriting the suspect away had to be done without drawing any attention.

But who was the witness? The clearest clue is in the claim that the witness was Jewish. Looking at the police files, there are three, possibly four, documented witnesses who saw the murderer and were able to describe him: Mrs Long in Hanbury Street, PC William Smith (possibly) and Israel Schwartz in Berner Street and Joseph Lawende at the entrance to Church Passage near Mitre Square. Unless Mrs Long and PC Smith were Jewish, and there is no evidence either way, but their names suggest they were not, then it falls to either Schwartz or Lawende who we know were Jewish. But which one?

I concluded that it must have been Schwartz. One reason I plumped for him was because Joseph Lawende made the sighting of the man with Catherine Eddowes from across the road, Duke Street. Neither of his two companions, Harry Harris and Joseph Hyam Levy, paid much attention to the couple and even Lawende's sighting was, he admitted, unsatisfactory. A description given by Lawende of the man he saw was set down in a report by Donald Swanson and published in the press. He was described as 'age 30 ht. 5 ft. 7 or 8 in., comp. fair, fair moustache, medium built, dress pepper & salt colour loose jacket, grey cloth cap with peak of same colour, reddish handkerchief tied in a knot, round neck, appearance of a sailor.'

According to Major Henry Smith, acting commissioner of the City police in 1888, he had apparently spoken to Lawende about his sighting at the time. Mistakenly describing Lawende as a German, Smith said in his 1910 memoirs that 'I think the German spoke the truth, because I could not "lead" him in any way. "You will easily recognize him, then," I said. "Oh no!" he replied; "I only had a short look at him."' It is difficult to believe that Lawende, who was always unsure about his ability to recognize the man if he saw him again, would be able to do so many months after the event, or that the police would expect him to.

I believe Lawende *was* called in to identify James Sadler, the companion and alleged murderer of Frances Coles in February 1891, but he was unable to do so. Some researchers have suggested that this identification, made at the *Seaman's* Home in Whitechapel, could have been confused in the minds of Anderson and Swanson with the passing of time, and unwittingly altered to become the Seaside Home. That said, it is difficult to reconcile this idea – Sadler, as far as we know, was not Jewish and yet both men had described the suspect as Jewish. And if Sadler is not Jewish, this negates the reason given by Anderson and Swanson for the witness's refusal to testify.

And of course the witness in the Seaside Home scenario identified the suspect as soon as he was confronted with him. Lawende drew a blank with Sadler, who could not have been Jack the Ripper anyway as he was at sea on the dates of most of the Whitechapel murders. Not only that, members of Swanson's family who knew him in later life confirmed that he was in possession of all his critical faculties right into old age and so it's highly unlikely he'd get this important point wrong.

With Israel Schwartz we have none of these problems. From a distance of only tens of feet away, he saw Elizabeth Stride being attacked by a man, just fifteen minutes before her body was found only yards from the scene. He is the ONLY witness to see a Ripper victim being physically attacked, a major reason for me feeling sure it was him. I believe the man even acknowledged Schwartz's presence, shouting 'Lipski!' at him, probably as an anti-Jewish insult aimed at Schwartz.

Once I went back to Alan McCormack with my reasons for choosing Schwartz, he corroborated my reasoning, then he explained about the identification. He said that a *confrontation* took place, as opposed to a line-up. It was not an unusual technique at the time, whereby a suspect or person of interest would be placed in front of, or shown to, a potential witness, not always necessarily to make a confirmed identification immediately, but perhaps to unsettle and intimidate the suspect who the police were sure was guilty in any case. This could provoke the suspect, believing he had been identified, to unwittingly give more information, or even break down and confess willingly. The scenario Alan put to me is the one suggested by Anderson and apparently confirmed by Swanson. This is my summary of it:

Aaron Kosminski was placed in a room at the Seaside Home. Israel Schwartz was led into the room by a police officer and confronted with Kosminski. He was then immediately led out of the room and asked if this was the man he saw attacking Elizabeth Stride on the night of her murder. Alan McCormack was adamant that there was what he described as 'an unhesitating ID'. After a gap of ten minutes or so Schwartz was taken into the room again, and again there was a clear affirmation that this was the right man. But then the police asked Schwartz if he would be willing to testify to the fact, and he refused on the grounds that he could not bear to have it on his conscience that he had sent a fellow Jew to the gallows.

Even though Aaron Kosminski had been clearly identified, the manner in which this identification was made was problematical, because to present it as evidence in court it would have to have been a full line-up of men from whom Kosminski was chosen. As a result, the police had the moral proof, but the *legal* proof was not good enough, a matter bemoaned by Robert Anderson who later said in his memoirs that if the British police 'had powers such as the French police possess, the murderer would have been brought to justice', meaning that such an identification would have been sufficient to officially arrest and charge Kosminski under the French legal system. Here, there were strict legal rules: there had to be a line-up.

The police had probably never anticipated Schwartz's refusal to testify against Kosminski or they would have staged a proper, legally watertight, identification. Alan McCormack stressed to me that there was no other evidence, and that there was never a conspiracy to keep the facts of the case hidden: the police simply could not proceed without Schwartz. I believe the fact there was a confrontation and not a line-up is the reason why Jack the Ripper has remained such a hot topic down the years: if Kosminski had been prosecuted and convicted, the Ripper case would be of interest only to experts studying serial killers, and would occasionally make a chapter in a compilation of historical crimes. It would not have spawned the books, films and whole Ripper industry that we have today.

Schwartz's position was invidious. As a Jew himself, he knew the prejudice against his race that was rampant at the time: if the Ripper was Jewish, it would feed into this growing anti-Semitism. And as far as his own community was concerned, he would possibly have been regarded as a traitor to have stirred up more bad feeling towards them all. He no doubt felt that, as the police were on to the right man, there would be no more deaths at the hands of this man, so his conscience would be clear on that account. He would not, as Swanson pointed out, have Kosminski's death on his mind for the rest of his life. He had helped the police nail their man: as far as he was concerned it was up to them to keep the East End community safe from him.

All criminal prosecutions rely on identifying the culprit. In some cases, it may be possible to establish identification through fingerprints, DNA or other forensic evidence, none of which was available to the police in 1888. Scotland Yard introduced its first Fingerprint Bureau in 1901. They literally had one eyewitness, who would not testify, and there was no other evidence.

Without a clear identification, everything else they had

against Kosminski was circumstantial, and there was little hope of getting more. His family may well have been able to help: it is hard to believe they did not at least suspect him. But if Schwartz would not testify against a fellow Jew, the siblings would certainly not testify against their own brother. Without enough evidence to arrest him and take him before a court, Aaron Kosminski was sent back to the home of his brother Woolf, after which he was watched day and night by the police until he was incarcerated in the asylum.

But how could a seemingly harmless mental patient like Kosminski be a brutal killer who mutilated prostitutes? There are two examples of potential violence, the first being the threat against his sister with a knife, the other being an attempt to hit an asylum employee with a chair. Aggressive acts in themselves, but apparent 'one-offs' which do not necessarily give such a violent portrait as the behaviour of somebody like David Cohen, Martin Fido's preferred suspect, who was also incarcerated in the Colney Hatch Asylum and proved to be a very difficult and violent patient to contain.

It is probable that Kosminski was schizophrenic. Various different factors contribute to the development of schizo-phre-nia, such as living environment, use of drugs and prenatal stresses, as well as, scientists today believe, a genetic pre-disposition. Kosminski was born when his mother was forty-five years old and life may have been hard, particularly after the death of Abram Kosminski when Aaron was at the impressionable age of nine years old. Soon after, Aaron was working in the family business, and some of his close family had already begun to leave Poland for the safety of London. There must have been a constant feeling of threat and insecurity among the Jewish population in Poland, and even as a child he would have picked up on the fears.

Immigration from areas of social adversity has been recognized as a significant factor in the triggering of schizophrenia. Any immigration into a new country and culture raises the incidence of schizophrenia by four to six times, and it is even higher when immigrants are living, in their host country, in poor social conditions and as a minority group.

The symptoms mentioned in the report by Dr Houchin are typical of schizophrenia. He said that Aaron 'declares that he is guided and his movements altogether controlled by an instinct that informs his mind' and that he knew 'the movements of all mankind'. These are the sort of delusions often experienced by sufferers from schizophrenia. In the early twentieth century, psychiatrist Kurt Schneider listed the forms of psychotic symptoms that he thought distinguished schizophrenia from other such disorders. They became known as 'Schneider's first rank symptoms' and have been described as delusions of being controlled by an external force, the belief that thoughts are being inserted into or withdrawn from the sufferer's conscious mind and the belief that their thoughts are being broadcast to other people. Other symptoms, known as 'negative symptoms', reveal similarities with Kosminski's deterioration while at Colney Hatch and Leavesden; these include blunted emotions, speech problems, asocial behaviour and lack of motivation.

The violence of schizophrenics is something that has been the focus of media attention in modern times, even though schizophrenics are statistically no more violent than the general population. When they are violent, it usually takes place during 'episodes', outside of which the individual may appear to be normal, and it attracts attention because it appears, to those who don't share the fractured delusions of the perpetrator, to be random, and therefore more alarming. Murder victims are overwhelmingly more likely to have been killed by a close family member or someone who knows them well, but it is the chance meeting with a deranged maniac that makes the headlines and fuels horror movies.

The episodic nature of psychosis is why many extreme serial killers are able to get away with their crimes for long periods, and why even those closest to them are not always aware of what they are capable of doing when their delusional state takes over. Many notorious killers have been diagnosed with schizophrenia or have shown behaviour that strongly suggests they have it. They include David Berkowitz, the so-called 'Son of Sam', who apparently suffered from auditory hallucinations; Ed Gein, the inspiration for Robert Bloch's Norman Bates in *Psycho*; Peter Sutcliffe, the 'Yorkshire Ripper' who murdered in response to voices from God telling him to do so; and Mark Chapman, who murdered John Lennon in 1980. Richard Trenton Chase, the 'Vampire of Sacramento', killed six people in the space of one month in Sacramento, California, sometimes indulging in necrophilia and cannibalism. He had been diagnosed as suffering with paranoid schizophrenia and sent to an institution in 1975, but responded so well to treatment that he was not considered a danger to the public and released in 1977 into the care of his mother. That year, he committed his first murder. There is an echo of Kosminski's experience, because he, too, despite showing signs of mental illness and later being declared insane, was at one point returned into the care of his family.

The eruption of schizophrenic episodes and the periods of

calm between them possibly explains why somebody like Aaron Kosminski could appear harmless much of the time (such as during his court appearance for walking the unmuzzled dog) and yet be capable of terrible violence. The choice of victims all from a certain class of women suggests that he felt compelled by his delusions to wreak out his fury on them. Prostitutes were all around him on the streets of the East End, and their presence fed these delusions. Later, when he was confined in an asylum, his delusions were not aggravated by them, which may partly explain his lack of violence once incarcerated. But he was not calm: his notes show that he was 'at times excited and violent', that he had 'episodes of great excitement'. Of course, in the harsh custody of the asylum attendants, his violence was contained, as it was not when he roamed the streets of the East End. The description of his behaviour in the scant asylum notes we have is consistent with what would today be diagnosed as schizophrenia.

Most serial murderers can consistently exhibit normal behaviour in certain situations, even in the presence of close family members, and their urge to kill can often lie dormant for many years. Two examples can be found: Dennis Rader, the BTK (Bind, Torture, Kill) killer, who had a number of periods when his killing spree paused for some time, on two occasions following the birth of his children; and Ted Bundy, a notoriously charming and cool character, who had a three-year hiatus from killing between 1975 and 1978.

The onset of schizophrenia typically happens between the ages of sixteen and twenty-five, and for young men is in their very early twenties, and follows a (typically) three-year stage where thoughts become more and more disordered. Aaron Kosminski celebrated his twenty-third birthday in September

1888, at the height of his killing spree, and when he was admitted to the asylum it was recorded that he had been mentally ill for six years: in other words, since he was twenty.

Although it is invidious to try to diagnose from the patchy information we have, this would appear to be a textbook case. In today's pharmacological world, anti-psychotic drugs can suppress the florid symptoms of schizophrenia, but these were not available then, and if his family ever hoped for help managing him, they would have been disappointed: permanent incarceration was all that was available then.

Schizophrenia if untreated can lead to accelerated physical aging, decline in social skills, poor self care, no motivation, and withdrawal from social contact. It also leads to declining mental abilities: memory, attention, intelligence. All of this bears out what we know of Aaron's time in the asylums, when he seems to have withdrawn, both physically and mentally.

My own theory, so far unproven, is that his psychosis may have been triggered by untreated diphtheria. Woolf's daughter Rachel died from diphtheria at the age of three, the year before the killings started. Aaron was probably living with Woolf's family at the time, and if not was certainly in close contact with them. There is, today, a substantial body of evidence associating schizophrenia with bacterial infections, such as diphtheria. The physical decline Aaron showed during his time in the asylums also correlates with untreated diphtheria. If we ever get the opportunity to exhume his body, we will, Jari believes, be able to test my theory.

When he died, Aaron Kosminski's family put a loving headstone on his grave. If they were aware of his earlier killing spree, they must have offered up thanks for his long incarceration and eventual death, safely away from suspicion and from any provocation to carry on murdering.

Looking hard at his life, I felt satisfied that he was the most likely candidate as the Ripper. We were confident we could isolate the killer's DNA from the epithelial cells. Now we just needed the last piece of the puzzle: I needed to find the DNA of Aaron Kosminski, to know that those cells were his.

CHAPTER TWELVE

CATCHING THE RIPPER

When I received news about the isolation of the twelve epithelial cells from the possible semen stains in December 2012, it felt like I'd won the lottery. At the very beginning, I had hoped to find some missing evidence that would solve the case, but when I bought the shawl, the most I thought could be achieved would be to prove that the shawl was genuine, that it had been at the scene of Catherine Eddowes' murder. I never dared to hope that, as well as her DNA, we would also have *his*. Yet here we were, in sight of the Holy Grail: the final, scientific identification of Jack the Ripper.

We now had samples to extract DNA material from and, luckily, it happened on the first attempt that David Miller made. I was relieved because the work on one vial had taken two months, so if that had failed, there was the potential for this to drag on for possibly another four months if he had needed to work on the other two vials. But my greatest feeling was one of huge excitement at what we had. The question was what to do with it? The answer was inevitable: if we had the DNA from the stains on the shawl which I believed were produced by the killer, we needed the DNA of the suspect, Aaron Kosminski, to prove I was right in choosing him.

It was a daunting prospect: it had been hard enough trying to work on the family tree of Catherine Eddowes in order to locate a living descendant and it was a lucky break that had taken me to Karen Miller, and my great good fortune that she had turned out to be such a generous, helpful person.

At this stage I did not even realize that I could get DNA from a descendant of a relative of Kosminski's: I thought it had to come directly from him, because he had no children and therefore no direct descendants. The only option, I thought, was to get it from his remains. I knew where he was buried and so I looked into what would need to be done, and whether there would be anything left of him from which to extract a sample. Yes, I was told: at the very least, his teeth would be in his grave, and would be a good source of DNA. To proceed I needed to get permission to exhume his body and I spent much of December 2012 trying to do it.

I approached the United Synagogue, which is responsible for the upkeep of eleven Jewish cemeteries, including East Ham Cemetery where the remains of Aaron Kosminski lie. As I knew from my research that it was the United Synagogue who had arranged his burial in March 1919, I contacted Melvyn Hartog, their Head of Burials. Again, I was aware that I was dealing with an extremely delicate situation and in approaching Melvyn I made sure that I did not come across as some morbid 'geek' or – worse – a potential violator of the grave, and that my intentions were clear and scientific.

Melvyn was very interested in what I had to say and knew a great deal about the Jack the Ripper story: after all, having the body of a major Ripper suspect under your immediate authority is bound to spike curiosity. He told me to send my proposal in writing, with a full explanation of how I had been working on the shawl and its significance to the case. Melvyn then passed the matter over to his superiors for consideration.

While I was waiting for the reply I began looking into exhumation companies, so that everything would be ready to go if I got permission. I found one company whose headquarters were based along a stretch of road that I had often driven along in the past twenty years because the scenery is so beautiful. The fact that this exhumation company was there, in a place I loved, made me feel as if fate was on my side, as if it was meant to be. Simon Bray, the owner of the company, advised me on how I should approach the situation. It came with a caveat: he warned me that the Jewish community would not take the idea of an exhumation lightly, owing to the religious strictures concerning burials. I had not really thought about any fundamental opposition to an exhumation on purely religious grounds.

Whilst waiting for the reply from Melvyn Hartog, Simon Bray made some suggestions: if the United Synagogue said no to a full exhumation, then we could go down the DNA extraction route. This means that the grave would be opened up, and as Kosminski was buried in a coffin nearly a hundred years ago, his coffin would have long decayed, leaving the body exposed. There would be no need to move the body to take a few teeth from the skull. DNA samples could be extracted from the pulp in those teeth and then they could be replaced. The body could be covered over and that would be the end of it. But there would only be one shot at this and as all the activity would have to take place at the graveside, it would require the forensic team, protective tent and all the paraphernalia needed to preserve the scene and acquire the samples with no contamination.

If the United Synagogue refused this idea, then the only other option would be to apply for a Ministry of Justice Licence to get legal permission to exhume the body. If this application was successful it would automatically bypass any refusal from the synagogue elders and they would have no choice but to cooperate. There was one problem: to apply for the Ministry of Justice Licence required the signature of a living relative of the deceased.

Just before Christmas 2012, the decision came through and, as I feared, the directors of the United Synagogue gave a resounding 'no'. I completely understand their decision: it would be a breach of their burial laws, which forbid the removal of corpses from a grave. They also vetoed the idea of uncovering the body to extract DNA samples from the teeth.

I now faced getting the Ministry of Justice Licence plan up and running. I needed a descendant and I needed their signature. Contacting the families of the Ripper victims seemed complicated and fraught with enough problems: it would be even more sensitive to approach the descendants of Aaron Kosminski. I anticipated that these people would be more reluctant to help than relatives of innocent victims.

I wondered if Alan McCormack at the Black Museum could help me with details of the Kosminski family, but when I rang the museum I discovered he had retired. His successor, Paul Bickley, agreed to look for any information the museum might have about the Kosminski family tree.

While mulling it over with Jari he told me something vital: if we could get a sample of DNA from a descendant of Kosminski's sisters, it would be enough to match with the DNA from the shawl. In other words, I needed to find a descendant in order to apply for exhumation, but if I could find a descendant down the female line her mitochondrial DNA would be enough to make the match, without digging up the body. Aaron Kosminski had the same mtDNA as all his siblings, and his sisters would have passed it on to their children, and it would have survived down the female line. I knew it would be hard to find, but it seemed a lot easier than applying for a licence to overrule the United Synagogue, which I instinctively did not want to do. I really did not want to transgress the burial rules of their religion.

So I began a different kind of digging. I subscribed to numerous genealogy websites and began work in earnest, focusing specifically on Aaron Kosminski's sister, Matilda, who had the rather distinctive surname of Lubnowski, and sometimes used Lubnowski-Cohen. After what seemed like an eternity of dead ends, I found a link. The information came from the genealogical research of one of Matilda's many descendants and it proved invaluable. Suddenly, my efforts at establishing a decent family tree were bearing fruit rapidly. I managed to find a marriage certificate for one of Matilda's daughters, which took me on a trail which, by coincidence, led me to Hove, East Sussex, only a few minutes' walk from the Police Convalescent Seaside Home.

I hoped this descendant would be able and willing to help, but I managed my expectations because I knew what a difficult thing I was asking for. Several attempts to make telephone contact failed when the calls went on to an answering machine, so I prepared a handwritten note and delivered it in person, knocking at the door on the off chance I would get a reply. There was no answer, so I pushed the letter through the letter box. There was no response to the letter either and I knew that, once again, I had hit a dead end. If this person already knew they were related to Aaron Kosminski, then they clearly did not want to be drawn into an association with the Ripper story. It was very frustrating: my best lead yet to find a female descendant, and my best chance of having this exhumation order signed if I had to go down that route, had come to nothing. In the meantime, Simon Bray from the exhumation company was calling, fired up to begin work and looking for good news: there was none to give him.

When I went on a family holiday to Egypt I took with me a book, *Jack the Ripper and the Case for Scotland Yard's Prime Suspect*, written by Robert House, an American writer who has long been fascinated by the Ripper case. The book argued the case for Kosminski as the Ripper and brought together much of what we know about his background and life, plus more that Robert House had painstakingly researched. It was an extremely thorough and responsible study, charting the history of Jewish settlement in London and the dangerous anti-Semitism in Eastern Europe at the time that led to so many Jews feeling compelled to leave their homeland. The book put the fate of the Kosminski family and therefore Aaron himself into context.

I went through the book, looking for any nuggets of information that might generate new leads in my search for a living descendant – after all, this was the first serious study dedicated solely to Kosminski, and House's research was impeccable and had unearthed much new material. In the end I could find very little information regarding the descendants of the Kosminski family that I had not already found out for myself. But when I read the acknowledgements I saw that the author wrote: 'my deepest thanks to the descendants of Woolf Abrahams, Isaac Abrahams and Matilda and Morris Lubnowski-Cohen.' Clearly the author had tracked down these people: it gave me renewed hope that I would be able to do the same.

I had a family tree, I even had names – and now with the help of a number of professional genealogists, I eventually had contact details for descendants who might be prepared to help me. There were some relatives in America, descended from Aaron's older sister Helena (Annie) Singer, and I was prepared to follow up this lead – perhaps, being American, the crimes would seem more distant and they'd be more willing to get involved – but first I had a few more British options to explore. I started with another female descendant of Matilda. I had no idea how receptive she would be to my call.

The first couple of phone calls I made went straight to voicemail, and I felt a sinking feeling in the pit of my stomach: was this going to be a repeat of my Hove experience? But the third time I got through, and explained who I was, and what I needed. As the conversation progressed, I felt she understood that I was not simply expounding a wild theory. She knew she was a descendant of the Kosminski family: it was apparently common knowledge in her family.

I arranged to meet her in the East End of London – it seemed appropriate. I am not naming her here, nor giving any personal information about her, because she does not want to be exposed to the cranks and weirdos who attach themselves to anybody whose name becomes public property today, through social media. I have promised to protect her identity, and I always will, so I am going to refer to her simply as M (and, no, that's not one of her real initials).

I was very nervous as I approached her, but I was as lucky with M as I was with Karen, Catherine Eddowes' descendant. I could not have hoped for two friendlier, kinder women. It is, understandably, much tougher for M. Although she knew she was descended from the sister of *one* of the suspects, I was now telling her that I wanted her help to prove he was *the* suspect.

She courteously and politely took me through all the arguments against her ancestor being the Ripper, as if, subconsciously perhaps, she wanted to prove it was not him. I was familiar with all the arguments, and able to refute them, but I understood why she wanted to make certain that I knew what I was talking about. She was fascinated by all the scientific work we had done on the shawl. Eventually I asked her the main question, the reason I was there: would she be happy to provide a sample of DNA?

I was very nervous as I asked. I didn't want to sound presumptuous and I did not want to be intrusive: but I needed her sample.

Eventually I broached the subject, and told her I had two swabs with me if she was willing to help. She said she was happy to.

I was so grateful. I phoned Jari there and then, because I knew he would be as excited as I was. I put M on to the phone to talk to him, and they had a chat about the work he was doing with the shawl samples.

It was one of those amazing days in this saga, a day when everything went right. Afterwards I took M and a friend of hers to Brick Lane for a curry at my favourite curry house, and then took her on my own Ripper tour: she had never actually traced the Ripper route before, and she did not know that Matilda and all her extended family had lived in what was now

Greenfield Road. As we walked along, side by side, I hugged to myself the incredible knowledge that I was in the company of a descendant of *his* sister and, what's more, she was willing to help me.

The next morning I jumped into my car and drove the familiar route to Jari's lab in Liverpool. There was no way I was going to entrust this precious DNA sample to the post. With the DNA from a direct descendant of Matilda Lubnowski, the Ministry of Justice Licence could take a back seat. We had what we needed to move forward: samples from the semen stains on the shawl and samples from a Kosminski family member down the female line. Everything was set for the final part of the story.

When Jari delivered the semen samples from the shawl to David Miller in Leeds, there were three vials of material, which went straight into David's freezer at his lab. He worked on one vial, and within a couple of months he had found the twelve epithelial cells which told us we would be able to get the Ripper's DNA.

So when it was time to work on the Ripper's DNA, Jari asked David for the remaining two vials back.

That's when we made a nightmare discovery. David's laboratory had moved, and his students were charged with packing up his freezers and unpacking them on to the new site. Somewhere in transit our vials had been lost. They had searched for them, thoroughly, but it was no good: they had gone.

Jari explained to me that in a lab like David's everything is marked with a standard code system and, of course, our samples were not part of the normal routine of this lab. They were marked with symbols which did not match the lab system, which is probably why they were discarded during the move. It's normal procedure in research and diagnostic labs to save space: if they do not recognize it, they do not know what it is, it cannot be used and it needs to go. David unpacked the freezers himself, with aid, to look for the vials, but no luck. I appreciate it was not his oversight.

I was on holiday, staying in a caravan on Anglesey, when Jari rang me with the calamitous news. The weather was bad, my mobile phone signal was rubbish, I was hanging out of the caravan window in the rain trying to make out what he said.

At first, I thought I had misheard him. I made him repeat it to me. Slowly it sank in: we had lost our raw material. It was catastrophic, and at first I was completely numb, too overwhelmed to really take it on board.

I had come so far, wandered blindly up cul de sacs, struggled to keep going against the odds. Finally, we had reached a really good place, only a short step from the most important development in the Ripper story since 1888. And now . . .

I was, to use a cliché, gutted. And another cliché: sick as a parrot. Devastated. I felt my stomach dropping away in sheer misery. We were, I thought, back at the drawing board as far as the Ripper part of the equation went. We could start again: Jari could take more samples from the semen stain on the shawl, but then David would have to process them again. We were lucky the first time when he found the epithelial cells, but there could have been a lot more trial and error repeating the whole process. I took the shawl back to Jari and he took more samples. It was dispiriting to have been so near and now so far. I was psychologically preparing myself for another long wait.

I was travelling by tube to meet an estate agent, Jeremy Tarn, in Commercial Road. Jeremy's company, a prestigious one, has been in Whitechapel since 1955, and I have been dealing with him for several years as I have been determined to buy a property in the area (which I have now, finally, done). I was changing trains, but the one I was about to board was held up, and the whole tube line was temporarily at a standstill. I decided it would be quicker to walk than wait. I walked down a back road by some arches, the arches filled with stall holders selling all sorts of exotic foodstuffs. It is an area where strangers don't feel welcome, and I attracted some uncomfortable stares. But I knew I was heading in the right direction. I had turned into Berner Street and was just passing the site where Elizabeth Stride was murdered – and Israel Schwartz saw the killer – when Jari's text pinged on to my phone screen, telling me that this latest sample was viable.

I stood still for a moment to read the text, more or less on the spot where he dragged his victim into the yard. When I looked up from my phone, everything around me felt unreal: the world seemed to be going at high speed, with everyone rushing past, and me marooned in it, walking very, very slowly. I walked along Greenfield Road, where he and so many of Kosminski's relatives lived, and I paused again, as the full eerie significance hit me like a ton of bricks. Here I was, on his territory, and Jari was telling me we now had, once again, a good sample to work from. It was something I could never have planned. It felt like a dream where you try to run but get nowhere: a weird, nonsensical feeling. I can't find words to describe it: I was so close to proving he was the Ripper, and at that same moment so close, physically, to where he had lived.

'I've got you, you bastard,' I said to myself, looking around at the street. Knowing so much about the Ripper story, and for so many years having to keep it to myself, whenever I am in the East End I feel like a ghost, an outsider, looking in at it all. When the chattering groups of Ripper tourists follow their guides around the streets he trod, I have wanted, at times, to shout from the rooftops the full truth of the story, but I have always had to bite everything back. And here I was again, getting such momentous news just yards from where he lived, and not being able to share it with anyone.

It was good news that the sample taken from the shawl was viable, but it still meant that we were a long way back in the process, and that this new sample would have to go to David Miller in Leeds and we'd be waiting for a few more months. Although I was relieved we had another chance, I was still disappointed to have taken several steps back in the hunt, in terms of the time it would take us.

But I hadn't reckoned on Jari's ability to find a way through any problem. The man is a genius, I can't praise him enough for the way he applies his mind to any problem and finds a solution.

'Do you know what?' he said. 'We have the microscope slides on which David found those twelve epithelial cells. I think there may be a way to get the cells from the slides.'

The slides had been fixed with a fixative and stained with Giemsa, a stain that was invented by an early German microbiologist, and one of its uses is to allow transparent cells to be seen with a microscope. Jari had to find a way to get the cells, which could only be seen with a 400x magnification microscope, off the slides. He explained to me that there was a huge risk of contamination in just scraping them off, and I tried to temper my hopes, because it sounded like a mission impossible. There was no standard scientific procedure.

'I was puzzling about it all the time,' he said, 'when I was driving, when I was relaxing, whenever I had a spare moment. When I was in bed before sleeping, and first thing when I woke up. I knew there had to be a way.

'Then I remembered using laser capture microdissection which I had been using in cancer research to isolate just single cells from microscope slides.'

The method is not used in forensics, but due to Jari's background and varied research interests he has a huge arsenal of methods up his sleeve, and just now this proved very useful. It was a ground-breaking development in forensics: isolating a single cell from a piece of evidence 125 years old, and then analysing the DNA of that single cell. It was a bit like looking through a telescope, finding a previously unknown planet from another galaxy, then zapping a sample of the planet down to earth to be analysed.

When Jari told me about laser capture microdissection (LCM) he had to explain what it was and what it could do: over the time we have been working together Jari has had to explain a great deal of science to me, and he has done it very patiently. LCM is a state of the art method of isolating and harvesting cells by cutting away unwanted cells or other debris. A laser is coupled to a microscope and focuses on the tissue. When the cells have been identified and isolated, they can be extracted from the slide one by one. The technique does not alter the form or structure of the cell, which is why it is invaluable in medical research.

So Jari had hit on a means by which we could extract the DNA we needed, but now the next big problem was: where was a suitable LCM microscope, and how could we use it? Jari knew of several universities and research establishments which had this very expensive piece of kit, but when he approached them they all said no: they were not prepared to allow their technology to be used for forensic purposes. There were protocols attached to its use, and we did not meet them. One university department would have allowed us to use their LCM, but only if Jari had undergone a day's mandatory special training in its use, and he simply did not have time in his already bursting schedule.

Again, I have great reason to be grateful to Jari. By this time, he was as much involved in the search for answers from the shawl as I was, and he refused to be defeated. He rang several manufacturers of the LCM, including the Carl Zeiss company in Germany, and from them he procured a list of all their customers in the UK who had the microscopes.

One name that came up was Epistem, a company which specializes in biotechnology and personalized medicine, with particular expertize in stem cells in the areas of epithelial and infectious diseases. It is based in Manchester, and does a lot of work in partnership with Manchester University.

Jari rang them, and after so many knockbacks we could hardly believe it when Dr Ross Haggart said yes, he could fit us into a gap in the LCM timetable. So I picked Jari up in Liverpool, drove to Manchester and we went to Epistem, which is located in the heart of the Manchester University area of the city. Jari, the scientist, was allowed to go in, but once again I was outside killing time, hoping everything was going well. I wandered into a church just round the corner: I have always been a spiritual person and I like churches, I always feel good when I'm inside a church. I prayed, selfishly I suppose, for the success of the work with the LCM.

Jari and Ross spent a couple of hours scanning the whole of David's slides in high resolution, and they were pretty sure they had located the cells, but could only confirm this by comparing it with David's original results. Jari said, 'We found lots of debris, plant cells, even a micro worm, which could have come on to the slide at any point. It was like having a map of London with no street names and having to find Big Ben. My eyes were sore from looking by the time we had finished.'

In the end what we had was a high-resolution scan of the microscope slides, a few hundred megabytes, and now this had to be compared with David's images of the epithelial cells. It was a mammoth task, like looking for a needle in a haystack in a field full of haystacks.

Back in Liverpool Jari set to work in the evenings. Because his family live in Bradford, he spends four evenings a week on his own in Liverpool, and was quite prepared to finish his day job and then start work on this.

It was laborious and time-consuming work, but after his first long evening he found a cell. 'I couldn't believe my eyes. It was exactly the same cell as David had found. I was staring at it, I could hardly take it in. Although I hoped I'd find the cells, I had a fair degree of scepticism about my chances,' he said later.

My phone pinged with a text to tell me he'd found it. I'd been waiting all evening, knowing he'd started the search, hoping we would get a result, but not daring to believe we would. It was after 1 a.m. when he sent me the message, but I was not asleep. It was a very intense time and I'd been picking up my phone every half hour or so, checking in case I'd missed a message. When it finally came through I was relieved and excited.

Jari carried on with the search for the next two evenings, spending more than six hours on it. Finding the first cell gave him a boost, plus he reckons he got better at recognizing what he was looking for.

Having identified them, we now had to go back to Manchester to capture them from the slides. Ross was very helpful again, but because of pressure on his lab we had to be there at 8.30 a.m. Jari caught the train from Liverpool and I picked him up at Eccles station on a raw, cold morning. I was there so early I slept in my car in the station car park until he arrived, then I dropped him back at Epistem.

He and Ross worked hard, examining the slides and deciding which cells they could capture. Some cells had no nuclei, a by-product of the staining process, so therefore would yield no DNA. They managed to capture thirty-three cells, having screened them as the right size, the right morphology (form and structure), and confirmed they had nuclei. (David Miller had stopped looking after he found twelve: he had only been trying to confirm that they were there, and when he found a sufficient number he was satisfied.) The cells were tagged by putting an electronic flag on the image (a bit like you do with Google maps) in order to find them again easily. They were then captured using the LCM and put in separate tubes, thirty-three in total. Finding thirty-three may sound a lot, but think how many cells are in a square centimetre of skin: approximately 110,000–125,000.

All of the cells except one looked like epithelial cells. The odd one looked like a kidney cell. I was tremendously excited when Jari told me this: it is not surprising, remembering that the Ripper removed Catherine Eddowes' kidney, but it was an unexpected bonus. To date, Jari has not had the time to work on this cell, so we have no confirmation that it is definitely from a kidney, but he says that the morphology very much resembles a kidney cell. (As a cautious scientist, he points out: 'It could be something else, but when I look at it the first thing that comes to my mind is a kidney cell.') When there is time, Jari will examine this cell to confirm what he suspects.

It was after midday when Jari emerged from Epistem, triumphant but exhausted, with the captured cells. I had filled in the tense hours that he was in the lab by walking around Manchester, calling in at a museum, trying to settle in a coffee shop. I was distracted and on edge until I heard the good news. I drove Jari back to Liverpool and we went to Chinatown for a meal. We were both shattered: we had been up very early, and Jari had been concentrating hard, while I was expending a great deal of nervous energy just hoping for a good result. We were so tired we were not jubilant: we spent the meal talking rubbish to each other, and afterwards, when I set off to drive back to Hertfordshire, Jari was genuinely concerned about me making such a long journey in my exhausted state.

So now we had the DNA from M, the descendant, and we had the cells from, we believed, her ancestor Aaron Kosminski. Now Jari's great experience and expertise came to the fore, yet again. He decided to do a whole genome amplification, a relatively new technique, on the cell samples. The WGA amplifies (copies) both genomic and mitochondrial DNA from the single cell to a level where we have enough material to do genetic profiling. We already had the DNA from the two descendants, Karen and M, and from the other main people who had handled the shawl, like me and him (to eliminate us).

Whole genome amplification means that tiny quantities of DNA can be amplified to provide a much greater supply for scientific work. According to Jari, five years earlier we would not have been able to use this method, and although it had been used in genetic sciences it was not routinely used in forensics. It is usually applied to a small number of cells that are in good condition. Here we were talking about one single cell, more than a hundred years old, and not in its best condition. (The other thirty-two cells were being stored in case we needed them in future.) Once again, Jari was working at the frontiers of science.

If a scientist has only one cell it is virtually impossible to do a whole genome profile from it, but if we can make multiple 100 per cent identical copies of the genetic material which is inside the cell, the task becomes possible. It was back to the lab for Jari, where he isolated single cells, added biological buffers to stabilize them, and then by adding a mixture of chemicals was able to extract copies of the DNA that was inside the cell. He explained it as a bit like a photocopying machine, which will make endless copies of one page of writing: through this technique he could make many copies of all the different DNA samples from the cell, giving him enough material to do DNA profiling and sequencing. Each segment of DNA was amplified about 500-million-fold. After this amplification step we would now, fingers crossed, have enough material for the actual profiling.

For the profiling, another amplification of the DNA was needed. This second step uses the polymerase chain reaction, which Jari explained to me was the same method used on the samples from Karen, me and him. With a little bit of luck, we would now get the mtDNA fragments amplified from just single cells.

It was a rainy Friday morning when I got the news that the amplification process had worked, giving us a massive resource to work from.

It was a major victory: now Jari had to start work amplifying specific segments, and then to do the DNA sequencing. He was about to start comparing it to match M's DNA against that of the Ripper, when he suffered a serious blow. His father died unexpectedly, back in Finland, and he had to fly there straight away.

His personal problems obviously took precedence at this juncture, and over the next couple of weeks he had to go back to Finland, twice, to sort everything out. It was a tough time for him, emotionally and physically. Neither he nor I were able to sleep, for different reasons, and we were texting each other late into the night. I really appreciate the fact that as soon as he was back at work, he started work on comparing M's mitochondrial DNA with that of the cells extracted from the semen stain on the shawl.

It was a very testing time for me, and I was living on nervous energy, knowing that he was back at work on this crucial stage. I wasn't sleeping, I lost half a stone in weight, and I was constantly checking my phone and emails for news of the test results. It was quarter past eight on a Friday evening when an email pinged into my inbox titled First Results. I hardly dared read it.

What Jari had found was a 99.2 per cent match when he ran the alignment in one direction, and going the other way it was a 100 per cent perfect match. These results were fantastic, mind-blowing for me. Jari was cautious, as ever, noting that there were two anomalies and further testing would be needed. He explained that the problem could be because the DNA had been amplified billions of times, and any mistake with the enzyme copying the DNA could also be amplified. The other possibility was contamination, although this was unlikely as he works in a pressurized room with special pipettes and ultraviolet light to eliminate unwanted DNA from other sources. But he was pleased with the result, and he was also pleased with the scientific work that achieved it. As he wrote in an email to me:

> There was a risk that we were genotyping dandruff from me or you. A fingerprint can contain more cells than we had as starting material, so I was really chuffed to see that the quality of the sample was so good. We created a decent sized DNA sample from a single microscopic cell isolated with a laser from the shawl prep (this could be compared with creating a standard size blood DNA sample from a dust particle). Then from this regenerated sample a segment of mitochondrial DNA region was amplified about 500 million fold. And the resulting sequence is 99.2% perfect. If we sequence in the other direction . . . the sequence is 100% perfect.

He even allowed himself a brief moment of pride and pleasure: 'I think this has been one hell of a masterpiece of work (quite proud of this) and it would not have been possible to attempt before 2006 as the technologies were not available.'

Later he said, 'Given the fact that we are working from amplified cells it is not outlandish that there would be one mistake.'

I, not as cautious as Jari the scientist, was thrilled: it felt as if we were home and dry. I looked at the attachment he sent me, a multicoloured sequence of blocks that aligned the DNA of M and our suspect, and I could see we had a near-perfect match. Jari explained that the anomaly did not mean there was a difference: it simply meant that the test did not take at that point in the sequence.

Not long ago, looking at a DNA sequence would have meant nothing to me, but under Jari's tutelage I can now scan the colours and see the match. I was bowled over, although at first I could not take it in fully. I felt a massive sense of relief and release. We had, I knew for sure, nailed Aaron Kosminski.

I had to delay my celebration to the following Tuesday, when I went to the East End – where else? I went to my favourite curry house for a meal: my good mood was infectious and the staff, who know me well, plied me with drinks. Then I decided to visit all the pubs and bars in Whitechapel that I had walked past for years but never been inside. It was my own private celebration but I felt I deserved it. Sheer persistence had paid off. I'd been living on adrenalin for years, and finally I was getting the right results.

But after that celebration, I had to put my excitement on hold as Jari carried on with his work. Now he needed to eliminate Karen (and through her, her ancestor Catherine Eddowes), himself and me, because our DNA was present on the shawl through handling it. A few weeks later this had been done, and we know for certain that the DNA extracted from the semen stains are not a contamination by either Jari or me, nor was it from the victim.

We also decided to test for ethnic and geographic background, although Jari cautioned me that we might not get a full profile from the samples we have. With good quality

DNA it is not a problem. Jari has done the testing on himself: 'I know that based on my mitochondrial DNA I am 96.3% Finnish, but the rest of me comes from Spanish farmers, which was a surprise. Somewhere in the past one of my ancestors might have married a Spaniard. I am looking into whether we have sufficiently good genomic DNA to be able to get the same precise information about our suspect, but we have to remember that it is very old DNA.'

So by the end of May all we were waiting for was, with luck, a geographic location of which area of the world Aaron Kosminski came from. Of course, we know the answer, but it would be great to have scientific evidence to underline it.

CONCLUSION

It was half past two in the morning when Jari's email came through.

He had established a 100 per cent match of the genome of our suspect's DNA to haplogroup T1a1. It sounded very impressive.

I had to wait until 7 a.m. to get a layman's explanation of what this means, and needless to say, I didn't sleep. What Jari emailed then gave me another, huge, 'wow' moment: the Ripper's haplogroup type is very typical in people of Russian Jewish ethnicity (with 'Russian' embracing Polish as well, as Jari later explained). With all the other DNA evidence we have, this is the cherry on the top of the cake: it matches Aaron Kosminski and his origins.

I can't pretend to understand the science of this amazing discovery, but as Jari explains it, in molecular evolution a haplo-group is a group of haplotypes (which are single nucleotide polymorphisms) which have the same mutations in all the haplotypes in the group, and therefore represent a clade, which is a group of people sharing the same common ancestry. In other words, DNA can be analysed to say which part of the world a person's ancestors came from. The process Jari used to establish this haplogroup for Kosminski is the same one that tells him he is Finnish with a dash of Spanish farmers: but, of course, working on his own DNA was easier because it is fresh – not well over a hundred years old like the DNA extracted from the shawl.

These mutations have different characteristics from the ones scientists use to track diseases, like cancer. They are not affected by disease, which is why they became common in a given population.

Jari compared the DNA sequences from the isolated cells to the collection of DNA databases stored at the National Center for Biotechnology Information (NCBI), based in Bethesda, USA. This database holds millions of sequences from various organisms, including humans. The answer took a while to compute, but the NCBI server came up with one perfect hit. This reference sequence, from someone who had exactly the same long sequence Jari had obtained from the shawl DNA, had only been entered a few weeks earlier, so once again luck was on our side.

The hit was for mitochondrial haplotype $T1a1$; it matched our sequence perfectly, and the ethnicity of the person it belonged to was recorded as 'Russian.' Jari read it three or four times before it truly sank in.

'I'd been dreading it would say something like "Jamaican" or "Polynesian" – then we would have had a problem.'

We'd got the evidence we needed to name Kosminski definitively as the Ripper, with his perfect match with his descendant M, but, like Jari, I knew that if this geographic profiling had shown him to come from a completely different part of the world, we might have had to rethink. But, thankfully, it backs up everything we already know. We had our belt, now we had the braces.

After the hit, Jari was also unable to go to bed, so wide-awake was he that he knew he wouldn't be able to sleep for thinking about it, so he carried on with the research. There we were, hundreds of miles apart, both with our minds racing. Jari knew that Russian Jews are known to have moved to central and eastern Europe, including Poland. A major study in the *Annals of Human Genetics* into mitochondrial DNA variability in Poles and Russians concluded that both countries have a similar DNA pattern, with all mtDNA haplogroups being represented equally in both nations (with haplogroup T1 very slightly more represented among the Poles). So when Jari came up with 'Russian', it embraces Polish, too, hence Jari's text stating Russian ethnicity.

As with everything on our quest, there were last-minute hitches, with a technical problem in the German lab which was customizing the oligonucleotides (short single-strands of DNA) for Jari, which he needed in order to carry out the laboratory analysis, making the DNA sequence (a string of text/letters) which he could then compare to the American database. Instead of a twenty-four hour turn around on our samples, we waited more than seventy-two hours. All edge-of-the-seat, nail-biting stuff for me, but I should be used to it by now . . . And we got the right result, so I'm not complaining.

There was more good news a few days later, when Jari was able to deduce more from the DNA. He had been doing tests to establish the hair, skin and eye colour of the owner of the cells and he was able to tell me that our man definitely did not have red or blond hair, but that his hair colour was likely to be dark (brown or black). He could also, to my amazement, tell that there was some very preliminary evidence suggesting that our man had acne. This may not prove to be the case – the science in this area is new and Jari was cautious about overstating this – but the fact that it could be possible to deduce this kind of detail is astonishing. As the research in this area develops, who knows what we might be able to tell from the cells in the future.

Israel Schwartz, the man I believe to be the best eye witness of a Ripper attack, had described the assailant he saw as having 'hair, dark, and a small dark moustache'. So although these new results did not amount to proof, they increased my conviction that we had the right man.

There is a feeling of deep satisfaction, knowing that I have solved the greatest murder mystery ever. It has taken a long time, there have been many lows as well as highs. I have come close to abandoning it more than once, and I have had moments of despair to counterpoint moments of wild jubilation. I have lost many hours of sleep over it, and my wife's patience has been stretched. Finally, everything I have done has been vindicated.

It has been an amazing journey. I have met some wonderful people along the way, and I have made good and lasting friendships. I have also discovered a great deal about myself, not least when, the day before Jari's final results came in, something surfaced from my subconscious that has helped me understand why I felt such a deep connection with the Ripper's victims, those unfortunate women who were forced to sell their bodies to pay for the basic necessities of food and a bed for the night. Yes, I had always empathized with them, partly because of my own short experience of being homeless. But this was something far bigger.

I recalled a conversation I heard as a child, something I had filed away, perhaps because I did not understand it fully at the time, and perhaps, also, because I did not want to understand it. I was about six years old, because I know we were living in the two-up, two-down terraced house. My Auntie Enid was talking to Mum about my grandmother on my dad's side, who I would only meet twice.

'She was a prostitute, that's what she was,' Enid said, her voice dripping with disapproval. Auntie Enid was a vivid redhead, married to my dad's brother Mickey, a milkman. She used to pop round from time to time to see Mum.

I had honestly never thought about this revelation until I reached the final chapter of my Ripper search. Why did it come back to me? A chance remark from a female colleague, in which she likened being the mistress of a married man to being a prostitute, sparked an irrational anger in me. The two things are not the same, but why did it annoy me so much that she conflated them? It was while I was trying to work out the answer that the conversation between Mum and Auntie Enid came back to me.

At the next opportunity I rang my mum, to check whether it was true. 'Yes,' she said, straight away. 'Your grandmother was a prostitute.'

She had abandoned her family when my dad was young, and he and his brothers and sisters had been brought up by Auntie Ruth, the oldest sister, because my grandfather worked driving lorries. There were six of them, and it must have been tough. When I was very small, when Mum and Dad were still living together, we lived on the tenth floor of a tower block, just a couple of streets away from the Liverpool docks. My paternal grandmother lived on the ground floor of the same block, but there was no contact between her and our family, and the only couple of occasions I met her were when we literally bumped into her, and she would say hello.

Unlike my other grandmother, who was warm and loving and everything a grandmother should be, this woman was a stranger: I don't even know her name. But I am still a descendant of hers, some of her genes are replicated in me, and this whole sense of family connection is something I have been made aware of through my scientific work tracking down the Ripper. I no longer have any connection with my dad's side of the family: he emigrated to Australia twenty years ago and I have only seen him once since then, and we didn't get on. But he, and this woman I never knew, are part of my ancestry, just as Catherine Eddowes is part of Karen Miller's.

With this personal knowledge, I find myself caring even more about the unfortunates, the women whose sad lifestyle made them prey for the man we have always called Jack the Ripper.

That name will never go away. But now, thanks to the shawl, the scientific brilliance of Jari Louhelainen, and my determination, persistence and refusal to be sidetracked, we have his real name. He is no longer just a suspect. We can hold him, finally, to account for his terrible deeds. My search is over:

Aaron Kosminski is Jack the Ripper.

ACKNOWLEDGEMENTS

I would never have reached the end of this special journey without the help of so many people, most of whom have shown me kindness, support and understanding over the years.

I initially wish to thank the experts and historians whose passion for the Ripper story gave me the grounding and information that helped me gain my first true understanding of the mystery. They are Paul Begg, Martin Fido, Stewart Evans and Donald Rumbelow.

Without Dr Jari Louhelainen's dedicated and painstaking forensic work on the shawl, my story wouldn't be where it is today. I wish to acknowledge his professionalism, support, understanding and kindness, and his utmost patience with me, a non-scientist. To Karen Miller and 'M', without whose contributions we wouldn't have had the DNA vital for the testing.

Andy and Sue Parlour, for the many years in which they have given me the will to keep going: their support has been tremendous. To my literary agent, Robert Smith, my sounding board, to whom I would turn at any time of frustration, anxiety and elation. He has always been there for me. My special thanks to my publisher, Ingrid Connell at Sidgwick & Jackson, who took a chance on me when I was halfway through my story.

To Jean Ritchie and John Bennett, who have provided me the

friendliest and most nurturing help in order to understand my life, Alan McCormack and Paul Bickley at the Black Museum in Scotland Yard, David Melville-Hayes, Chris Phillips, Pat Marshall, Robert House, Diane Thalman and Darren Nicholhurst.

To the institutions who were so helpful and informative: the National Archives in Kew, the London and Metropolitan Archives in Farringdon, the Public Record Office, the London Hospital Museum in Whitechapel, Cambridge University Library, Sotheby's, Christie's, the Huguenot Society, the Victoria & Albert Museum, Encyclopaedia Britannica and Lacy Scott & Knight Auctioneers.

PICTURE ACKNOWLEDGEMENTS

All images © Evans Skinner archive excluding:

Section One

Page 1 – top and bottom: © Lacy Scott and Knight Auction Centre; 2 – top right: © Mary Evans/Peter Higginbotham Collection; middle: © Mary Evans Picture Library; 4 & 5: courtesy of Library of the London School of Economics & Political Science, LSE/BOOTH/E/1/5

Section Two

Page 1 – middle: courtesy of Andy and Sue Parlour; 4 – top: © Adam Wood and the Swanson family; middle: © Mary Evans/Peter Higginbotham Collection; 5 – top and bottom: © Mary Evans/Peter Higginbotham Collection; 6–7 – © Dr Jari Louhelainen; 8 – top and middle © Dr Jari Louhelainen

Integrated

pp. 46–7 Stanford's Map of Central London, digital reproduction © MAPCO 2006; p. 135 Letter: courtesy of David Hayes

Appendix

London Metropolitan Archives, City of London

APPENDIX

7.367.

LONDON COUNTY ASYLUM,

COLNEY HATCH.

Lunacy Act,
1890,
Sec. 25.

This is to Certify That *Aaron Kozminski*

aged *29* a Patient discharged

from this Asylum to-day, has not recovered, and I am of opinion that

he is a proper person to be kept in a Workhouse as a

Lunatic.

Dated this *19*th day of *April* 189 *4*

W. J. Seward M.

Medical Superintendent.

29   **MALE**

Registered No. of Admission. **7367**	Name *Kozminski Aaron* Date of Admission. *19th April 1894*	Age. *29*	Parish. *Mile End*

Married, Single, or Widowed   Previous Occupation *Hairdresser*   Religion. *Jew*

When and where under previous care and treatment } *Colney Hatch*
   as mentally affected

Whether previously under treatment here, and, if so, is it a }
   new attack or a continuation of the old attack ? }

Number of previous attacks   Whether subject to Epilepsy *No*   Whether suicidal or dangerous *No*

Name and address of nearest known relative, } *Mother, Mrs Kozminski, 63 New Street, New Road, Whitechapel, London E*
   and degree of relationship

Causation.

   (*i.*) Predisposing (*e.g.*, hereditary influences, congenital defects, previous attacks, change of life, &c.)

   (*ii.*) Exciting (*e.g.*, alcohol, epilepsy, mental anxiety, worry, &c.)

Facts indicating insanity

Family History.	**Bodily condition on admission.** Temperature.
Age of parents, if alive	Height weight
Cause of death	Marks or injuries
History of insanity, epilepsy, or paralysis	
,, intemperance on either side	Cleanliness
Syphilis	Head, shape of
Consanguinity of parents	measurements
Number of brothers and sisters alive	
,, ,, dead cause of	Colour of hair eyes
Mental and physical condition of brothers and sisters	Pupils
	Teeth Palate
Personal History.	
Labour (*i.*) natural or otherwise	Digestion Appetite
(*ii.*) instrumental or otherwise	Tongue Bowels
Has pt. suffered from (*i.*) morbilli	Urine
(*ii.*) Pertussis (*iii.*) varicella	Catamenia
(*iv.*) Variola (*v.*) otorrhœa	Circulation
(*vi.*) Scarlet fever	
History of fall, injury, or fright	Pulse
Walked at age of	Respiration
Talked ,,	
If educated . Where, and for how long ?	
	Viscera
History of present attack.	
	Skin
	Genitalia

Hamlet of Mile End Old Town.

ADMISSION ORDER.

Dated this _19th_ day of _April_ 18_94_

To Dr. _Case_ Medical Superintendent of the Metropolitan District

Asylum at _Leavesden_ .

Admit the Person named and described as below, from the Hamlet of Mile End Old Town, in the said District.

NAME.	Age.	Calling, if any, and Occupation for which suited.	Religious Persuasion.	Name and Address of nearest known Relative. The full Postal Address to be inserted.		
				Degree of Relationship	}	_Mother_
				Name		_Mrs Kozminski_
Aaron Kozminski	29	_Hair Dresser_	_Hebrew_	Full Postal Address	}	_63 New St_
						New Rd Whitechapel

W. Thacker Clerk to the Board of Guardians.

MEDICAL CERTIFICATE

CASE REGISTER.

Mental condition.   Diagnosis.

Dementia Secondary

OBSERVATIONS.

Transferred from Vol. 9 Page 47

Dementia Secondary

16.9.10 — Faulty in his habits, he does nothing useful & cannot answer questions. Simple manner. Bod. poor.

29.9.11 — Patient is dull & vacant. Faulty & untidy in habits. Does nothing useful. Nothing can be got by question. B.H. best.

15.4.12 — Noted but negative. Off

6.9.12 — No replies can be got; dull & stupid in manner. Faulty in his habits. Requires constant attention. B.H. weak.

16.1.13 — Patient is morose in manner. No remark reply can be got by question. He mutters incoherently. Faulty & untidy in his habit. B.H. weak.

16.7.14 — Incoherent & excitable: troublesome at times: Hallucinations of hearing. Untidy — B.H. fair.

14.2.15 — Pat. merely mutters when asked questions. He has hallucinations of sight & hearing and is very excitable at times. Does no work. Clean but untidy in dress. B.H. fair.

2.2.16 — Patient does not know his age or how long he has been here. He has hallucinations of sight & hearing & is at times very obstinate. Untidy but clean, does no work. B.H. good.

CERTIFIED COPY OF AN ENTRY OF DEATH

GIVEN AT THE GENERAL REGISTER OFFICE

Application Number 780216-1

| REGISTRATION DISTRICT | | | | | WATFORD | | | |
| 1919 DEATH in the Sub-district of Abbots Langley | | | | | in the County of Hertford | | | |

Columns:-	1	2	3	4	5	6	7	8	9
No.	When and where died	Name and surname	Sex	Age	Occupation	Cause of death	Signature, description and residence of informant	When registered	Signature of registrar
99	Twenty fourth March 1919 Leavesden asylum Watford RD	Aaron Kozminski	male	54 years	Mile End Union formerly a Hairdresser	Gangrene of left leg Pru certified by Frank Ashby Elkins MD	Frank Ashby Elkins medical Superintendent Leavesden Asylum Watford	Twenty ninth March 1919	J Calvert Deputy Registrar

CERTIFIED to be a true copy of an entry in the certified copy of a Register of Deaths in the District above mentioned.

Given at the GENERAL REGISTER OFFICE, under the Seal of the said Office, the 10th day of December 2008

DYC 153105

See note overleaf

3010233 14131 0405 7045PSL 01/9/07

TMF

To the Steward of the Leavesden Asylum,

Please deliver to Mr. Friedlander

Undertaker,

of Duke St. United Synagogue. London. E.

the body of Aaron Kozminski

Signature I. W. Abrahams

Address The Dolphin, Whitechapel Rd. E London

Date 25th March 1919 Relation to deceased Brothers

NOTICE TO UNDERTAKERS.—The body must be removed before the hour fixed for its removal from the Institution.

INDEX

Note: all street names are in London unless otherwise stated.

INDEX